WITH THE BATTLE CRUISERS

By FILSON YOUNG

NARRATIVE HISTORY

Christopher Columbus and the
New World of his Discovery
The Relief of Mafeking
Titanic

ESSAYS AND BELLES-LETTRES

Ireland at the Cross Roads
Memory Harbour
Letters from Solitude
Venus and Cupid
New Leaves
Mastersingers
More Mastersingers
The Joy of the Road

NOVELS

The Sands of Pleasure
When the Tide Turns

POETRY

The Lover's Hours

MISCELLANEOUS

The Wagner Stories
The Complete Motorist
With the Fleet
A Volunteer Brigade

Rolling Home.

(From a sketch in oils by the Author.)

WITH THE BATTLE CRUISERS

By

FILSON YOUNG

(Late Lieutenant R.N.V.R.)

CASSELL AND COMPANY, LTD
London, New York, Toronto and Melbourne
1921

First published *April* 1921
Reprinted May 1922

To
THOSE WHO DIED
AND THOSE WHO LIVE
FOR ENGLAND

Thou wast made glorious in the midst of the Seas

PREFACE

THIS book is not a chapter of naval history. It is, however, a study of naval life in war from which the material for a chapter in naval history may some day be derived. The Navy and its life must remain to a great extent *terra incognita* to the public that owes so much to it; and it is as much due to the public as to the Navy that an explorer like myself should give some account of his adventures.

Although the book covers so short a period of the North Sea warfare the period is vital in that it embraces the discovery of nearly all our naval shortcomings, and the initiation of the means taken to overcome them. The point of view—that of the spearhead of the British Naval forces—necessarily includes a wide angle of outlook, in which the detail of things must diminish in proportion as they recede from the view-point. But just as one full and intimate picture of the life of one ship for one month would give the reader a more human insight into the Navy than a general survey of the whole Fleet for four years, so the narrative of an eye-witness whose place was for six months on the very point of that bright spearhead should have a value apart from, and supplementary to, the official and technical histories which are being com-

Preface

piled. My aim in this narrative has been to draw as few conclusions myself, and to present as much material from which others may draw them, as is humanly possible.

As the Admiralty in its wisdom has refused[1] me access to documents by which I might verify my facts, the sources from which that material is drawn are limited to (1) my own observation and memory, which are trained for such a purpose; (2) the few notes and records of fact, valueless to an enemy but important to us, that I have been able to preserve; and (3) the published works of officers high in English and German commands. No one but myself is responsible either for my facts or my deductions; but having waited for five years after leaving the Navy and for two years after the end of the war before putting pen to paper, I shall not, I hope, be accused of rushing into print with a hasty or ill-considered record of my impressions.

My book is written primarily for the public and not for the Naval Officer; but I know him well enough to be sure that he, who will best understand the difficulties encountered in writing this book, will most generously forgive its defects. In my brief temporary membership of the " band of brothers " I came to hold the brotherhood as permanent.

Filson Young.

London, *March*, 1921.

---

[1] See Appendix D.

CONTENTS

LIST OF ILLUSTRATIONS

List of Illustrations

List of Illustrations

CHARTS

WITH
THE BATTLE CRUISERS

CHAPTER I

THE YEARS BEFORE

OF the half-great men, or great half-men, of our time, in whom lack of scruple in the pursuit of large ends is held to be a positive virtue, Lord Fisher was probably as near the whole man as any; and this story may as well begin with him, since it was through talking with him that I came in the years before the war to understand where the centres of effort and of resistance ,would be when the hurricane fell upon Europe. No man of our time, with the possible exception of Lord Haldane, has been so inaccurately measured as Lord Fisher; by the Navy, because they saw in his methods a grave disloyalty to certain deeply cherished standards; by the public, because he has been chiefly presented to them by a Press which, according to its spectacles, saw in him either an angel or a villain. He was neither. He was a simple and guileful man, cast in a very unusual mould, of which the only other product I have seen was that minor masterpiece of simplicity and cunning, the late President Kruger. Both were essentially simple men, and the element of greatness in both rested on that. Both were inspired by a profound

B

The Years Before

patriotism—the one for the smallest, the other for the greatest, of modern States; in both the simplicity of character was expressed in a brain convoluted and patterned with the oblique philosophy of the Old Testament; both were strong and fearless, and both were unscrupulous in their methods of attaining great ends. Kruger with his theory of the tortoise putting out its head, Fisher with his obsession (expounded to me on one of the blackest days of the war) of the armadillo attracting the ants—as applied to a battle cruiser in the Atlantic and enemy cruisers—here was the same kind of simple guile, dangerously attractive to the unprofessional, above all to the literary, mind. Both were tried in the test of war, and both had to look for justice beyond the judgment of their contemporaries. Beyond that point it is not worth while here to pursue the comparison; but the few others living who had personal experience of the two men may find it interesting and illuminating.

I fell under the old man's spell on an autumn evening when, arriving at Kilverstone to spend the week-end with him, the car was stopped at the entrance gates by the sturdy, impressive old figure of my host, who haled me forth of the car and had me deep in talk of the Navy before we had reached the house. My chief and lasting impression of that week-end was of a personality passionately inspired with one idea and purpose; a monomaniac, if you will, for whom the universe was one storm cloud; who had no thoughts of peace, or the ends for which war is waged, but only of war itself and the preparation of the British Navy to take the decisive and destructive rôle in that war. This war cloud was then no reality to me, and I marvelled that so strong and able a mind

Lord Fisher

should be so completely obsessed by it. But I learned
to think differently, and, like so many others with whose
temperament such preoccupations were incompatible, to
remember with a shudder the mental indifference that
had made me turn my face from the writing on the wall.
In those long monologues, with their background of
garden pleasaunce or Norfolk stubble, I learned the secret
of this lonely life spent so mysteriously and consistently
in the pursuit of one aim; mysteriously, because though
all his talk was of the sea and sea power, I never could
associate Lord Fisher in my mind with the sea, or think
of him as a sailor, or imagine him on the quarter-deck
or signal bridge. The slow, ponderous personality, utter-
ing itself in aphorisms laboriously quarried from the stuff
of solitary thought; the simple, childlike modesty that
pretended to no knowledge on many a subject apparently
indispensable to his purpose; the equally childlike pride
in and reliance on the results of his own experience,
meditation and original thought; the very winning and
flattering appearance of deference to what one thought
or said oneself—these seemed more in accordance with
the character of a prophet or apostle than of a man of
action. If it was true (as I have heard) that even in his
sea days he was no tactician, and but a poor handler of
a squadron, it was because ships and squadrons were too
small for him; he thought in fleets and in seas, and where
another man might think of firing a salvo he would want
to launch a division. It is characteristic of this large
view that the only charts I ever saw in his room at the
Admiralty were of the smallest available scale to the mile,
and if they did not include an ocean or a sea or two were
of no use to him.

3

The Years Before

He was at that time presiding over the Royal Commission on Oil Fuel, and had evolved, and would expound with pride in conversation, the remarkable theory that England was miraculously favoured by Providence in having no natural supply of oil. The seas were our oil reservoir and oiling station; there were umpteen millions of tons of oil fuel always in transit on the seas; the wireless charts showed the daily position of every tanker; and all the warship had to do in war-time was to intercept the nearest oilship, fill her bunkers and proceed refreshed. It did not at all work out like that in the event; but the theory was characteristic of a mind that foresaw developments with wonderful precision, and in material matters made the right deductions, but often failed to foresee the actual conditions in which the developments would take place. His vision was of the smokeless, funnel-less and therefore practically invisible warship; and though he dated the war with absolute accuracy, he did not foresee that the use of smoke as a screen would be a greater feature in tactical warfare than the absence of it as a tell-tale.

But if there was nothing of the conventional sailor about him, and if he lacked the breezy charm of his arch-detractor, Lord Charles Beresford, there could be no doubt that he was a master of his subject, and for that reason, if for no other, a delight to listen to. Naturally he was obsessed with a sense of the tremendous effort of his own years at the Admiralty, and with doubts as to his successors' worthiness of their heritage. No man who had toiled as he had toiled, and fought as he had fought, could think lightly of the toil or the warfare. Thus his conversation was largely retrospective; things that he had

A Meeting

said, things that he had done, stood out like milestones on the way, and marked for him the history of the modern Navy. I remember his showing me at Kilverstone the bound volumes of his despatches to the Admiralty when he was Commander-in-Chief in the Mediterranean—all printed on foolscap on board ship, and set up by a man specially trained in a graduated system of type-setting, in which the *damns* and other expletives were set in various grades of display type, and in three colours of ink, according to the emphasis required by the context. I don't know what the Board of the time thought of these highly unconventional despatches, but the days of their arrival must have provided their Lordships with some highly entertaining reading. I hope they will be published some day.

At that time Winston Churchill had just entered on his career as First Lord of the Admiralty—a period in which, although it ended in clouds, he rendered his country greater service than he has achieved in any other office. On the few occasions when I saw him then he was always interesting and inspiring on the subject of his trust, and obviously found the handling of it the greatest of his many adventures. And it was through him one day in 1912 that I first met the third and most remarkable of the three men who were to exercise so far-reaching an influence on our naval destinies, and whose actual work in war I was to see so close at hand. We had been discussing some subject, and Winston said: " But the man who can tell you all about that is my Naval Secretary." And opening a door at the end of his room he took me in and introduced me to Admiral Beatty.

I had been accustomed to regard Admirals as very

The Years Before

senior and indeed venerable beings, those whom I had known being mostly of great age, and retired, living amid a kind of property background of spy-glasses, boat-cloaks and sea rime. I was therefore the less prepared for the appearance of the man, young, distinguished-looking indeed, but more with the distinction of Pall Mall than of Plymouth Hoe, who turned to greet me. Youth and high physical training were written all over the figure and shone in the clear eyes; but there was something in the heavy lines of the face (they are heavier to-day) that seemed to contradict the sense of youth, and, like the deep voice, gave an impression of weight and gravity to a personality that I perceived at once to be remarkable. The meeting proved to be one with much of destiny in it for me; and (what is not always true of such moments) I felt and was sure of it at the time. Here was the man for whom, in a dim but persistent way, one had been looking as a sea-leader; here surely was the realization of one's dream of the fighting sailor. It was not until after months of friendly intercourse that I began to know what good ground I had for that intuition, and not until after years of trial that it was to be made clear to the world; but I am glad to think that it was clear to me in that dim room at the Admiralty nine years ago, and that in those years my certainty of it never wavered. I little thought then that I should wear the uniform of his service and stand beside him in battle; but I made up my mind that his was the career to be watched and studied, and his the mind from which one could accept the truth amid the conflicting voices then engaged in debating the essentials of naval supremacy. Here, then, was the ideal type for which Lord Fisher in our conversations had so

6

Naval Divisions

often sighed; and I was secretly disappointed when, on my mentioning Fisher's name, Beatty merely smiled. And I was still more crestfallen when, a few days later, I spoke of Beatty enthusiastically to Lord Fisher, he gave me a blank, sour look and said: "Really? Never met him."

I did not know the Navy as well in those days as I know it now, or I would have been less surprised than I was that the obviously ablest men in control of naval affairs were far from seeing eye to eye with one another, and even (what was more remarkable) neglected to make any real study of one another's aims and potentialities. Naval thought, where it existed, was divided into camps, each one regarding victory over the others as essential to victory over the Germans. Thus Lord Charles Beresford, whose best work in his retirement was his untiring public advocacy of naval efficiency, gave one in private a most alarming impression that the Navy was already practically in German control; and one of his mildest views of Lord Fisher was that he was a madman who, on the eve of war, had deliberately scrapped the majority of our cruisers. Winston Churchill was at one time probably one of the men most disliked by the Navy at large; but when one tried to discuss his administration seriously, one was told stories of his bad manners: as, for example, of his going on board a ship, entering the ward-room, ringing the bell and sending for the Commander —a solecism the gravity of which one must have lived in a wardroom to appreciate. And yet, one felt, it was not quite an argument against his efficiency as an administrator. But all the naval officer saw was a man to whose power our sacred naval traditions were com-

The Years Before

mitted, and who apparently knew or cared so little for
the smallest of them that the greatest might well be in
peril at his hands. The anti-Churchill camp was a very
strong one. He, on the other hand, seemed to regard
Lord Fisher as a dangerous genius to be caught, chained,
tamed, and made careful use of; Lord Fisher regarded
him (I am speaking of the two years before the war) as
a politician to be fought or flattered, made or destroyed,
according to his degree of adaptability to the great
purpose. Sir Percy Scott was regarded either as the
fountain of truth or as a self-advertising madman.
All of them regarded the principal non-official students
of naval affairs as tiresome meddlers in a scheme of things
that they could not be expected to understand; if they
could be enlisted in any particular camp, well and good;
otherwise they were dismissed with lofty contempt. Mr.
Arthur Pollen was looked upon, not as a student and
inventor who had proved his value to a Navy that should
know how to use him, but as a man who was disappointed
because some of his inventions (the principle of which
was hastily adopted when experience confirmed his foresight) were not employed. All of his criticisms were
supposed to be inspired by bitterness—a most childish
and costly mistake. Commander Bellairs was merely a
naval partisan. J. L. Garvin, whom personally I found
the wisest and most inspiring, as well as the best informed,
of all, was regarded as a tragic crier of "Wolf!"
Viscount Curzon was supposed to be trying to make a
name for himself by mischievous questions in the House;
he also has been abundantly justified. H. W. Wilson,
who is probably one of the best informed men in
England on naval development over the whole world,

The New Command

was regarded (because he had once been author of a
standard work called "Ironclads in Action") either as
a naval expert on the period of the Flood or of Tarshish,
or, because he wrote in the *Daily Mail*, as a dangerous
young chip of that scarcely older block that could never
be relied upon to keep its heavy guns trained on one naval
camp at a time. Yet all these laymen were far more
right than the professionals in power.

But the mark of Lord Fisher was, for good or ill,
stamped on the material of the Navy; the *Lion*, the
latest development of his maxim, "Speed is armour,"
had lately been commissioned, and was at the head
of the new Battle Cruiser Squadron; Admiral Jellicoe,
the predestined commander of Lord Fisher's choice,
had for years been preparing and fashioning at the
Admiralty the weapon which he would have to wield
in war. The high commands were all more or less
settled, with the exception of the Battle Cruiser
Squadron, the formation of which had just been completed by Sir Lewis Bayley, its first admiral. It is
to Winston Churchill's credit that, in spite of murmurings
and heart-burnings, he handed this magnificent arm, the
super-cavalry of the sea, to the youngest admiral on the
list (the last to be entitled to it by the laws of seniority)
because he believed that Beatty was the man who would
use it best. And it is interesting to note that of the
three great naval reputations made in the war—those of
Beatty, Tyrwhitt and Keyes—none of them was a Fisher
man, or indeed belonged to any camp; all had passed
bad examinations and done as little office work as possible,
and none was predestined or trained by the Admiralty
for the work he was to do. And it is proof of the lament-

The Years Before

able fact that the Admiralty was too deeply absorbed in administering the Navy to think of preparing it for fighting, that when Beatty took the Battle Cruiser Squadron to sea in the spring of 1913 for training, he found that there were no instructions from the Admiralty as to what it was to be trained for, no policy formed as to the nature of its employment in the Fleet. No one had thought of that, and Sir Lewis Bayley's period of command was too short to permit of his remedying the defect.

There could be no clearer example of the deplorable lack of a Staff, a mere thinking department, to think out even the general lines on which the weapons so laboriously prepared were to be used. The weapons were there, in a high state of edge and polish, thanks largely to Lord Fisher and to the stuff and spirit of the Navy itself; but the most formidable weapon of all, the collective, co-ordinating brain, was simply not in existence. Brains were at a discount both in the Navy and the Admiralty, as they are in every organization of our national life; officers who made any real study of war from the point of view of Staff work were regarded as cranks or lunatics, hunters of soft jobs; and the gin-and-bitters school were quite content to be left to the guidance of their splendid but not always highly trained instincts. As it had been at the beginning, so it would be now; only let us sight the enemy, and the rest would follow. There was no Staff organization to think out and prepare the gallant men for the set of facts with which they would be confronted, or to warn them that "sighting the enemy" would be a privilege reserved for very few of them, and that the main part of their work

The Lack of a Staff

would have to be done far out of sight of an enemy. For the individual officer, discovering or fearing some defect in design of the weapon, there was no untrammelled technical Staff to whom his criticism could be immediately referred and dispassionately investigated. If he was not shut up by his immediate senior, if he risked ridicule or unpopularity, there was nothing for it but a laborious thrusting up of his ideas through one superincumbent rank after another until they emerged at the top to receive the frigid snub which it is the pride of the Permanent Official at all times to administer, and which the Mandarin known as the Secretary of the Admiralty had brought to a kind of desolate perfection. Thousands of the best men that England ever produced perished in the North Sea uselessly and needlessly because the Admiralty in 1914 had not grasped the simple truth that there is no weapon in the world which is not the more deadly for having brains behind it. But to talk of " brains " in all but a small section of the Navy was, I really believe, considered indelicate; the word smacked of the slaughter-house rather than of the battlefield; and Intelligence was regarded as a thing to be put in pigeon-holes rather than as a spirit informing the minds of men.

I will give one example of this total lack of foresight as to war conditions, because I was the means of getting it definitely and officially demonstrated at the time. It was the custom of the Admiralty, when the Fleet was mobilized for manoeuvres, to invite certain newspapers to send representatives as guests, one to each of a dozen or so picked ships, and to give these guests a week of voyaging and entertainment before the actual manoeuvres began. It had formerly been the practice to take some of them on the actual manœuvres, but the Silence and Secrecy policy (which hid from criticism the defective design of our turrets, that lost us the *Queen Mary* and other ships, after it had become known to the Germans) stopped at that. I had been one such guest on board the *Agamemnon* in 1912, with Captain (now Rear-Admiral) Hayes-Sadler, and a very delightful visit I had; but I saw enough to realize the futility, if not the danger, of this method of advertising the Navy through men whose knowledge of its affairs was often of the slightest or altogether non-existent, and from whom in consequence it was necessary that everything of a confidential nature should be concealed; and also of the inevitable danger that would arise in war-time if there was no organization for the intelligent distribution of information. I expressed these views to Beatty one day, and suggested that a kind of corps of naval war-correspondents should be formed, of men whose character and discretion could be trusted, who could go on manœuvres for purposes of study instead of publicity, and who in actual war could take their place in the Fleet so that the traditions of the Navy (which would be a poor heritage to-day if they had depended on official records) might be handed on enriched by the narratives of trained eye-witnesses, and published, if necessary, not until the close of hostilities.

But Beatty, who in some matters is as conservative and conventional as in others he is original, shook his head. The idea of anything like organized publicity was obviously against all his instincts and training. The Admiralty would never stand it, the Navy would never stand it. (I was to hear the same arguments three years

The Press and War

later from Lord Fisher, within six months of the Admiralty launching on a perfect orgy of, I am bound to say, extremely amateurish Press advertisement.) Everything would take place in the most impenetrable secrecy; the North Sea would be closed, and the very mouths of the fishes, I supposed, sealed. Still, as I was so persistent, he suggested that I should put my views in the form of a letter, which he promised would at least be considered by the Board.

The letter was written, and I suppose exists somewhere in the Admiralty archives. The tenor of it was that in a European war the Press would be an element the force of which no one could calculate beforehand, but which would probably be greater than any other unorganized power in the country; that the Press would have news, somehow or other, and that no official organization could prevent it if it had public opinion behind it; that if it were forced to piratical and unauthorized efforts to get news, the effects might be disastrous; and that the advantage of having trained and trustworthy persons to describe such technical matters as naval actions would be considerable; and that the way to train them was to recognize their status beforehand, and both educate and test them by allowing them to go to sea on manœuvres in war conditions.

This letter was circulated at the Admiralty and the suggestion in it unanimously turned down. Winston Churchill himself told me it was impossible, that I did not realize the extent to which the Fleet would be enveloped in secrecy; that the confidential knowledge involved would be so vital that *no one* could be trusted. I told him that the secrecy could never be preserved for

The Years Before

more than a short time, and that people would have to be trusted. We both lived to hear the movements of the Fleet discussed at Mayfair luncheon tables before the orders had reached the bases, and to see Scapa Flow and the Firth of Forth turned into a kind of holiday rendezvous for hurrah-parties of people whom any of our many Departments had an interest in pleasing.

But on the whole the two years before the war were an interesting and stirring time in the world of naval affairs, and looking back on them, I seem to remember very little except my increasing interest in that world as I found it expressed in these three men—Fisher, Churchill and Beatty. Lord Fisher, except on the rare occasions when one met him in society, which he generally avoided, I almost always saw alone, and my intercourse with him was rather like that of a pilgrim who should visit an idol in a shrine, or an oracle whom he desired to consult. He wrote some interesting and characteristic letters, which I am sorry I have not kept; but our correspondence chiefly took the form of an interchange of Biblical texts, especially those having reference to Smiting, or Coming Swiftly from Behind, or the ruthless and remorseless dealings of Jahveh with his enemies, or the disagreeable things that happened to people who were not found Watching. But with the other two, my contemporaries, intercourse was on more level and less exacting terms, and through the Beattys I came into contact with some of the more advanced school of naval men—captains well up on the list, but young for their seniority, and generally regarded as being in the running, who combined devotion to the Navy as it had been with a desire to make it something better. One of these was Captain Osmond de B.

One of Lord Fisher's Postscripts.

Captain Brock

Brock,[1] more conveniently known as O. de B.—who was destined to rise on the war-wave to a position corresponding to his abilities, as so many junior men, alas! were not. He was and is a singular contrast, or rather complement, to his chief, and undoubtedly proved a great strength to him in administrative tasks. Where Beatty was vehement, Brock was quiet; where one struck sparks, the other could blow up the fire; where one was instinctively right, the other could discover why. At once a profound student and practical master of tactics, he filled many gaps that were inevitable in the training of one whose career had been a series of forward dashes with a *minimum* experience of paper lore and the tiresome methods of offices; and he always provided the solid background of loyal support and cool patience so essential to the finely-tempered nature that is inclined to break its heart if things glaringly necessary cannot be done or obtained out of hand. O. de B. was a great reader, and had the sense to recreate his mind, when it was not professionally occupied, with things that are greater even than the British Navy; and his cabin had always the refreshing peculiarity of being like a branch of Mudie's Library. One met other officers of Beatty's future staff at Brooksby in those days, and I remember one night, when Winston Churchill was also there, a great discussion raging on a question of gunnery tactics—I think the point at issue was the masking of gunfire involved in a certain turning movement. The chief protagonists were Reginald Plunkett,[2] Beatty's Staff-Commander, the Admiral, and the First Lord. Argument soon waxed

[1] Now Rear-Admiral Sir Osmond de B. Brock, K.C.B., K.C.V.O., etc.
[2] Now Captain the Hon. A. R. Plunkett-Ernle-Erle-Drax, D.S.O.

The Years Before

hot; sheets of paper and matches were requisitioned, and the discussion reached a point (not uncommon in naval discussions) when the junior had to admit that the First Lord could not be wrong, while secretly convinced that he was incapable of being right. I asked Winston about it the next morning. "Of course I was right," he said, "but these are things that the average naval mind" (Oh, Plunkett!) "cannot grasp." I asked Plunkett. He said, "I am afraid you could hardly expect Winston to grasp a fact which, however elementary, does make a faint demand on common sense." I asked the Admiral. He said they were both wrong. And there, for the time, my study of naval tactics ceased.

On March 1, 1918, Rear-Admiral Beatty hoisted his flag in H.M.S. *Lion*. The ceremony of taking over a command is, where a ship is lying in a dock-yard, one of the least impressive in the world, whatever its inner significance may be. A gentleman in mufti gets out of a cab, picks his way across the dock-yard lumber to the brow joining the jetty with the ship, and with a salute to the quarter-deck, disappears below. A little later an officer in admiral's undress uniform stands, with the ship's company at attention, while the white cross of Saint George slowly ascends the foremast; there are a few papers to be signed, a brief chat in the wardroom, and a gentleman in mufti goes ashore and catches the train back to London. But the Navy is never wrong about its ceremonies. When splendour is required it can be provided in more true magnificence than in any other environment; but in the ceremonies that have to do with the endless routine, the

A Naval Occasion

passing of responsibility from one hand to another, that are but a moment in a working day, and herald a task that has yet to be done, everything but what is necessary for dignity is omitted. The frills and cheers are reserved for achievement; and an occasion like this depends for its impressiveness on the hidden possibilities that lie in it and the destiny that may await what is so quietly begun.

CHAPTER II

THE BATTLE CRUISERS

TOWARDS the end of May, 1918, I received an invitation from Admiral Beatty to spend a few days with him on board the *Lion*, then in Cromarty Firth; and on the last night of the month, at the end of a busy London day, I was speeding northward on a journey that was afterwards to become very familiar—Edinburgh, Aviemore, Inverness, Dingwall, and then the Admiral's coxswain on the platform at Invergordon, the walk down to the water, the trim blue steam-barge, and the dash down the waters of the firth to where the five great battle cruisers, *Lion*, *Princess Royal*, *Invincible*, *Indefatigable* and *Indomitable*, lay like leviathans basking in the afternoon sunshine. And for the first time, little knowing what the future held, I came up the gangway and saluted the *Lion's* now historic quarter-deck, and was taken below to the Admiral's quarters. These, in battle cruisers of this type, are extensive, and the chintz, the fine engravings, the old furniture, enlivened by flowers and books, looked very homely and charming in the heart of this steel citadel.

It is hard to realize that they were once as unfamiliar to me as they are to the reader, that every detail was a thing of curiosity and interest, and every incident a practically new experience. An admiral and his staff,

An Invitation

although so closely identified with the flagship, have in fact nothing to do with it as a unit; they are merely guests on board, have their own quarters, live their separate life, eat their separate food, and are waited upon by their own servants. The only real link between them and the ship is the captain, who is also a member of the admiral's staff; but even there the connexion is often a slight and merely social one, and when he leaves the admiral's cabin and enters his own quarters, he turns to a duty entirely separate, in which he is supreme—the command of the flagship and its whole complex life. This is a life of many departments, and the more familiar you become with it the more elaborate and complex does it appear. Thus a ship, although technically a unit, is humanly an aggregation of small communities or states, each with its own laws, its separate customs, its particular duties. The wardroom is another world of its own, into which neither the captain nor the admiral any more than the lowest rating in the ship would dream of entering without invitation or permission. And so with the gun-room, that strange school of adolescence and command, the warrant officers' messes, the great bureaucratic world of the petty officers, the democracy of the mess decks, and so on. All this was not so familiar to me in May, 1918, but that it added a spice of interest to a situation sufficiently agreeable and memorable in a quiet life; so after I had been made welcome in the wardroom and paid my respects to Captain Chatfield and the Commander, I made the inevitable round of the ship and traversed the streets of that steel town with the mingled fascination and bewilderment that are inseparable from a preliminary survey of even the least complex

The Battle Cruisers

of warships. A walk with the Admiral, a small dinner party which included Captains Chatfield, Brock, Sowerby, Seymour and Kennedy, followed by a cheerful rag in the wardroom, finished the day, and I went to bed in an august apartment on the port side of the ship known as the Admiral's spare cabin, the counterpart of his own on the starboard side. And not through the small round scuttle associated with the sea cabin, but through generous window spaces open to the violet sky, the salt and scented airs of that unforgotten summer night flowed in upon me.

The next few days were spent at sea exercising the squadron in its manifold duties of day and night firing, signalling, and manœuvring ; and it was possible to study the process of welding together into one coherence all the diversity and variety, both human and material, comprised in five such ships with their captains, officers, and complements. For every ship has its own character and individuality ; the greater its efficiency, the more definite is its character. Externally almost indistinguishable by a layman, three ships less alike in character could hardly be found than the *Lion, Queen Mary* and *Princess Royal ;* and during the war, and as the years advanced, the differences grew more definite, even while the invisible unity that bound them to one another was strengthened. Just consider. Each of these ships, containing innumerable complete weapons, was in itself a complete weapon of war, by whose condition and efficiency the captain of each was to be judged. It was the Admiral's task, and the object of these exercises, to combine these five great weapons into one further and greater weapon, namely, the Battle Cruiser Squadron, which in its turn was to be

Admiral Beatty on the Bridge (1913).

combined with the greatest ever wielded by human power —the Fleet. And Beatty's task at that time was rendered easier (for an unacademic sailor like him) in that the duties of a battle cruiser squadron at sea had in no wise been laid down either by the Admiralty or the Commander-in-Chief. There was, indeed, a definite school of naval opinion which held that battle cruisers were of no use at all. It was thus left to its commander to invent duties for it, as well as train and exercise it in the performance of them. All of which had been the subject of much silent thought and study on Beatty's part during the preceding year, and when the squadron was handed over to him he had but to put into practice certain definite principles that he had arrived at and to devise, in consultation with his captains, methods of training which should apply these principles to North Sea warfare. As laid down by Beatty, they were of the simplest kind. The main uses of battle cruisers were twofold : to provide on occasion an independent scouting force, and to act as a provocative or decoying force to engage the enemy's heavy ships and, by the use of superior speed, bring them within reach of the main Fleet and so force them to action. In war generally, apart from actual battle, their functions would be fourfold :

(a) Reconnaissance with fast light cruisers on the enemy's coast at high speed,[1]

(b) Supporting a blockading force or a patrol of armed cruisers,

(c) Forming supports between such a force and the Battle Fleet when cruising,

---

[1] The Germans used their battle cruisers effectively in this way in their "tip-and-run" raids on our coast towns.

The Battle Cruisers

(d) Forming supports to a cruiser force watching an enemy's fleet at sea,

while in a general action they would form a fast division of the Battle Fleet, probably on its flank. The soundness of this conception was to be proved in the course of a year or two, although in the early days of the war this absolutely indispensable arm of the battle cruisers was used for far different purposes, and its very existence risked by employment on duties that should have been performed by smaller ships which the Admiralty, in the absence of a Staff to think and foresee, had failed to provide.

In the private record of those days I find notes of a talk we had, during a long walk ashore, on this subject of training for war. To practise firing at high speeds;[1] to cut down expensive deadweight to the last possible degree (such as torpedo-nettings and the vast supplies of salt provisions, based on the requirements of days before steam and of long ocean voyages, which even during the first part of the war ships were required to carry); to substitute offensive material such as coal, oil and ammunition; to eliminate the elaborate signalling of orders—it is not so long ago since the signal " On boots " was made, as an " evolution," from the flagship to the whole Fleet —and put independent and co-ordinated responsibility in its place; in a word, to restore and stimulate initiative, which Admiralty policy had steadily discouraged; and, most revolutionary of all, to insist upon leave being given

---

[1] This, owing to a penny-wise stinginess in the provision of ammunition for practice, was never done, and our fleet went into war having never fired its big guns at anything faster than a target towed at six knots. Even that was a recent innovation on a target firmly anchored so that it *could not* get away.

The Fighting Spirit

and taken on every opportunity, instead of being doled out, like a dangerous drug, in homœopathic doses. Beatty's policy was to work his people hard while they were at work, and chase them off to recreate and enlarge their minds when work was over. All of which is commonplace now, but it was highly unorthodox then.

One other thing which became apparent to me in those wonderful days of sea breeze and nights of study and talk in the North Sea was the spirit that underlay all the work and study and discussion. It pervaded all exercises and manœuvres, and spoke in every line of the Admiral's brief memoranda to his captains. The principle which embodied it was that the coherent action of the squadron should be (if one may use the term) automatic; that if the principles governing its employment in war were thoroughly grasped, then, in the event of certain things happening, the action to be taken followed logically and should not have to be a matter of signals and orders. And there was never any doubt in the Admiral's mind as to what was to be done with the enemy. Beatty's strategy and tactics, given the superiority of force which would enable him, and not the enemy, to select the battle ground, might each be summed up in a sentence : one, To get at the enemy; the other : To destroy him or lead him to destruction. No other considerations would lightly be allowed to qualify these ends ; and to attain them no risk was too fine, no cost too great, even the cost of annihilation to oneself. These principles are really the key to Beatty's career as a commander at sea, and every action of his, tested by and examined in the light of them, will be found clear and consistent. They are the principles, profound as instincts, of every

The Battle Cruisers

man with a natural gift for organized fighting. I mention them thus early because he was already labouring (as I think he never ceased to labour throughout the war) to instil into his people that, roughly, in the situation in which we should be, it could never be wrong to go for the enemy when you saw him, and that if this principle were thoroughly grasped the details of tactical action would be reduced to great simplicity, should never be a matter of doubt, and therefore need not be the subject of elaborate orders and signals. The lesson was at once too great and too simple to be universally apprehended; here and there someone failed him, now from too much thinking, now from too little. Beatty's ideal squadron would have turned and manœuvred and fought like one man, without a word from the flagship; and once it had got its teeth in an enemy it would never have let go so long as one of them remained above the water. Of course he never achieved his ideal, but there were moments when he came very near it, and probably he was never so near it as on the great day that covered the battle cruiser Fleet with glory, and robbed it of some of its best and finest elements.

We came home majestically down the east coast, putting in for a night to the Firth of Forth, where in the opalescence of a dead calm summer morning I watched from the bridge of the *Lion* the squadron turning together sixteen points after weighing; and the low-lying mist, shot with the colours of the sunrise, hid the calm water and made sea and sky into one glory, so that the ships were manœuvring as though on the floor of heaven. And in that unimaginable splendour we passed down what was to be our historic war-beat, from Inchkeith to May

Speed or Armour?

Island, round the corner of St. Abb's Head where a certain manœuvre was to be tried for the first time in the history of naval warfare.

The main characteristics of the battle cruisers, apart from their size and powerful armament, was speed. The extra displacement, or weight, which was used in battle-ships to provide heavier armour and an extra pair of big guns, was in the battle cruisers devoted to boilers, bunkers and engine-room. One of Lord Fisher's aphorisms was that "speed is armour," and the main difference between our battle cruisers and the Germans' was that the Germans sacrificed a little speed to greater armour protection. Our battle cruisers were supposed to be the embodiment of the "speed is armour" theory; and I think that when they came to be proved, they were found to be defective only, but exactly, to the extent to which that dangerous aphorism applied. The thinness of their armour was a practical disadvantage on several occasions, as we shall see, and the knot or two in speed in which we were superior could be secured in other ways. The greater hitting power of our guns, if the ammunition was sound,[1] could be relied on to reduce the speed of an equally fast fleet less heavily armed. We never really caught up with the German battle cruisers when they were running away from us at full speed. It takes a long time, and a huge distance has to be covered, if a ship going at high speed is to be overtaken by a slightly faster one of which she has the start. In the case of a ship steaming at 24 knots, having a 20-mile start of a ship steaming at 26 knots, it would take just five hours, and 180 knots would have to be covered in

[1] Which it was not.

The Battle Cruisers

a stern chase, before the twenty miles were reduced to ten—the beginning of effective gunnery range. And the North Sea did not, in fact, prove big enough for the faster ships to secure their theoretical advantage. The difference was not great enough; but the armour protection which had been sacrificed to secure it made in several cases the difference to the Germans between being sunk and getting home.

It was the speed that was the really untried element in manoeuvres with ships of such a size. The fastest squadron of the battle cruisers was at the most capable of 28 knots; and although the four "cats" (*Lion, Tiger, Queen Mary* and *Princess Royal*) all claimed to have exceeded 80 knots at some time or other, I am doubtful whether any of them, with the possible exception of *Tiger*, ever attained that speed. But 28 knots, for a ship of the vast dimensions of these, was, of course, an entirely new element in naval tactics; no one had any experience of how it would work out; and the manoeuvres of destroyers (practically the only craft that had ever attained a similar speed in the water) gave no idea whatever of the effect of speed in a squadron of these enormous ships. Therefore, great was the interest which attached on this June day in 1918 to a manoeuvre involving a meeting of battle cruisers at these unprecedented speeds on opposite courses. The *Indomitable* had been sent off in advance to a point a hundred miles out in the North Sea whence she was to return at full speed towards the English coast, the other battle cruisers meanwhile spreading in order to locate her and bring her to action. Steam for four-fifths speed had been ordered in the whole squadron, which then scattered and searched the sea for

A Striking Experience

their objective. The dark smudge of smoke on the horizon, which is the first visual intimation of friend or enemy alike, was located; the squadron formed into line ahead and stormed through the smooth waters towards the *Indomitable*. The organization which controls the firing of the guns was kept busy, for, although the guns were not fired, the whole intricate routine by which the ranges and bearings, telephoned constantly down to the transmitting station in the bowels of the ship, are worked out and signalled up to the turrets in terms of opening or closing ranges, was gone through. Never before had the crews of heavy guns had such an experience; for the speed at which we and the *Indomitable* were steaming towards each other gave a closing rate of something approaching a mile a minute, and the distance of fifteen miles, at which the enemy was first sighted, was demolished in seventeen minutes, after which the exercise was over. The impression of speed, apart from our own hustling rush through the water, was chiefly conveyed by a sense of the rapidity with which the target grew in bulk, and from being a blot of smoke visible only through powerful glasses gradually took the form of a ship, visible to the naked eye, increasing in size with every second. It was a very striking experience, and although it seems a small thing in the telling, the lessons learned in that short manœuvre were many and far reaching and gave food to the keen professional technician for many a day after. We then continued for eighteen hours at the same speed—an engine-room test out of which I remember that the *Invincible*, the slowest ship of the squadron, came with honours, being visible, although far astern, when the manœuvre finished the next morning. At a

The Battle Cruisers

more moderate and economic speed we jogged southward
through the summer afternoon, turned the corner of
England somewhere in the dark hours, and dropped
anchor at Portland next afternoon.

This, then, was my introduction to the battle cruisers.
Brief though it was, it was made in such favourable and
intimate conditions that to anyone interested as I was
in the sea science in which they were so important an
element, it was enough to give a general insight into the
complex nature of that science and the tremendous issues
attendant upon the degree in which it was mastered by
those who would have to use it in war. And, side by
side with the technical things that I had learned, there
remained an impression of a vital human organization, of
splendid human material, and of a spirit of fellowship
and enthusiasm which is the pre-eminent characteristic,
from an outsider's point of view, of the whole British
Navy. With these impressions also, as I returned
through the lush Hampshire landscape (already strange
after even so short a sojourn on the blue floors of the
sea) there was, and remains to this day, a memory of
wonderful things seen on land and sea in the summer
of the far North, where about the firths and headlands
our five giants had played and manœuvred in midnights
that were almost as bright as day, where the glory of
the stars and the undying glow in the sky made even
the lighthouses, with which those wild coasts are jewelled,
seem dim and ineffectual. It was to be different when
I saw them next, when in the black darkness of howling
winter nights we glided out through the " gate " at
Cromarty on our grim quest. Then the lighthouses were

The Lightkeepers

quenched, or only showed a feeble glimmer at a pre-arranged hour to guide us out or in. How one longed then for the suns and stars that had wheeled and blinked at us through the golden June nights, and how often one thought, sometimes with envy, of the lightkeeper sitting beside his shaded lamp as we rushed by to the unknown. Few people who live inland think enough of the work of these men who are, nevertheless, of all silent, invisible, unobtrusive servants in the sea service the most deserving of occasional remembrance and tribute. Those engaged on shore stations live with their families the life of a man, but those who keep watch in lonely towers on rock stations or remote islands live like no other men; their house is in the air, founded on a rock, with the sea all round it; but they have neither the liberty of the air, the variety of the earth, nor the freedom of the sea. They are prisoners of all three elements. In monastic groups of three, cut off from all the world for weeks at a time, silent, liverish, irritable, exact, patient, conscientious and responsible, they perform their monotonous but glorious duties with a precision and efficiency unexcelled in any other service.

Where I am writing this it is far from the sea, but the night is bleak and the wind is rising as though to salute the passing of an angry year with a desolate curse. To-night, as every night, England sleeps in a glory, ringed with a crown of stars of these men's kindling. From the Wolf to Skerryvore, from Stroma to Fair Isle, from the Bell to the Eddystone, they will see the New Year come in between two flashes of their mirrored lights, between two thunderclaps of bursting seas, between two shouts of the gale. And every night someone,

The Battle Cruisers

delivered from the weariness of the sea, is coming home to his roof and fire because of them. Ever since those starry nights at Cromarty and the starless ones in the winter of the year that followed, when the wind keeps me awake at night I think of them sitting each beside his star, and am grateful.

CHAPTER III

BREAKING INTO THE NAVY

THIS book is not a history of the Naval War, and therefore no description will be attempted of Winston Churchill's great *coup*, the Test Mobilization, so happily timed that at the declaration of war the Navy was found completely manned and equipped, and at a single word was scattered to its far-flung stations. I was not there, and knew only what the world knew—that the Fleet had vanished and that no word of its whereabouts or doings would be vouchsafed. I saw Winston Churchill in the first few days, and was told by him, very kindly but quite convincingly, of the absolute impossibility of my being with the Fleet in any capacity whatsoever. He was good enough to say that if anyone had been allowed to be a recorder in the interests of history, I should be allowed; but that it was the one thing which was just as impossible as anything could be in a world of impossibilities.

This was in the days when even the Army did not want volunteer officers, while the Navy treated the idea with ridicule. One's great preoccupation was to get to the war, in any capacity whatsoever wherein one might be of use; and I spent six strange weeks deeply involved with the affairs of a voluntary hospital which I helped to organize, and at St. Nazaire saw the firstfruits of the

Breaking into the Navy

great retreat and of the battle of the Marne in the shape of train-load after train-load of wounded and dying men. One's duties were anything, from forcing hospital supplies out of unwilling depôts and chasing the Commander-in-Chief half across France to ask the impossible, to giving anæsthetics at major operations and helping to bury people. Even that had its lively interest; but the rush passed and left us idle there, far from the war, far from England, amid the stagnant intrigues of a remote base. I could not stand it. If I was to be useless, I had better be at home; and accordingly I returned, in October, 1914, to a London that seemed even less concerned with war than St. Nazaire had been. To know anything one had to go out to lunch, and I am bound to say that at such houses as the late Lady Paget's and Mrs. J. J. Astor's the information was generally up to date and accurate. The well-fed oracle from the War Office, carefully waiting until the servants had left the room, with a peach and a glass of port before him and his, "Well, I can soon tell the little I know," remains a type of those days. He would be so deep in the imparting of his information that the return of the domestics with the coffee and cigarettes was never allowed to interrupt it. Strange little scenes are etched on the memory. Lady Cunard giving a detached but admiring Mr. Balfour her advice on Russia; Lady Beresford's views on Lord Fisher; those indefatigable lunchers, Sir John Cowans and Colonel Repington, analysing a G.H.Q. battle—such things were interesting once or twice, but soon palled.

I was suffering from a home-sickness for my friends in the Navy. I wanted nothing better than to be with them and to share whatever might befall them. This was no military zeal—it was just inclination. The muddy glories of the battlefield repelled rather than drew me; for, whatever I may be, I am no soldier. It was only because all my friends were at war that I wanted to be at war too; and amid scenes in London that had formerly been so congenial to me my spirit became more and more an alien. I did not trust the women who seemed to be running the war at home, and when a great lady, at whose table the possibility of a successor to Lord French was being discussed, and someone had mentioned the name of Douglas Haig, announced with a formidable concentration of purpose, " *Never*, if *I* can prevent it," I felt it was time to quit those scenes.

I had written to Sir David Beatty after the affair of the Heligoland Bight, and had received a very cheery letter from him in which it appeared that in spite of wrestling with the Admiralty he was heartily enjoying himself. This increased my longing for the clean spaces of the sea, but it was a letter from Lady Beatty, in reply to one I had written her expressing something of such longing, that sowed in my mind the daring idea of attempting the impossible. Why didn't I go and join him, she said. She was sure he would like to have me; and So-and-so, who knew far less of sea affairs than I did, had just joined the Grand Fleet with an R.N.V.R. commission. I immediately journeyed to the Crystal Palace and saw Commodore Williams-Bulkeley; he was kindness itself, and put my name seventy-fourth on the list of those waiting for an R.N.V.R. commission. He said he did not think any more would be required at present. I wrote again to Sir David Beatty, asking him

D

if he could do anything. He replied: "I will help you all I can, but where I am I am powerless. You must tackle someone on the spot. Surely you could manage an R.N.V.R. commission if you went the right way about it; and if you were sent to the battle cruisers we would find a place for you somewhere." A few days before Lord Fisher had been called to the Admiralty as First Sea Lord, and on a mere friendly impulse I had written him a line of congratulation and good wishes. At that moment came a reply in his well-known angular hand: "I am exceeding busy scrapping parasites. Come and see me. I will try and find a spot for you."

The infection of unscrupulousness was already upon me. From that moment I began to scheme as to how these two perfectly innocent and good-natured utterances could be combined to procure a passport for me into the forbidden land. In a letter from which I have just quoted Beatty wrote, *à propos* of Lord Fisher's appointment: "He is the best man for the job, but I wish he were ten years younger. He is the man for you to tackle to get you a job afloat." And so I tackled him.

I employed the old and very simple trick of the man who comes to you and says that he has a promise of work in Canada if you will give him ten pounds for his passage, and writes to an employer in Canada that there is somebody who will pay his passage if he will provide him with a job. I went to Lord Fisher, but he was deep in an Admiralty Board meeting, and I could not see him. Captain Tom Crease, his henchman there, said, "You may as well tell me what it is you want, as I shall be the one who will have to do it."

I told him that I wanted a commission as lieutenant

Ritz Hotel.
Piccadilly.
London. W.

TELEGRAPHIC ADDRESS
RITZOTEL-LONDON

My dear Tibor Yag

Heaven Bless You —

Forgive me!

I'm *exceeding* busy!

I'm "Scrapping" parasites!

Facsimile letter from Lord Fisher. (1)

I Break In

R.N.V.R., as Beatty said he wanted me. Slightly over-stating the case, you see, but not enough to cause my statement to be repudiated by its author. I was immediately given a note embodying this request, and told to take it to the Admiral Commanding Reserves, in Victoria Street. After being kept waiting three-quarters of an hour, I told the Admiral's clerk that I must now return to the First Sea Lord and explain that the Admiral was too busy to read· his letter. Slight over-statement again, you observe. I was instantly ushered in to the Admiral, who looked hostile and asked what I wanted. I said I wanted nothing, but that I believed the First Sea Lord wanted something which was set forth in the letter I had brought. He said there were great difficulties in the way of my being given a commission; that I ought to have done this, and that, and the other thing. I said it was a matter of indifference to me (slight over-statement again), but that if he wished I would return and tell the First Sea Lord what he had said; upon which the over-driven man gave me an ill look and said that he would see what could be done. My commission arrived by special messenger on the evening of the next day.

Here was success beyond my dreams, but it behoved me still to walk warily. I had not yet got an appointment, and appointments I knew to be one of the most jealously guarded of Admiralty privileges. I was now in their Lordships' power, and might be ordered anywhere. But I remembered another sentence in Beatty's letter which said, "If you are in any difficulty, go to Dennis Larking at the Admiralty." Dennis Larking and I had often met at Brooksby and Hanover Lodge, but I did not know that on the outbreak of war he had been appointed to an Admiralty post which involved the carrying out of the Second Sea Lord's intentions with regard to appointments. After a brief visit to my tailor, therefore, I went and saw Commander Larking. Like every other innocent victim of my sharp practice (excepting the Victoria Street Admiral), he was delighted to help. What did I want? I told him—again stretching a point —that David Beatty was good enough to let me go and join him; that I had been given a commission for that purpose (it was in the *Gazette* that morning), and that I wanted to get off as soon as possible to join him. Now the personnel of an admiral's staff is laid down by regulations; it cannot be increased except by special Admiralty Order, and the war was as yet far too young for emergency conditions to be at all recognized or to make it possible for one admiral to have a larger staff than any other of his rank. Commander Larking could not appoint me to Sir David Beatty's staff, but what he could do, and did with great ingenuity on the instant devise, was to have me appointed to *Lion* on Special Service. What I did when I got there was to be my affair and the Admiral's—to say nothing of the Captain's; but it was enough for me. I was told that I should be attached to the staff, and had better take an aiguillette with me—little guessing at the time how helpful that golden adornment to one's breast would be in defining an indefinite position. I departed and gave an additional order to my tailor, and then went home rejoicing, but rather alarmed by what I had done and by the comparative ease in which great crimes can be accomplished by a cool and unscrupulous hand. " Silence and secrecy," said I to myself, and kept very carefully away from the

I've just told Garvin that War is "Great Conception" and "Quick Decision" Think in Oceans! and Shoot at Sight! yours Fisher

Facsimile letter from Lord Fisher.   (2)

Special Service

Admiralty, and especially from Winston Churchill, for the next few days, and lay very low indeed. I did not feel anything like safe until my warrant was exchanged for a ticket to Invergordon by the booking-clerk at Euston.

The ways of secrecy are strange. It was a serious offence to give away the position or station of any ship in the Fleet. I was not allowed to tell my mother where I was going, but every booking-clerk was quite gratuitously informed on every warrant the base of the ship which the warrant-holder was travelling to join. And they used to wonder how these things got about!

I was duly gazetted to the *Lion* for " special service," the date being November 9, 1914. A great many people wondered—they have since wondered, and are still wondering—what the " special service " was for which I was appointed. I did not know, and I am very sure nobody else knew either. I have heard it variously explained. Because I ultimately produced a camera with a telephoto lens and used it, in spite of an Admiralty Order to the effect that all cameras had to be surrendered to the captains of ships, it was supposed by some that I was officially appointed to take photographs, although it was to be years before the idea of official photographs occurred to the Admiralty. Certain base spirits, showing an ignorance of the character of the vice-admiral which did very little credit either to their intelligence or their sense of humour, affected to believe that I had been appointed in order to keep the doings of a certain branch of the Fleet in the public eye. The fact that no sentence of any subject whatsoever was ever written for publication by me, from the moment I thought of entering the Navy

37

until more than a year after I had left it—and then only at the request of the Admiralty—would no doubt be surprising to such people; and the fact that I was with him at all is a sufficient guarantee to those who had the slightest knowledge of David Beatty that he could trust me perfectly to abstain from writing about naval matters and also to forget for the time being that I had ever been a writer at all. I fear I cannot credit him with any desire to help me even now.[1] The facts were just as I have stated, and they followed upon each other with such rapidity that the Admiral had no time either to think out any other destination for me or to know what my " special service " was before I was upon him, in perfect reliance upon his friendship and good nature to fit me in somewhere. There was plenty of room later on for undefined " special service " in the Fleet, but at that time, and in the very heart of what was by far the most sought-after branch of the Service (with the possible exception of destroyers and light cruisers), it was a tall order.

Before I left, however, I had an interview which gave me a somewhat grim view of how my possible duties might be regarded. Having told Lord Fisher where I was going and that I should like to come and say good-bye to him, he sent for me the evening before I left London, and saw me, after what had evidently been a long and tiring day, in his room at the Admiralty. I remember the grim and yellow aspect of the old man as he sat at the blue cloth-covered table. He told me a great many things that I had not known, chiefly of the tremendous programmes of construction which he had instituted.

[1] See Appendix D.

A Useful Afterthought.

A Mysterious Remark

He accounted with pride how he had been fighting contractors all day and had come out victorious, with a promise of (I think) sixty destroyers by the end of the year. He also told me—what surprised me more—that he had sent off *Princess Royal* into the Atlantic to intercept a German cruiser which was suspected of hostile intentions on the Atlantic traffic. When I expressed some surprise at the battle cruiser force being deprived of so valuable a ship at such a moment, he would have none of it. He was full of one of his theories—the armadillo and the ants. "Don't you see? You send out the armadillo; the ants come round to eat up the carcase, and the armadillo eats *them* up." I did not see, but was discreet enough not to say so. He then asked me about Beatty, as to whom his views had evidently been slightly modified.

"Everyone tells me he is a first-rate chap. I called on him on board the *Lion* at Spithead in July. He is a smart-looking fellow. Well, you are going to have a very interesting time. You are going to quite the most interesting part in the Fleet, and you are sure to be in the middle of whatever is going on." Then, after a pause : "Now, there is always something to be learned from a fresh point of view. An outsider sometimes sees more than the trained man. If you hear anything that's interesting, or see anything going on that you do not think quite right, just drop me a line; you can always send a letter to me by the Admiralty bag marked 'Private,' and no one else will see it."

Such were the old man's words, and I confess my heart sank when he uttered them. What was it I had so often heard about him from people who admitted no good in him whatever, and who accused him of having attacked the finest traditions of the Navy by introducing a system of espionage and reports from junior officers upon their seniors? I had never believed it before, and I am not obliged to believe it now. Upon no instance, excepting this, did it ever come within my personal knowledge, and these words may deserve no more serious construction than the lightest which could be put upon them. But I remember the kind of check which they gave me, and the chill upon faith and enthusiasm.

" Well, give him my love and let me know how you get on," said Lord Fisher, as I took leave of him; and I then and there resolved to fulfil both commands in a way of my own, and to have a very clear understanding with my Admiral on taking up my appointment.

I broke my journey for a day going north, and resumed it in the snow and darkness of the November night, through the strained, disjointed, uncomfortable ways of the railway world of England at war. Sleet and darkness and a drear whistling wind on the freezing platform at Wigan, where we waited for hours whilst train after train, laden with coal for the Fleet, rumbled and clanked through the station; and then at last the blessing of a sleeping-car and comparative oblivion as far as Edinburgh. How different was this journey from my last journey north to join the same ship at the same port! Then I was going for the most delightful holiday I ever spent. Now I was going through one unknown to another, on what might quite possibly prove to be the last journey I should ever make.

The war doings and war conditions of the Fleet were then absolutely unknown to me, and I had a very real

Journeying North

sense of adventure. In my new uniform I was even unfamiliar to myself, and had that uncomfortable sense of masquerade which anyone with the smallest knowledge of the significance of that uniform could hardly avoid. It was one thing to be going where one was definitely ordered to go, or to someone who had definitely invited one to come; but I knew very well that the order (although I carried it in my pocket on official paper) was very largely a matter of my own invention, and did not represent the will or wish of anyone at all; and that, as far as the invitation was concerned, it was, strictly speaking, non-existent. Yet through that long drawn-out journey, becoming more and more naval in its personnel as the train dragged farther north, I was supported by the memory of the friendly family towards which I was journeying, remembering that I was not going to it as a stranger. And, as it turned out, I was not mistaken; but on arriving at Invergordon I had a very early insight into one of the most practical of reasons why the staffs of commanding officers are strictly limited. At the hotel to which I had taken my luggage while waiting for a boat, I heard a group of sub-lieutenants in a corner of the room discussing their grievances; one of them was saying, "I have to turn out of my cabin and sling a hammock because there is an R.N.V.R. fellow coming on the ruddy staff. Why the——" etc. etc. I hastily made myself known with the best apologies I could. He was a high-spirited, dare-devil youth, the life and soul of the *Lion's* gunroom, who never suffered from any grievance very long, and in ten minutes he had forgotten all about this one. But it was one more reminder to me of the eternal difference

Breaking into the Navy

between sea warfare and land warfare. On board ship the space is limited. There is simply not accommodation for all the trained people who might be of use, and to occupy a part of any such space with comfort one must feel sure that one is doing work, not only which is useful, but which cannot be done by someone else.

Somewhat sobered by these reflections, I hurried down the long lane that leads to the wharf at Invergordon, and saw a familiar figure, just landed from a smart blue-painted barge with a polished brass funnel, stepping over the snow-covered baulks that littered the wharf. The moment had come. I hurried up, saluted, and, in a formula which has now become classical, said, "Here I am."

He looked at me in my naval disguise with an expression of astonishment, followed by an inscrutable smile. "Well, I'm damned!" he exclaimed; and added, "You'll find the barge there, if you're quick; you had better let her take you off to the ship. I am going for a walk; see you when I come back," and with a hail to the barge, which was just about to shove off, he hurried on.

Before me, across the narrow stretch of black water, lay the snowy hills, and three great, grey, untidy looking brutes of battle cruisers in the foreground. Behind me was all my life, personified in my brother who had come to see me off and was waving farewell from the roadway. I stepped on board, said "Carry on" for the first time with authority, and began my new life.

CHAPTER IV

INVERGORDON AND THE NORTH SEA

The corn was turnin', hairst was near,
  But lang afore the scythes could start
A sough o' war gaed through the land
  An' stirred it to its benmost heart.
Nae ours the blame, but when it came
  We couldna pass the challenge by.
For credit o' our honest name
  There could but be the ae reply.
    An' buirdly men, fra strath an' glen,
    An' shepherds fra the bucht an'
      hill,
    Will show them a', whate'er befa',
    Auld Scotland counts for some-
      thing still.

Half-mast the castle banner droops,
  The Laird's lament was played yestreen,
An' mony a widowed cottar wife
  Is greetin' at her shank aleen.
In Freedom's cause, for ane that fa's,
  We'll glean the glens an' send them free
To clip the revin' eagle's claws,
  An' drook his feathers i' the sea.
    For gallant loons, in brochs an' toons,
    Are leavin' shop an' yard an'
      mill.
    A' keen to show baith friend an' foe,
    Auld Scotland counts for some-
      thing still.

The grim, grey fathers bent wi' years
  Come stridin' through the muirland mist,
Wi' beardless lads scarce by wi' school,
  But eager as the lave to 'list.
We've fleshed o' yore the braid claymore
  On mony a bloody field afar,
But ne'er did skirlin' pipes afore
  Cry on sae urgently to war.
    Gin danger's there, we'll thole our share,
    Gie's but the weapons—we've the will,
  Ayont the main, to prove again
    Auld Scotland counts for something still.

CHARLES MURRAY, in *The Times*.

I READ these verses, among the best which were directly inspired by the war, in a newspaper on my way north. They fitted with the sombre mood of those days; and I place them here because they remain for ever associated in my mind with this strange return to Scotland and her intimate association with the essence of all that England had ever meant at sea.

Invergordon and the North Sea

There was something very desolate, grim and warlike about the aspect of Invergordon on that waning November afternoon. Ships that when alive in their element partook of the cleanliness and the movement of the sea, seemed strangely dead, untidy and dirty amid the litter of these dark harbour waters; and when you add to this apparent confusion the indescribable atmosphere of war, with implements and thoughts of death crowning the whole scheme, the general aspect, both on the surface and beneath it, was at once gloomy and terrible. Nothing that I had thought or imagined that I would see was at all comparable with the grimness of the reality. The little rural harbour town seemed to have lost all its innocence, all its partnership with the beautiful landscape in which I had last seen it. It was like a small peasant child living in silence and fear in the shadow of the monster which had come to occupy its home, and when one climbed the Jacob's ladder that hung over the *Lion's* low quarter, amid an unfamiliar raffle of steel nets, hawsers and other gear, one felt that the world one was entering had somehow indescribably changed from that of not much more than a year before. And, in the writer's plain life, the fact that the first quarter-deck which he saluted in uniform was the *Lion's* could not fail to add a touch of solemnity to the moment. In the wardroom, however, there were many old friends and familiar faces, and the kind of welcome that is and can be found nowhere else but in the wardroom of one of His Majesty's ships.

I had come from France, from London, feeling that now at last I should learn something about the war and

44

The Duty of Ignorance

what was going on. To my astonishment I found that it was I who was being asked for news, and, above all, for naval news. It was the first astounding revelation of the way in which the men on whom everything depended were being kept in the dark, not only as to the war in general, but as to the way in which it intimately concerned the naval arm and their own part of it. The absence of *Princess Royal* being referred to by someone with puzzled indignation, I naturally made some reference to her mission in the Atlantic. It was my first lesson. A dead silence followed my remark. Someone said : "We are not supposed to know that," and the conversation was as soon as possible changed. But the effect had been produced. What had been talked quite freely about in London was not known here, and when accidentally made known was not further discussed. I remember at the time being even more deeply impressed with the bleak, noble attitude of the naval officer towards whatever his superiors decreed to be his duty, than by the utter stupidity of this extreme application of it. Not three people in that wardroom had known of the destination of *Princess Royal* until I spoke, and they had not communicated their knowledge. Yet the absence of *Princess Royal* was at that moment by far the most vital concern of the Battle Cruiser Squadron, and might conceivably have been at that moment the most vital concern of the war. Instead of the six ships, of which at that moment in the Admiralty mind the Battle Cruiser Squadron consisted, were only three—*Lion*, *Queen Mary* and *New Zealand*—the latter, of course, a slower and less powerful ship. *Princess Royal* was absent, as we have seen; *Tiger* had not yet joined the squadron, and was to prove far from ready when she did join; *Indomitable* and *Indefatigable* were in the Mediterranean; *Invincible* and *Inflexible* were at the Falklands. Up to a week or two before the battle cruisers had been without any home or protected base, and had been roaming about on various duty in constant peril of submarines; and the boom defence at Cromarty, which was then quite a novelty and had not been thought of when the war began, had only just been completed. Even then the battle cruisers lay at anchor with their torpedo nets out, in doubtful security.

I had a long talk with the Admiral on these and other matters that evening after dinner. I found him the same serene and buoyant personality, but obviously very deeply concerned at the general position and at the innumerable things in the naval organization which were all too palpably neither foreseen nor understood by those responsible for the conduct of the war. It was the old story which I had had before, which I was to hear again *ad nauseam*, and which I can testify is on the whole a true story : of the unaccountable indefinite gap between the Admiralty and the Navy, which no one in the history of either has ever yet bridged. The naval officer, whether in peace or war, had the sense that the Admiralty cared very little about his interests, did not wish to hear his point of view; and, what concerned him a great deal more, seemed to care very little whether the Navy was or was not properly equipped for the work it had to do. This may seem incredible, but it is true. The Admiralty's point of view was that everything was safe in its hands, and that all the naval officer had to do was to keep quiet and to do what he was told. The naval point of view was, as I have said, that the Admiralty regarded the

Admiralty Failings

Navy as an appendage, and the naval officer was a person to be kept in his place by a system of freezing officialdom and heart-breaking insistence on the literal interpretation of petty regulations, as being the whole duty of naval man. I have seen the Admiralty at work and the Navy at work, and I do not hesitate to say that during the war (in which, having *carte blanche*, it was presumably to be seen at its best) the Admiralty as an organization was partly unworthy of the great trust reposed in it. First-rate men were there, and doing first-rate work; that also was obvious to anyone who had the slightest acquaintance with the Admiralty. But the spirit informing the whole was a narrow and lifeless spirit, expressing itself everywhere in the policy that the means were more important than the end.

That first night at dinner in the Admiral's mess the Admiralty was the principal topic of conversation, as I suppose it was in every admiral's mess all over the Grand Fleet; and the next day at lunch and dinner, and every day through the long months during which I sat at that table the same topic always came up sooner or later. The significance of this should be understood. It was not dullness of mind, or paucity of interests, that made this subject recur so regularly. These six men were in every way representative of the best of the Naval Service (or they would not have been where they were). They were all not only dead keen on the war (that goes without saying), but keen on their profession; and their collective intelligence and experience of life could, and did, provide discussions on any subject which were well above the average of wit and common sense. Can you suppose that they really liked talking about the ineptitude of Admiralty administration? They had quite enough of it in their working hours, and the interest with which extraneous subjects were discussed was quite enough evidence that they were glad enough of any relief to the necessary monotony of their occupations. But the pre-occupation was there; men whose one idea was efficiency at every point and to the highest degree could not but chafe and be indignant when that mysterious deadness which you may call stupidity, ineptitude, swollen-headed-ness, pettiness, or merely narrowness of outlook, con-tinually imposed itself between them and what they knew to be necessary. To convey demands for vital necessities through the cold form of official correspondence is a hard enough discipline for the eager soul; but to find the necessities forgotten and your strength involved in a mere contest of official correspondence is apt to break the heart; or, if it does not break the heart, it inevitably breaks and blunts the fine point of enthusiasm for the Service, and often beats what should be a bright sword wielded against the enemy into a shield to ward off the pin-pricks of official annoyance and the blows of official stupidity. Of all the burdens laid upon Beatty and other men in naval commands during the war, I am convinced that there were none so heavy as these; and just because they represented the younger school in the Navy, animated by newer and less conventional ideas than those in control, the effort to push against the dead weight of official opposition was all the greater. It gives some measure of what the Navy is and might be to say that *seventy-five per cent. of its efficiency was absorbed by the Admiralty, and that with the remaining twenty-five per cent. the enemy had to be fought.*

First Impressions

If this narrative is to have any value it must be true, even at the cost of dullness; and these reflections come rightly into their place here because they are the principal impressions left upon me by that first evening in the *Lion*. I do not know what I had looked forward to, but it was quite different from the reality. I had seen in London more than enough of the world of self-seeking, intrigue, and hearty desire to make the war serve personal instead of national interests; and in coming to the Navy I had felt that I was leaving all that behind me, and going to a world where the sword was bright and the moment swift. And so I was; but I could not realize it on that first evening.

It is not to be supposed, however, that the atmosphere in which I found myself was one of gloom or depression. The attitude of the Admiralty towards naval officers, which shocked me so much, was nothing new to them. They were accustomed to it, and took it as a matter of course. The real tone was one of high expectation that at any moment the enemy might come out and the long-anticipated fight take place. There was a conference that evening after dinner as to what was to be done with me, and it was decided that I should take my share of the work in the Intelligence office, to which I was conducted by the Secretary and the Flag-Commander, and duly initiated.

There was not then, nor was there I believe throughout the war, any real Intelligence service in the Fleet. The prejudices of the Navy were against all such innovations; in fact it must be admitted that the very idea of an efficient Fleet Intelligence was far in advance of the point to which our naval ideas had advanced. But, thanks

E
49

chiefly to the Secretary and the Flag-Commander, an attempt was made in the *Lion* to organize the information with which we were being supplied into as full and useful a form as possible. The proper use of an Intelligence service one would suppose to be the collection of information and the distribution of it to the quarters in which it would be most useful; but we never got quite so far as that. The naval idea of Intelligence at that time was to collect the information and sit upon it, and the man who had the most secrets was the most efficient Intelligence officer. In our case, of course, this office was merely a repository for the extremely confidential material which was constantly being supplied to the Admiral, and which was far more than any one man could deal with; the work was done in watches by members of the Admiral's staff, and was primarily intended to be of use to him personally. In our keeping were, among other highly confidential matters, the secret ciphers, which never left the office and for the safety of which each of us was responsible during his watch. As signals were received by the ship in cipher in the wireless room they were brought by messenger to the officer on watch in the Intelligence office; he deciphered them, and the translation, sealed, was sent to the Admiral, by whom it was destroyed as soon as read. Logs and records of all such signals were kept by us, but not in a form by which they could be identified with the sheets bearing rows of figures on which the wireless operators transmitted them to us. It was perhaps the most interesting place in the ship. Everything there was to be known as to what was going on we knew, and the only hardship connected with the service consisted in the strict necessity

Intelligence

under which we lay to keep all such information absolutely dark, even from those officers whom it might be supposed to concern. It was characteristic of the naval point of view that the Intelligence office, with its collection of secret books, confidential documents and its necessary knowledge of everything that the Commanders-in-Chief or the Admiralty had to say to our chief or he to them, was regarded rather with amusement by the wardroom, as a kind of hush-hush department by means of which staffs and other hot-air merchants strove to justify their existence or add to their importance.

In addition to being initiated into my duties I had a talk with the Admiral that night which perhaps went some way to justifying my presence on board. I told him of my interview with the First Sea Lord, and of Lord Fisher's mysterious parting words. In some ways naval life is as formal as that of an embassy or Foreign Office, and there is no avenue by which an officer, once appointed to a high command, can freely discuss with his chiefs at home matters relating to the efficient carrying out of his command. The official letter, stereotyped as to its very wording, was the only recognized means. Since I had been invited to communicate my views to Lord Fisher, it seemed that I might make myself useful by conveying such views to him as my chief might wish, but which perhaps were not sufficiently urgent or defined to be the subject of an official communication. And in the light of my mysterious instructions I made it a condition that I should write nothing on any subject to Lord Fisher which I did not first show to my chief. This pact being faithfully observed, several quite useful recommendations were made in this way, some of which received the desired attention; although I imagine that Lord Fisher very soon became aware of the nature of my correspondence with him, and that he was not likely to hear any views from me which were not those of my chief. There was danger, indeed, of its becoming a kind of game among the staff to endeavour to express their own views to Lord Fisher on various Service matters with considerable force through the medium of my unsuspecting pen. These views were generally so sound that it was a matter of regret to me that I was not innocent enough to oblige.

A more useful turning to account of my informal relations with the First Sea Lord was my suggestion to Sir David that he should himself enter into an informal correspondence with the old man. As far as material things went, Lord Fisher could do what nobody else could do. I had given the Admiral his friendly message, and suggested that he should reply to it that evening in a similar tone and so break the ice; for these men had never written to one another, and had only seen each other once for a few minutes. It was absurd that, both being so vitally concerned in naval affairs, and both being unconventional men, they should have no means of communication but the formal and impersonal official letter. The Admiral thought it worth trying; he is as interesting and vigorous a correspondent, in his own quite different way, as Lord Fisher was; and the result was a very friendly and interesting correspondence that existed as long as Lord Fisher was in office, and was, I think, productive of nothing but good. Lord Fisher and Sir David Beatty were too utterly dissimilar in nature, breeding and ideas ever to like each other, nor do I think that Lord Fisher ever understood Beatty or appreciated the

best of his qualities. I think that Beatty understood Lord
Fisher better, and admired as much as anyone his strength
and his pugnacity.

The moment was in one way not the most favourable
for initiating a friendly correspondence. The Admiral
was deeply concerned at the withdrawal of *Princess
Royal*, and I soon understood why. As far as we
knew, the Germans had four battle cruisers ready; we
had for the moment only three to meet them with.
They were expected to come out at any moment. In
fact the Admiral could not understand why they did not
come out; for in those days—if they had only known—
they had opportunity such as was never to be vouchsafed
them again.

"If they come out," said the Admiral, "I shall
consider it my duty to engage them irrespective of odds,
and I shall possibly lose my squadron. And all because,
etc., etc. . . ."

He had represented his views as strongly as he could,
only to be told that he must not be alarmed, that all
would be well, etc. The idea that Beatty was likely
to be "alarmed" at the prospect of a losing fight
was, of course, absurd; but he had no love or ambition for losing fights; he felt they were not the
business of his side; and he knew that with all our
advantages a losing fight would be a disgrace. It was
not alarm that moved him, but genuine concern that the
situation was being completely misapprehended by the
Admiralty, in that they were capable of denuding the
Fleet at this vital point of attack for the sake of accom-
plishing a few odd jobs on the other side of the Atlantic.[1]

[1] I refer to the quite problematical quest of *Princess Royal*.

Invergordon and the North Sea

And for a good while we lived under the shadow of a possibility of the tragedy of Admiral Cradock being repeated on a larger scale, and of the greatest mobile weapon we possessed being thrown away through a mis-reading, which seemed to us inexcusable, of the vital elements of the situation. And I think it is due to the memory of Lord Fisher to say that when these points were put before him strongly by Beatty he expedited the return of *Princess Royal* by every means in his power.

The first few days at Invergordon I spent in getting the general hang of things and of exploring the wonderful new element in which I was living. The reader can imagine how exciting it was to land at one jump into the heart of the naval organization at sea; for though the Grand Fleet lay in all its majestic strength at Scapa Flow, we pitied rather than envied the lot of our brothers there, for the view that was then held, almost universally, was that they might have to spend a whole year of war and never see the enemy at all. It was the extremists, of course, who took that view. A month or two was the most the majority of us ever allowed for the continuation of the existing situation. A fortnight's inactivity in harbour was at that time, for the battle cruisers, the equivalent of being put into the Reserve; and the great topic of conversation was always the possibility of going to sea, for with that was coupled the possibility of a fight.

The naval mind was in the position of, let us say, a swimmer who has trained and practised for a contest, brought himself to the pink of condition, and stands, stripped and ready, on the edge of the diving-board waiting for the word to go—and is expected to continue holding himself in that attitude of expectation for three

We Go to Sea

or four years. Nothing more trying to the spirit could possibly be devised, and I think there is nothing in all the history of our Navy that stands more to its credit than the fact that this intolerable situation did not in the least affect the spirit and efficiency of the Battle Fleet, which had none of our excitements or adventures to keep them fresh. But at moments it was very trying, even for us.

My arrival was considered lucky in that three days afterwards came the longed-for orders to go to sea. At that time it was the custom of the Fleet to make occasional sweeps across the North Sea, in the course of which there was always a possibility that the enemy might be encountered; but as the Intelligence work at the Admiralty became organized this costly and dangerous practice was discontinued, and we never went to sea (except for exercises in remote regions) unless we had news that the enemy was out, and that therefore there was a chance of cutting him off. This expedition in November was, I think, one of the last of these combined operations; but it had a special interest for us owing to the reduced strength of our squadron. I went ashore in the afternoon with the Admiral for a walk up towards the hills behind Invergordon; and at six o'clock, in a pitch dark night and bitter cold, we weighed anchor and proceeded to sea.

I had always seen the departure of a Fleet in peace time as a matter of considerable circumstance, accompanied by much signalling in the form either of streams of colour from the signal yards or a kind of gala illumination of searchlights and Morse lamps. On that drear winter night it was very different. The orders had all

been given before. Nothing could be seen in the blackness except, perhaps, the blinking of one very subdued
signal light from the flagship; and at the appointed hour
the capstan engines began their work and, amid a row
of dim silhouettes on the fo'c's'le of each ship, the huge
cables would come creeping home link by link.

I remember going up on deck on this first night to
see our departure—although see is hardly the word. I
felt my way up the spiral stairway leading from the
Admiral's lobby, where all our cabins and offices were,
to the upper deck, and thence by ladders, the position
of which was known but not seen, to the searchlight
platform below the signal bridge. The *Lion*, which had
led the way in and was anchored farthest up the harbour,
led the way out, and so had to pass the other ships.
There was no quiver or sign from the turbine engines
when they began to move; no shouting or utterance of
orders such as herald the getting under way even of small
craft. Only, in that cold night air, a colder air began
to flow and blow upon one's face; the air became wind;
so one knew that the ship was in motion. Presently in
the darkness ahead showed a denser blot of darkness,
unillumined by any gleam from scuttle or war-light, and
with only the glimmer of a pocket torch on the fo'c's'le
head to suggest that the mass was inhabited at all. This
dark shadow passed and was received into the darkness
astern, while another emerged out of the darkness ahead.
This also we passed, with a sense of incredible stealth
and secrecy; the wind on one's face increased, and the
darkness ahead was not broken. I went below for a
moment and glimpsed the life of the ship. The dynamos
hummed and whined, the ventilating fans roared; the

The First Watch

whole complicated whisper and rustle which is the noise of machinery in a great warship filled the lighted, white-enamelled spaces that stretched in their perspective to other and unseen centres of organized effort and activity. In the wardroom men were sitting and talking; the orderly and organized life of a human community was everywhere going on. I returned on deck as we passed between the Souters, the entrance to Cromarty Firth. The speed had increased; the blackness flowed and pressed upon one's body so that one had to lean forward against it. A pale glimmer from a lighthouse on the headland was all that signalled our departure from the land; and so in the November night the battle cruisers went forth upon their terrible quest. And even while thrilling to the sense of the dread significance of the moment, one rejoiced.

We dined early that night as soon as we were clear of the land. It was my first watch.[1] Soon after eight o'clock the ship had settled down into the routine of her nights at sea. All along the lighted alleyways were hammocks slung in bunches, so that one had to stoop almost double to walk under them, wherein a part of the watch below, as well as such of the marines as were not sleeping at their gun stations, took their rest amid snores and sighs. The ship was very quiet, and but for that somnolent sound and the purring voices of machinery there was no sound except the rustle of the waves on the other side of the steel wall, and no movement but a rhythmic though almost imperceptible heave to remind one that one was in a ship at sea. A few ciphers came in, and for the first time I was alone and responsible,

[1] The first watch at sea is from 8 o'clock until midnight.

Invergordon and the North Sea

and, of course, thoroughly enjoyed it. Signals drifted
in bearing on various matters connected with the Fleet;
not all of them concerned us; one was just listening to
the secret night talk from the Commander-in-Chief to
his children concerning their duties or their movements.
There was a great chart of the North Sea behind me with
the ship's eight o'clock position to be marked upon it
and other tracks that recorded the whereabouts of enemy
submarines to be plotted out. There was a little flag
for every squadron in the Grand Fleet, which showed
where the Fleet was disposed, and there was another
little flag, signifying the *Tiger*, which had been slowly
moving around the chart from the west of Ireland north-
wards and was now approaching our own position from
the direction of the Shetland Islands. This represented
our new and formidable sister which was about to join
us, and was a matter of special interest in the circumstances of the moment. The Admiral looked in on his
way down from the bridge somewhere about eleven. He
had been up there in the windy dark looking after the
night disposition of the Fleet. Whenever we were at
sea he slept in a small apartment, inscribed "Admiral's
sea cabin," in the superstructure, above which rose the
signal bridge and the compass platform, and so was
always within instant call. With a cheery, "Well, how's
the First Watch getting on?" he came in and lightened
my solitude with a word or two, and departed to turn in.
With one's various duties and occupations the four hours
soon flew by, and I went to my own cabin, having
awakened and handed over to my successor, to sleep the
soundest sleep that I had known for many a month.
There was always the possibility that daybreak, when it

H.M.S. *New Zealand* in Harbour.

The Intelligence Office, and the Secretary.

Enter the *Tiger*

came, would show us the enemy; we always turned in at night at sea with that hope; and all through the squadron ships' companies were at action stations with the break of day.

Next morning when I awoke and came on watch again at eight o'clock we were somewhere off the coast of Norway, making rendezvous with the First Light Cruiser Squadron, under Commodore Goodenough, and the Second Cruiser Squadron,[1] which consisted of the *Shannon* and two other ships of her class, which we were not particularly glad to see owing to their slow speed and small fuel capacity. At noon on that day, after a great deal of wireless talk about our respective positions, the *Tiger* joined us and fell in astern of *Queen Mary*, her unfamiliar rig and formidable appearance being viewed by us with much curiosity. There was a scare that afternoon that a German submarine was in the vicinity, but had got away from the *Leda*, who was chasing it; otherwise the day was uneventful. My night was divided into three, as I had the middle watch,[2] and I turned in before and after it. That is a very quiet time at sea. The very ship seems to be breathing as though asleep; apart from the silent, attentive group high up on the navigating platform and on the signal bridge below them, there is no one above decks at all, and few awake below decks. There were very few ciphers; the messenger dozed on his perch outside the door; the snores of the marines mingled as usual with the voice of the ship, and the atmosphere below deck steadily thickened. This

[1] Readers interested in the composition of this and other squadrons will find details in Appendix C.

[2] From 12 o'clock until 4 a.m.

Invergordon and the North Sea

is always the longest of the sea watches, and from three to four A.M. the longest hour of the twenty-four. But the glad moment comes when you can go and rouse from his sleep the unfortunate officer who is to relieve you and, turning in, fall asleep yourself with a suddenness unknown in any other life.

I remember there were all sorts of excitements in our floating world the next morning. The weather had stiffened and there was a heavy sea—too much for the destroyers, who were sent home to their base. The *Tiger* had disappeared in the night, and reappeared with rather a dissipated air in the course of the morning, alleging, in reply to urgent signals, that she had lost visual touch with the squadron. Reproof was duly administered. I even remember the wording of it: "Your extraordinarily bad lookout will cause a disaster." By lunch time we were off the Muckle Flugga, a wild and forlorn rock, one of the most utterly desolate spots in the Shetland Islands. We were doing target practice with 4-inch guns, and the *Tiger* again came in for reproof because she was late and kept us all waiting: "If you do not get on with your practice you may be torpedoed, etc., etc." She certainly came in for a good deal of scolding on her first day with us. After luncheon we fired our big guns at Ramna Stack, a square looking rock in that lonely sea which was well adapted for the purpose, and constantly used by the Fleet until in some newspaper or other the fact of its being so used was mentioned, thus depriving the Fleet of a useful target, for when the next ship went to do practice there, they found a German submarine waiting. I remember on this day the trivial fact that for the first time, not without secret misgivings,

From the Foretop

I climbed into the foretop, where my action station had
been allotted to me. As I would have no particular duties
when the ship was in action, I had petitioned for a place
where I should get a view, and I certainly got it there.
But I had certain qualms. I have no head for heights,
and access to the foretop was obtained by means of a steel
ladder placed vertically up and down the fore-mast; and
there was a nasty gap at the top of it which had to be
spanned by striding across on to a small foothold below
the cross trees, reaching for a handhold above, and hauling oneself up until one could get a knee on the edge
of the trap in the steel floor of the top. Knowing that
I would have to do this sooner or later, I thought I had
better try it now. It was a very unpleasant climb. The
wind seemed to have a malignant force and one's hands
to be doubtful instruments with which to hang to smooth
steel grips. Although the view was magnificent, I was
very glad to be back on the comparatively humble
elevation of the signal bridge, and decided that I would
not go up again until it should be actually necessary.
That night I had not very much sleep, since it was my
turn to be awakened at the dread hour of 4 A.M. and to
shake myself into wakefulness for the morning watch.[1]
This was the watch that I always enjoyed most, once
the terrible business of awakening had been gone through.
As far as ciphers go, it was the quietest watch of all for
us in the Intelligence office, as apparently at that hour
even the active minds from which the ciphers originated
took a little rest. One put on one's uniform over
pyjamas, drank a little cocoa, and settled down to read,
or write, or work.

[1] From 4 a.m. to 8 a.m.

Invergordon and the North Sea

Even in those winter nights so far North there began to be a promise of day towards seven o'clock, and long before that the ship had begun to awaken to her daily life. The coming of day is proverbially a welcome thing to those who are watching through the night, and surely never more so than to those who have watched at sea. It was pleasant when the quartermaster entrusted with that duty came along and unscrewed the steel deadlight that obscured the scuttle and when, the scuttle itself being opened, one saw the touch of the sunrise tipping the crests of the breaking waves with saffron colour, and could breathe great lungfuls of the salt air after the cooked atmosphere of the night. It was pleasant to go up on deck for a moment, feel the wind in one's face again, and see day warming over the North Sea swells, and all our companions and satellites, each with a bone in her teeth and each in her appointed station, planing over the grey fields. Pleasant undoubtedly to occupy the last half-hour of one's watch in shaving, bathing and dressing, and scenting, with a sea appetite, the first subtle odours of breakfast from the dining cabin. But if all this was delightful in mid-winter, how much more so was it when spring came, and the opening of the scuttle would glorify one's cabin with the rose and gold of morning, and when the perfumed breath of spring at sea would fill the spaces of the ship! There were many moments when it was good to be at war.

On the morning of Friday, November 20, we were anchored in Scapa Flow, and I had my first view of the vast wild harbour, land-locked by ranges of mauve hills, and containing an area of sea so great that even the

Third Cruiser Squadron.

H.M.S. *Tiger* at Sea.

In Scapa Flow

Grand Fleet with its innumerable dependent and satellite craft seemed almost lost in its fifty square miles. A mile away from us lay the *Iron Duke*, and it was possible through glasses at certain hours of the day to see, pacing her quarter-deck, the solitary figure on whose shoulders the responsibility of the whole was laid. On the next day we did torpedo practice in the harbour, and I remember that one of our torpedoes, after keeping its course for about a mile, turned in its tracks and came straight for us—a homing manoeuvre which, however much it facilitated the recovery of the weapon, was rather depressing in the light of its destined employment. And that evening when we were back at anchor I had an experience which made a deep impression on me; the picture of it remains clearly written on my mind. Let me try to reproduce it.

The ante-room temperature had reached the height normal to it on a winter evening in harbour, when the scuttles were closed, the radiators aglow, fire blazing, and pipes, cigarettes, and voices in full blast. A wardroom argument had developed through the first three regular stages—assertion, flat denial, and personal abuse of a highly pointed nature; and had then reached the final stage, when everyone was talking at once and no one listening. The tall Blue Marine, who was the Wireless Officer, on board, pushed his way across the thronged deck mopping his forehead. "It is a wonderful night for wireless," he said, in that rather shamefaced and apologetic way in which men in the Service refer to their own particular job. It was born of an atmosphere where enthusiasm had to be expressed to the last ounce in action, leaving none to be expended in verbal demonstrations, all

63

Invergordon and the North Sea

of which were compendiously grouped under the contemptuous epithet of "hot air," and were apt to be received with ribaldry. Yet among the younger men there were always a few ardent souls whose imagination was still kindled by the wonders which they handled, and who found something responsive in the unabashed enthusiasm of the new-comer, to whom everything was not yet a matter of course.

" A wonderful night for wireless—you can hear all sorts of things going on. If you want to have a look down below, you could not have a better night." It was in fact a horrid night, both muggy and cold, but there was something in the atmospheric conditions which responded exactly to the requirements of those mysterious powers which man has invoked without understanding them, and to whom he must behave like a lover to a capricious mistress, studying what their tastes may be, swiftly accommodating himself to them, as swiftly avoiding what seems to offend them. That night the goddess was in a benignant mood and consequently the wireless room, which took its benefits thankfully without bothering too closely to account for them, was in a good temper.

Of course I accepted the invitation, and we stepped and wriggled our way along the deck, where in the full glare of electric light and the publicity of the main thoroughfare of the ship scores of men were, according to routine, slinging their hammocks and preparing to turn in. Down the steel staircase, across the ship, along the mess-deck and down another and steeper ladder, we came at last to the white-enamelled door on which were inscribed the important words, " Wireless Office." One

H.M.S. *Iron Duke* at Scapa.

Submarine Look-out.

Wireless

had seen such places ashore, spacious areas of polished mahogany, in the design of which silence and elbow-room were the chief considerations. This, through which came all the wireless business of the most important unit afloat, was different. There was no space and no mahogany. A little cabin crowded with knobs, bars, and switches in brass and copper and vulcanite, and furnished with one or two tiny desks; in the midst of it a great cage or shrine. In this was isolated the cable, the great tap-root of the plant that climbs up through the deck, branching into spans of gossamer web, and blossoming at last into the infinite ether—truly something like that life-tree Igdrasil, which has its roots down in the kingdoms of Hela and Death, and whose boughs overspread the highest heaven.

Round the shrine of this deity were seated its ministers, arrayed in the same blue serge uniform that, with the slightest variations, covered all the service of the sea from cooks and butchers to bosuns and gunners. It is only to a stranger that there would be anything incongruous in the sight of bluejackets and petty officers sitting amongst all this delicate and scientific apparatus. It is only the popular imagination that pictures a bluejacket as always heaving a rope or tossing an oar. He is much more likely to be carrying a pencil behind his ear, a spanner in his hand, or an armful of ledgers. A pair of pliers is of more use to him than an oar; he has much oftener a piece of paper than a rope in his grasp; and a tin of Bluebell polish is a more familiar implement than a marline-spike. Here, in the wireless room, one saw him in one more of those highly technical and specialized settings of which the Navy affords an endless

Invergordon and the North Sea

variety; and among that glitter of polished metal and black vulcanite, dealing with an invisible and deadly power that spoke with its own voice to him in a jargon which, although he could transcribe it, it was no part of his business to understand, he was as much at home as when dealing with sheer brute force in the cable holds and stowing the monster, link by link, as it came dripping down to him, or standing clear when it roared out in a thunderstorm of sound and a cyclone of powdered rust.

" What have you got now, Webb? " asked the officer, as we stepped behind the C.P.O. in charge. " Just finishing the Poldhu, sir," he answered. " But you can hear practically everything to-night; we ought to have Nordeich in a moment." Nordeich was the high-power German station, corresponding to our Clifton and Poldhu, from which the daily Press message was sent out to ships at sea. The chief had his eye on the clock, whose minute hand was approaching the hour of nine. " He is very punctual, sir, is Nordeich; you can set your watch by him. I dare say he is just knocking out his pipe now; he'll start in a minute. If you take the receiver you'll hear him." I fitted the receiver over my ears. A black vulcanite disc which regulated and tuned the wave-length to synchronize with one of the many voices in the air, was set to a certain number. I listened; there was a very faint and ghostly chorus of indistinct whines and buzzes, like that coming from a colony of insects disturbed in some affair. Punctually as the minute hand rested on twelve, a strong, clear and strident note broke forth into the buzzing. " There he is," said the chief, who had a duplicate set at his ear. Nordeich began, as everyone begins, by making his call sign, advertising to all whom

Voices of the Air

it might concern that he was about to begin his daily recital of that version of the news which Germany wished the world to believe. I listened for a little to the strong, clear tones beginning their untruthful recital; and could not but think it a symbol of what was happening in the world of action, where the truth was being proclaimed in confused and sometimes diffident chorus, and where for the moment wrong and untruth were speaking with a single and clear voice.

"Now listen to Poldhu," said the chief, turning the dial to another number. The strident tones died away, and in their place a deep, gruff muttering dominated the air. When I was listening to Nordeich, Poldhu had been among the little minor chorus of whines and buzzes; when the dial was revolved, Nordeich sank to join its voice in that background of insect songs, and the rough voice of Poldhu—the deepest of all the voices—took up the solo. Another turn of the handle and the gruff voice finished, and in its place a musical note, small and bell-like, took up the tale. "That is the Eiffel Tower," said the operator; and my imagination, which had been fixed on that tall group of masts that rises above the heather and gorse on the downs beyond Mullion, transported itself to the night streets of Paris, and that busy network of steel girders among whose interstices a little living, breathing human figure was sitting and pressing a key.

Again we turned the indicator to another wavelength, but on its way past one of the contacts a momentary loud voice broke in on the murmur. "Ah! you've got the Commander-in-Chief," said the chief, turning back the handle. I wished to hear that august voice coming from the ship that was lying not ten cables'

length from us, and I turned back the pointer until the
loud note broke in again. Of course it was much more
powerful than the others, being so close. Even when
we were listening to Poldhu, or Nordeich, the commanding tones would break in and, to my ear, interrupt the
message, although the trained operator easily concentrated his sense of hearing on one voice and disentangled
it from the babel of the rest, much as some people can
read a book in a crowded room quite oblivious to all
interruptions, holding their attention to the printed
page.

But those were not all the wonders shown to me in
the wireless office that winter night in the Northern Seas.
It was indeed a " wonderful night for wireless," almost
unique in the experience of those to whom I was speaking. We heard all kinds of things on that night which
are seldom heard together and under the same conditions.
We heard the Russian Commander-in-Chief in the Baltic ;
we heard Madrid ; we heard the German Commander-in-
Chief, from his fastness across the North Sea ; and it
amused me to turn the wave-length back and forward
between the German and British commanders—the two
voices that meant so infinitely much to us all—to contrast
their tones, and to imagine what they were saying. We
heard the British Commander-in-Chief of the Mediterranean. All these, of course, were call signs known and
recognized, but there were many others, coming, no
doubt, from places as diverse and remote and as kindling
to the imagination, which we did not know or recognize.
Yet they were for the most part voices only—voices and
nothing else. To the men who took them in they were
voices representing groups of figures or letters, and there

The Invisible Tether

their interest in them in any case ceased; but even to us who had access to the codes and ciphers many of them still meant nothing, just because we lacked the key to the particular ciphers of letters or figures which turned the jargon into illuminating sense. Not that it would necessarily have been interesting or exciting. What one did recognize was far from exciting—just the infinite detail of a vast organization which never spoke except for business. As I was turning away a bitter cry came from somewhere between Iceland and Ireland: " Daffodil to Ranunculus: 2,000 lb. of marrowfat peas intended for me addressed to you at Happyhaven. Request you will, etc."

Wireless telegraphy was the youngest of all the sciences that were serving the Navy in the war, and it is not too much to say it was the chief. An organization barely ten years old, which has for the most vital part of its material the unknown, it is remarkable for the efficiency with which it sustained the enormous burden thrown on it, never failing, never breaking down. It did more to change the conditions of fighting than any other single thing. It meant the abolition of independent action and the consummation of highly organized and concerted action. It gathered information, distributed information; it gave orders, it made dispositions, scattered ships to the four quarters, and concentrated them to within ten minutes of a given time on a single point on a blank chart; and it did more wonderful and fateful things than these. In the olden days a captain of a ship could get out of touch with his squadron and act independently. The admiral of a squadron could set sail, and once he was over the horizon he had nothing to consult but his own ideas, and nobody to consider but himself. The Admiralty, once it had formed and equipped the Fleet and appointed the Commander-in-Chief, had little further part in the strategical and tactical dispositions; war was made by the Commander-in-Chief. But in this war the wireless tentacles reached everywhere, and there was no element in which a commander was free from the supervision of the Admiralty. If he flew up in the air it could follow him there, and if he dived down to the bottom of the sea, although it would not dive after him, it would be waiting for him when he came to the surface inquiring where he had been and why. Even the Commander-in-Chief had the Board of Admiralty ever at his ear; and an idea conceived in a Cabinet or War Council in London might be transmitted to and imposed upon the Fleet far away at sea within an hour.

As to all this, it may briefly be said that its advantages were obvious to the men at the Admiralty, or transmitting end; and that its disadvantages were obvious to the men at the seaward, or receiving end. It took much of the burden and privilege of initiative away from the sailor, and placed it in the hands of the administrator or statesman. With that burden and privilege went also the great responsibility which rested upon those who had this initiative reserved to themselves. Whether the Navy would have done better in this war if left to itself, or not so well, is not for me to say; but it is quite certain that it would have done differently.

At this time every day brought a new experience. On Sunday, the twenty-second, I saw my first church service at sea in war time, and I am bound to say that

Devotional Exercise

I was not greatly impressed with the Church's part in the naval organization. A more uncomfortable or unsuitable place for the exercising of religion than the mess-deck of a man of war, with its low head room and interruptions of vision caused by air-trunks, pipes and deck supports, can hardly be imagined. Of the four or five hundred men there, not more than half could either see or hear the parson, and there was that restless, fidgety atmosphere which one associates with Sunday schools and other places where little children are expected to be quiet even though they are bored and uncomfortable. The Admiral and his staff, the Captain and the officers of the ship, occupied chairs in front, the rest of the congregation being packed on mess benches. The singing was led by that dire instrument, the ship's harmonium, which was totally inadequate to prevent the unison singing from falling at least a semi-tone flat in every hymn. The Admiral and the Captain read the Lessons. Of the sermon little need be said, except that it would have needed a man with greater gifts than the gallant preacher possessed to forge any link between the environment and circumstances of the congregation and the subject of Christian evidences as applied to the last Sunday after Trinity. One felt that there must be simple and heartening things that could suitably have been said in such a time and place. But for all its assumption of spiritual pre-eminence the Church of England has to take a very minor place in the scheme of the British Navy afloat. The mere orders: " Hands rig church," " Marines up harmonium," " Up hymn-books," " Two seamen from duty part of the watch rig pulpit," and so on, are themselves eloquent of the temporary and transitory nature of the tabernacle. And the fact that the priest ministers ever under the eye of the Commander, at whose stern command, " On caps," immediately following the blessing, the serious business of life is proceeded with, brings the whole affair —necessarily, of course—into the mere order of ship's routine. The chief incident of that service remaining with me is that the Admiral, before the singing of the last hymn, admonished the congregation on their lacka- daisical and dragging praise, adding, " I want to hear the *Lion* roar." And the last hymn being " Fight the good fight," known to the more earnest section of the Oxford ecclesiastical world as " Fighters," it did roar, in a very painful and distressing manner.

A naval chaplain has probably a more difficult position than any man of his cloth ; and most of those that I have known had the sense to cut down the pretensions of their priestly order to a minimum and to content themselves by being real friends and counsellors to such of the men who needed them. And no mere onlooker would presume to judge or estimate the value of that intimate and hidden service. Undoubtedly the opportunities it presents to the right man are very great.

And so to sea again the next day, this time in com- pany with the whole of the Grand Fleet. Our objective was the Heligoland Bight, and the first morning at sea was occupied with two of those elaborate Fleet exercises known as " P.Z.'s." The Battle-Cruiser force was separated from the Commander-in-Chief and did some exercise or other ; I have forgotten what ; I was too much absorbed in the actual mechanism of command on the signal bridge to study, or even understand, the nature of the evolution. To the layman, however accustomed

On the Signal Bridge

to the sea, nothing is so bewildering in naval manœuvring as the loss of sense of direction caused by continually turning. Our course for the morning generally was about south-east by south, but under the grey, sunless sky, and within the unbroken circle of the horizon, we were steaming sometimes north and sometimes west. At one moment the squadron would be in line ahead, apparently steaming towards Germany. Up would go a hoist to the signal arm, repeated by every ship; and as at the single word of command the flags came down, every ship would turn at a right angle to port, and one would find oneself in a new formation, line abreast, hurrying towards Norway; and a few minutes later we would be on a course for Scotland.

The signal bridge of a flagship is a busy scene at such a time. There does the Admiral handle his whole Fleet; and the officer of the watch in the flagship herself, directing her movements from the compass platform overhead, observes and obeys the signals as though they come from another ship. I never ceased admiring the mental dexterity with which a highly trained flag-lieutenant translates an order given to him in plain English instantaneously into the letters and numerals of three or four codes, nor the physical deftness with which a leading signalman would snatch out the necessary flags from their pigeon-holes, bend them on to the halliards, and hoist them. A couple of hours of such work in a strong wind makes no light call on the muscles of the back and arms, and naturally the slightest hesitation or slowness—to say nothing of an actual mistake—even if the Admiral turns a blind eye to it, evokes immediate and stern comments from the Signal Boatswain and the

Invergordon and the North Sea

Flag-Lieutenant. And, as well as the visual signals, other signals were being exchanged on the short distance wireless, which would be telephoned up to the chart-room a few minutes before they came up in the form of a written message.

It is true, at any rate in the writer's experience, to say that any hour spent with David Beatty, either at work or play, was pure delight; but it was never better than on the bridge of the flagship on a fine day at sea when things were going well and when, surveying his kingdom scattered over the blue-grey waters, he could admit that it was not so bad after all. There was never a dull moment, and he never lost an opportunity for a lesson or an experiment. I remember a second P.Z. which we did on that day and in which we played the part of the enemy to Sir John Jellicoe's force in the Grand Fleet. The exercise took the form of a contest in manœuvring for the most advantageous position in which to engage; it was exciting while it lasted, but it was brought to an end by Beatty making a daring 16-point turn to starboard. "Risky but successful," said the uninstructed; but the Admiral knew very well what he was doing. The risk was only apparent, and the manœuvre was characteristic of a brilliant tactician who never, in fact, did anything rash at all, but who knew how to wait for his opportunity, and seize it when it came. We were not, I remember, allowed to enjoy the full fruits of our victory, for the moment its success became obvious the signal, "Negative P.Z.," was made by *Iron Duke*, the "Secure" was sounded, and the hands went to dinner.

The object of our sweep towards Heligoland was to

The Admiral's Back.

Faulty Dispositions

support a contemplated air raid on Cuxhaven, and we woke up on the 24th in the highest spirits and assured expectation of a fight. But alas! it proved to be one of a series of endless disappointments to which, although they continually recurred, we never grew accustomed. During the forenoon watch a signal was received from the Admiralty saying that owing to the strength of the enemy's light forces in the neighbourhood of Cuxhaven the contemplated air raid would not take place, and the seaplane carrier was ordered back to her base at Harwich. Since we had come so far, however, it was considered advisable to take a look at the Bight, and the First Light Cruiser Squadron and the Second Cruiser Squadron were sent on. An excitement was caused by a signal from the Commodore (T),[1] in command of the Harwich Destroyer Force, to the effect that he was in touch with the enemy; but the enemy turned out to be our light cruisers, of whose presence in those waters the Commodore was ignorant—a characteristic result of the Admiralty Staff work of the time. He should, of course, have been informed of the movements and probable position of any of our own forces in the same waters. It was a perfect day for fighting, with calm sea and long visibility; but I remember that the operation filled the Admiral with disgust. The Second Cruiser Squadron was in a uselessly risky position and one in which, owing to its inferior speed, it might quite easily be cut off by the enemy. Commodore (T) reported a great deal of smoke behind Heligoland, and the Second Cruiser Squadron went in far enough to sight the island and be fired on by them

[1] Commodore Tyrwhitt. (T) after such a title signifies Torpedo craft, and (S) Submarines.

75

for, I think, the first and only time in the war. The danger indeed of such reconnaissances in slow ships was quite obvious. Such an operation should take the form of a dash in and out; but we were hanging about, a bait for submarines, from seven o'clock until eleven, and the Commander-in-Chief with the Battle Fleet was too far astern of us to have been of any assistance to the Second Cruiser Squadron if it had been attacked. In spite of this tempting bait, however, the Germans did not oblige us by coming out. We had it all out on the bridge after we had turned for home, and at dinner that evening, and came to the conclusion that risks had been run for nothing and a fine day wasted. So back we went north-westward again, employing the shining hour by doing some more P.Z.'s, and it struck me as a fine manifestation of our occupation of the German Ocean that, having gone to look for the Germans in their own waters and not finding them, we employed the time by doing exercises and having a sham fight amongst ourselves—since there was no enemy to fight. And the next morning, the 26th, after a rough night, found us at anchor again off Invergordon.

There we remained until December 15. That fortnight in that desolate harbour was the dark hollow of the year's wave, the middle of the tunnel of winter through which we seemed to be journeying towards the spring and fulfilment of our hopes. Outside of the ship there was absolutely nothing to do; all our interests were within and, except for an occasional walk ashore for the sake of exercise, there was no variation of the monotonous shipboard life. It was dark at four o'clock in the afternoon, when the scuttles would be screwed down and the ship

Photo: Russell.

Rear-Admiral H. B. Pelly.
(Captain of H.M.S. *Tiger* 1914.)

had to say good-bye to daylight and fresh air for a good fifteen hours. One day Captain Pelly came to lunch and gave us an entertaining, if disquieting, account of the *Tiger's* journey from the Clyde, where she had been built, around to the English Channel. She was hustled out at very short notice, and in the hurry of departure it appeared that no confidential books had been issued to her. This was discovered when she was well out at sea. Search was made, but the only thing found was a large parcel marked, "Secret; not to be opened," so it was not opened. The unfortunate ship got as far as Plymouth without disaster, but on attempting to go in there to procure the necessary information, she was promptly hustled out again, as there were reports of enemy activity. Passing through the Channel in the darkness of night, she suddenly found herself illuminated by the searchlights of a strange warship, making a recognition signal which the *Tiger* did not understand. Fortunately, her identity as a French ship was established before either of them opened fire; but it was an awkward and indeed scandalous position that a new and valuable battle cruiser should be sent into the Channel without escort and without an officer being in possession of signals being used in his own Fleet. Of course the missing books were found to be contained in the mysterious parcel.

The walks ashore were the best part of Invergordon, although when one had the Admiral for companion they were apt to be somewhat strenuous. I remember that on one afternoon we landed at two o'clock and walked inland and upwards towards the hills in a gale of wind and rain at an exhilarating pace. My companion was in good form, and kept me entertained for three and a half hours of fast walking with yarns of his Egyptian campaigns, river fighting, and certain lurid incidents in the battle of Atbara, one of which had for its climax the sewing of a head on to a dead body. It was pleasant up there among the hills, walking over the hard frosty roads or beside the bed of a burn, brown and swollen, whose music was refreshing after the clangour of the ship. We reached the boat at 5.80, and must have walked thirteen miles that day; and a walk with David Beatty is real walking, not strolling. Hard exercise is a necessity to him, and even when we were at sea he would tramp his daily mileage at the same eager pace.

A less strenuous walk, often taken with various companions, lay along the shores of Nigg Bay, a wide and desolate tract of shallow water unvisited by any craft, with the lonely road running along beside the beach. There was an old topsail schooner lying at a deserted quay, which used to make a convenient objective for an afternoon walk; and often in the dusk of a winter afternoon we have stood and listened to the wind moaning in her neglected rigging and the soft lap of the water against her forefoot, which was probably destined never to furrow the waves any more; and our thoughts would run on the melancholy ending and sea-death of a poor old coasting tramp such as this, to whose probably waning activities the war had given a final blow. Some of us will remember that old ship when we have forgotten far more important things; although it is possible that when the submarine campaign became acute she may have been patched up sufficiently to crawl forth again on the coasting trade and earn some substantial dividend for her owner. At any rate we will hope so.

CHAPTER V

SEA DOINGS

DECEMBER 9 provided a welcome break in the monotony of our lives. I remember that Cyril Ward (he was then a Commander R.N.V.R.) had come to dinner with the Admiral—in itself almost a guarantee of cheerfulness; but as we finished our rubber of bridge, the news came of Admiral Sturdee's victory with his battle cruisers off the Falkland Isles. We all of us carried the news personally to the wardroom, where there was an immediate uproar, more champagne, people fetched out of bed who had turned in, and general high spirits. The bosun's mates were sent round the mess decks bellowing out the news in chorus. There was much ragging afterwards of a very light-hearted and boyish kind; furniture was broken, people not in their cabins were locked out of them, and the few fortunate ones that were in theirs were locked in, and certain young gentlemen from the gunroom joined, on the wardroom table, in the venerable game known as " running torpedoes," the torpedo being the unfortunate midshipman, who is hurled, face downwards, along the whole length of the smooth table by the combined available forces. The " torpedo " generally enjoys this game; but if he does not, it is repeated and continued until he does.

Sea Doings

In this comparatively long spell in harbour I had ample opportunity to become acquainted with what had been happening since the Fleet went to sea in August. I heard all about the action in the Heligoland Bight which, like most of the other actions described in the war of which official accounts were published, by no means took place exactly in the form suggested by the published dispatch. This was an operation conducted by the Admiralty, and conducted so sketchily that, owing to our submarine commanders not having been informed of the forces at sea, they very nearly torpedoed our own battle cruisers. Everybody's information was so insufficient or ill-timed that if it had not been for a piece of pure intuition on Admiral Beatty's part in turning back when he did, the battle cruisers, which were steaming away under the impression that everything was over, would never have been on the spot where they rendered such signal service to our light forces. One incident of that affair was the return to Scapa. For long afterwards it could not safely be mentioned in the presence of the Admiral. It seems that as the squadron entered the anchorage at Scapa and passed down the line of our battleships, they were cheered —which annoyed the Admiral, as he did not consider the sinking of a few very small ships by battle cruisers a matter for Fleet cheering. But imagine his feelings when, having reached the end of the line, a bungle on the part of one of the battle cruisers in taking up her position for anchoring made it necessary for the whole squadron to turn back and come down the line again as though inviting more cheers, which cheers were heartily given, the Admiral being in a state of livid fury on his bridge. But the cheers expressed, naturally enough,

The Floating Pianos

the enthusiasm of the Fleet on our first contact with the enemy.

I heard also of the various extraordinary scares in Scapa Flow, the wild scurrying of the Fleet from its base to lochs on the west coast of Scotland, of the ever-increasing anxiety of the Commander-in-Chief as to the insecurity of his position in indefinite Scapa. I heard all about the beginning of the war, and how ships went up the Channel stripping themselves for the fight which was expected to take place at any moment, and of the numerous tables, pianos, arm-chairs and many other kinds of inflammable furniture which were to be seen bobbing about in the waves of the Channel. I should have been interested to have seen the floating pianos. But such was the keenness of the Navy that in a great number of ships the officers thus stripped themselves of every comfort, so eager were they to be ready for the fray; and it was not until it appeared that they might have to wait a month or two before a general Fleet action took place that furniture was gradually and shamefacedly restored to its appointed place. I knew one cruiser flagship whose Admiral was of so gallant and keen a disposition for fighting that he vacated his quarters altogether and lived, not only for weeks, but for months in the chart-room, where he fed his unfortunate staff exclusively on cold foods and non-alcoholic beverages.

We were less extreme, though not less efficient, in the *Lion*. Ships, as we know, have their character, and the character of the *Lion* was very definite; although she was a most amazingly efficient ship, she was inclined sometimes to be a little gloomy, not nearly so cheery as the *Princess Royal*, and not a " wonder-ship " like the *Queen Mary*

Sea Doings

and the *New Zealand*. Although, as has been seen, she had her moments of mirth, the wardroom was inclined to be serious—much more so than the Admiral's mess. No company presided over by David Beatty could ever be dull, and the *Lion* had not fallen into the mistake of over-austerity, nor of supposing that in order to fight the enemy efficiently it was necessary to be uncomfortable.

It is one of the charms of naval service that you live your own life, in your own house, and in your accustomed way, until the moment of the battle; and can rise from table to go to a fight as naturally as to go to a concert. The Admiral's mess always dined, when we were in harbour, in undress mess uniform, and was probably one of the very few messes that did so at that time. Three nights a week the band played outside the Admiral's cabin during dinner, and the remaining nights in the wardroom flat. All of which was pleasant and made for efficiency.

By far the most serious effect of the Admiralty's lack of foresight in preparing for the conditions which were to obtain in North Sea warfare was the complete absence of submarine defences in the North Sea bases at the beginning of the war. Sir George Callaghan and Sir John Jellicoe had done what was possible in the way of improvised gun defences at Scapa, but nothing in the nature of a boom, or of submarine nets, was achieved before the beginning of November, when Cromarty Firth was provided with this defence. The position at Scapa, with its three entrances and storm-swept waters, was much more complicated, and had been causing the Commander-in-Chief the most acute anxiety. Time and again he had had to take the whole Fleet out to the

Rear-Admiral Sir Lionel Halsey, G.C.V.O.,
K.C.M.G., C.B.
(Captain of H.M.S. *New Zealand* 1912-1917.)

A Policy Wanted

westward, and Lamlash, Loch Ewe, Loch-na-Keal and Lough Swilly were all at one time or another in process of preparation for more or less permanent occupation by the Grand Fleet. Just before my arrival, at the beginning of November, the Fleet was still based at Lough Swilly, and its distance away from the scene of action gave rise to not a little thought and discussion. The Commander-in-Chief's organization of and provision for the Fleet in all material ways, his care for the interests of the officers and men under him, were most cordially recognized throughout the Fleet; it was felt that these matters could hardly be in better or safer hands. But the whole question of the governing policy with regard to the main business was already, even in those days, a matter of considerable speculation and bewilderment. It was assumed that the Commander-in-Chief's hands were tied. There did not seem to be any definite policy at all. We were already suffering from German mine-laying activities and from the threat of enemy submarines, but there did not seem to be any definite idea at headquarters as to how these serious menaces were to be dealt with. There was no organized hunting for submarines, because we had not got the light craft to hunt with. As for mines, it is known now that at the beginning of the war we had none worth the name, and that when we began slowly to produce them they turned out to be more dangerous to us than to the enemy. And there was no policy, that I could ever hear of, as to even the elementary strategy which should govern our own use of such methods. At one time the idea was to mine the Germans in, so that they could not come out—a necessary preliminary to a naval campaign in the Baltic. But the Baltic project was

Sea Doings

overruled, and it was then pointed out that unless the Germans came out we could not fight and defeat them, upon which the mining policy in the Heligoland Bight was for the time abandoned. Also we had no mines. The enemy's mining activities were apparently being prosecuted without interruption. Admiral Beatty was always uncomfortable when he was in harbour, as their obvious policy should have been to mine *us* in, so that *we* could not come out. On the other hand, to be always at sea was not only to be exposed to the submarine danger, but also would involve an excessive strain on the fuel supply and wear and tear of material and personnel.

It was quite clear that the Commander-in-Chief's principal anxiety was to protect his Fleet from danger; and the lengths to which he was willing to go in this direction may be deduced from the fact, as stated in his own book, that on returning to Lough Swilly on November 3 after a conference at the Admiralty, and finding that the Fleet was under orders to proceed to Scapa at once, he immediately had these orders cancelled, and instead took his Fleet out to the westward of Galway Bay, thus placing two islands and a couple of seas between himself and the enemy. Action like this, on the part of a man whose personal courage was beyond all question, on whose part indeed it must have required considerable courage to pursue a line of action so foreign to the spirit of our Navy, shows the extent to which the tenets of Whitehall were influencing him. And his strategy was not a little puzzling to that part of the Fleet which was operating in the North Sea itself, and hoped for nothing better than to come to immediate grips with the enemy.

The same attitude of mind seemed to be observable

Turning Away

in the Commander-in-Chief's tactics, in so far as they could be judged when we met him at sea carrying out Fleet exercises. On several such occasions, when he and the battle cruiser forces were opposed to each other, Admiral Beatty launched destroyer attacks at him, to avoid which he invariably employed the method of turning his ships away. I remember that the first time I saw this happen from the bridge of the *Lion* a staff officer near me said : " If he does that when the Germans attack he can't be defeated, but he can't win." The turn-away is, of course, one of the recognized methods of avoiding a torpedo attack, but it is not the method usually advocated by experts as desirable to be employed by the stronger force or by a force determined on victory, even at a heavy cost.

It is fortunately not within the scope of this book, nor does the writer regard himself as competent, to enter into subjects in this connexion which have since become matters of keen controversy. I only touch upon them here to show that this attitude was already attracting the attention of serious students of war in the Fleet as early as November, 1914, and that in the Fleet itself there were many keen critics of the policy which may be described as the defensive-offensive. It seemed to me then, and seems much more clearly now, to be a necessary result of what has been well termed the " material mind " in naval affairs.[1] Lord Fisher had the material mind and, although he personally was nothing if not pugnacious, and had not one ounce of timidity in his composition, he had not the kind of mind that could use the staff necessary to carry

[1] See "The Battle of Jutland," by Commander Carlyon Bellairs, M.P., p. 42 *et seq.*, for a masterly analysis of this subject.

Sea Doings

out his magnificent but formless conceptions in terms of strategical and tactical warfare. He was preoccupied with the power of the weapon, but assumed that it would be handled with a spirit like his own.[1] Sir John Jellicoe, who was a product and disciple of the material school, and Lord Fisher's own choice, was obviously deeply impressed with the power of the weapon, but seemed to be preoccupied with a sense of its value preserved intact. To use it might be to endanger it, and therefore the instinct was in the direction of preserving it intact for use on some day or other when it could be used without any risk—a day that might never come.

This preoccupation of safety, which was characteristic of the material school, and which involved the Commander-in-Chief (holding the views he did) in such very real difficulties, has its analogy in the world of people who have amassed great wealth—which nearly always brings an exaggerated idea of the importance of money. A millionaire may be prodigal of his hundreds and thousands, but the sovereigns and shillings are handled far more carelessly by the man with a thousand a year than by him with twenty thousand. The only real value of money is that it can be spent and exchanged for the things that are desired, and surely the chief value of ships *in war time is* to win battles with them. Napoleon speaks somewhere of admirals who were always "seeing pictures," and whose minds were obsessed with the idea of the terrible things that might happen to them, rather than of the terrible things that ought to happen to the enemy. It was so with our material school, hoarding its

---

[1] "Those men in war who get there and then don't do anything—*cui bono?* A fleet magnificent, five times bigger than the enemy, and takes no risks!" Fisher, *Memories*, p. 115.

Material Defects

material like a miser. And the tragedy of the material school was that the material was not always good. Our mines, our torpedoes, our ammunition, were all inferior to those of the Germans at the time of which I write; and it was not until a great while afterwards that the Commander-in-Chief, excellent as was his organization and his provision for, and equipment of, his Fleet, could regard that magnificent weapon as being at all secure in the waters of Scapa Flow. These reminiscences come into the picture here; but the reader would be far wrong in supposing that there were any divisions, or frictions, then or at any time, in the Fleet. Sir John Jellicoe might be right or wrong, but he gave and received unqualified loyalty. He and Sir David Beatty represented diametrically opposite schools of naval thought, but this difference was never reflected in their always cordial relationship, nor was allowed to affect for a moment their co-operation in the attainment of the large purpose.

Up to the beginning of November the battle cruisers had constantly been used for a purpose which filled Admiral Beatty with misgivings, namely, the stopping and examination of merchant ships encountered on the trade route. This, of course, was a duty which should have been performed by cruiser patrols consisting of fast ships with large fuel capacity especially designed for the purpose; in no circumstances should it ever have been performed by capital ships. And even when it was performed we had an uncomfortable suspicion that the main purpose, of preventing material of war from reaching the enemy, was not always being fulfilled. A week before I joined one such flagrant case had occurred. A ship, stopped and examined, was found to be carrying iron ore

Sea Doings

from Norway to Rotterdam. Her captain was quite frank about the destination of the iron ore, which was nominally consigned to a company in Rotterdam, but on arrival there was unloaded over the side into lighters and sent up the Rhine to Krupp's at Essen. Stopping a ship like the *Lion* at sea in war time was, of course, running a dangerous risk of submarine attack, as a ship which is stopped can hardly be missed, and a submarine detailed on this duty would only have to follow a merchant ship and wait until the examining cruiser came up. We can therefore imagine the feelings of the Admiral and the Captain and every officer on board when a battle cruiser had to be used for this purpose. In this case, however, there seemed to be some result, and the Norwegian ship was taken in to the examining station at Kirkwall. A few days later orders came from the Admiralty that she was to be allowed to proceed. Having regard to the nature of the captain's admission, the Commander-in-Chief protested as strongly as he could, but with no effect. The ship had to be released, and the ore went on to Germany, to be turned into weapons directed against the lives of the brothers of those who had risked theirs in stopping the ship that carried it. When we found that on the board of the company owning the ore mines in Norway, a shareholder in the company that owned the ship, and a large shareholder in the firm in Rotterdam to which the ore was consigned, was a millionaire, holding a high position in English social life, and deep in the counsels of the Government, we felt that desperate measures were necessary. Desperate measures were taken; what they were only four people in the world accurately know; but they had results.

CHAPTER VI

THE RAID ON HARTLEPOOL AND SCARBOROUGH

IN the small hours of Tuesday, December 15, I was aroused by the sound of our torpedo nets coming in; and when, at 4 A.M., I went on duty, I found that we had suddenly been ordered to sea and were to sail at five. A German force was reported to be leaving the Ems this morning, and our orders from the Commander-in-Chief were to rendezvous with the Second Battle Squadron and the First Light Cruiser Squadron from Scapa and the Third Cruiser Squadron from Rosyth, in latitude 57.20 N., longitude 0.10 W., at 2.30 P.M. on December 15. There had been a succession of heavy gales, and the destroyers at Scapa could not accompany the Second Battle Squadron owing to the tremendous seas running in the Pentland Firth. *Boadicea* and *Blanche*, the light cruisers attached to the squadron, were so damaged by the heavy seas encountered in the Firth (*Boadicea* losing several men overboard) that they had to return to their base for repair.[1] To take their place all the available destroyers from Cromarty were ordered out, also two flotillas from Harwich; but this latter force, owing to complications due to its being directly under the command of the Admiralty, never got far enough to the northward to take any part in the subsequent operations. Only seven destroyers were available at Cromarty

---

[1] Jellicoe, "The Grand Fleet," p. 176.

The Raid on Hartlepool and Scarborough

—*Lynx, Ambuscade, Unity, Hardy, Shark, Acasta* and *Spitfire;* and the shortage of destroyers was to prove a very important factor in the occurrences of the following day.

As things were very quiet in the Intelligence office I went up on deck as we passed in the dark through the boom defence at Cromarty, and stayed there until we had passed out beyond the Souters, when we encountered a very heavy sea which caused even the *Lion* (usually but little affected by heavy weather) to roll and screw in a somewhat disquieting manner. Daylight found us out of sight of land on a south-easterly course and in weather which promised to add considerably to whatever excitements might be in store for the small craft accompanying us. At noon we received the following signal from the late Vice-Admiral Sir George Warrender, who was commanding the Second Battle Squadron and was therefore the senior officer at sea; his squadron consisted of the battleships *King George V.* (Flag), *Orion* (Rear-Admiral Sir Robert Arbuthnot), *Ajax, Centurion, Conqueror* and *Monarch.*

" V.A. Second Battle Squadron to V.A. *Lion:*
  "German squadron of four battle cruisers, five light cruisers and three flotillas leave Jade River daylight to-day, returns Wednesday night. Am proceeding to rendezvous 54.10 N., 3.0 E., 7.30 A.M. 16th. Hope to get news from Commodore (T) and join him. If nothing heard at 7.30 shall steer 90° till 10.30 and 270° till 1.30, speed 14 knots, then turn north. Considering your strength do not get more than five miles from me. Steering 90° I want you astern, otherwise ahead, with 3rd C.S. and 1st

90

The Dispositions

L.C.S. under your command. I think raid probably
Harwich or Humber. If you get engaged draw
enemy towards Battle Squadron. If Commodore
(T) does not join up I fear enemy's destroyers only.
On joining 3rd C.S. to take station one mile from
your port beam. 1st L.C.S. one mile on starboard
beam opening to five miles to-night, closing daylight.
They are then under your command to engage
enemy's light cruisers and head off destroyers as you
may direct. Battle Stations by 7 A.M. and steam
for full speed at midnight. Warn cruisers to beware
of mines floating or dropping astern. Have you any
suggestions? As soon as you understand take station
five miles ahead. If this weather continues if possible
engage enemy to windward and steer to hinder
destroyers. 11.41.''

This signal did not add greatly to the Admiral's
knowledge of the situation he was likely to encounter
next morning. Fortunately—or unfortunately—he did
not know then that the Harwich destroyers, although
at sea, would be 60 miles to the south of us at the
critical time, and that for scouting purposes we should
be dependent, in what promised to be very heavy weather,
on four light cruisers and seven destroyers. However,
the junction with the Rosyth and Scapa forces was duly
made that afternoon; and we proceeded in the formation
directed, with slight modification as to the positions in
which the scouting craft were spread. The order taken
for the night was that the battle cruisers took station
five miles ahead of the Battle Squadron, with the First
Light Cruiser Squadron disposed five miles to starboard
and the Third Cruiser Squadron five miles to port, the
destroyers being astern of the Battle Squadron.

The Raid on Hartlepool and Scarborough

In spite of the disadvantages in the composition of our force we were in high spirits and full of anticipation of a fight the next morning. Great preparations were made in the way of stripping cabins of all movable gear, removing as much woodwork as possible and generally preparing for action. The Admiral paid one of his rare visits to the wardroom before dinner, and found everyone full of hope and lively anticipation. Those who were not on duty turned in early that night. I had the middle watch, which was absolutely quiet as far as signals were concerned, but was full of unfamiliar sounds made by the huge ship straining as she was driven into the heavy seas. These moderated as the night wore on, and when I turned in at 4 A.M. there was prospect of smoother weather. I awoke at 6.80 and, on going up to the bridge, found that various signals had been received during the last hour, indicating that destroyers were engaged astern of the Battle Squadron. Strong Telefunken signals were reported from the wireless, and several undecipherable German signals were intercepted; and the continuance of this throughout the morning, as well as the meagre and often mangled nature of some of our own signals which we took in, seemed to indicate that the Germans were using their wireless for the purpose of confusing and interrupting ours. *Ambuscade*, *Lynx* and *Hardy* were all damaged by enemy fire, the two latter withdrawing to the Humber under escort of *Spitfire;* and the destroyers generally, in the absence of a flotilla leader, were often scattered and were unable to give much information. Action was sounded off in the *Lion* at seven o'clock, and very soon after the fine sunrise and clear sky gave promise of a welcome improvement in the

Daybreak—December 16, 1914.

Isolated Engagements

weather. At 7.80, the destroyers being evidently in severe trouble, we altered course to the westward of north in order to get into touch with the enemy reported. At this time (7.80 A.M.) the light cruisers were spread to the northward at a distance of five miles, and the Third Cruiser Squadron spread five miles astern.

Presently, as the daylight increased, we sighted the Battle Squadron ahead and received the signal: "Are you going after *Roon*?" This was the first we had heard of *Roon* (a German cruiser), and the obscurity of the situation was deepened rather than lightened by the question. The Admiral replied that he had heard nothing of the *Roon* and asked what course the Battle Squadron was steering. A few minutes later, at 8 A.M., a signal was received through *King George V.* from *Shark*, timed at 7.5, or nearly an hour before: "Position 54.22 N. 8.20 E.; am keeping touch with large cruiser *Roon* and five destroyers steering East. 0705." On receipt of this signal at 8 A.M. the battle cruisers and light cruisers altered course to the eastward to cut off the *Roon* and worked speed up to 24 knots, the Third Cruiser Squadron, which was limited to 20 knots, being ordered to preserve station on the Battle Squadron. The difficulties of the situation were very real. We had to bring our force from a base thirty-six hours away and hit off the enemy within an hour, for, according to the information furnished, if we did not succeed in reaching him in that time we should not reach him at all.

The next excitement was at 8.80, when *Shark* signalled: "Am being chased to westward" (interruption) "54.84 N. 8.48 E. 0815." Apparently, therefore, the course of the enemy was now west; but as yet we

93

The Raid on Hartlepool and Scarborough

had no information as to the position of his main forces. At 8.42 we intercepted a signal from the coastal scout *Patrol*, who did not give her position and whose signal was obscured by German interference, stating that she was heavily engaged with two enemy battle cruisers, upon which course was altered to the north. Ten minutes later the climax to this puzzle was provided by a signal intercepted from the Admiralty to the Commander-in-Chief: "Scarborough being shelled."

I remember receiving this signal by the chart-room telephone (it came through the first time as "Scapa being shelled," but even that could not add very much to the confusion). However, it gave us at least two definite points of enemy activity, and course was immediately altered to the westward in order to cut off the enemy's return from Scarborough. Soon after we had intercepted the signal to the Commander-in-Chief we received a signal from Sir George Warrender: "*Scarborough being shelled; I am proceeding towards Hull.*" Beatty's reply to this was characteristic. I forget the wording, but the effect of it was: "*Are you? . . . I am going to Scarborough*"; and to alter course himself to the westward in the direction of Scarborough. I think it was before this, or at any rate very soon after, that a signal was received from Sir George Warrender, who knew his man, practically telling Admiral Beatty to use his own judgment.

It now appeared that the enemy's main forces were to the westward, and not eastward, of us. The weather promise of the early dawn had not been fulfilled; mists were driving over the sea, visibility was reduced to about five miles, and the spray caused by the heavy seas made

We Make for the Coast

gunnery conditions poor for light craft. But we felt that we were really on the enemy's track now. We were not more than one hundred and twenty miles east of the English coast, and somewhere between us and that coast were the Germans. Another element entered into the situation which seemed to add to the advantage of our position. A belt of enemy mine-fields, some ten miles broad, lay in a north and south direction over the east coast of England, with a gap in the centre of it, the position of which was known to lie between 54.20 and 54.40 N. By this time we had heard that Hartlepool had also been bombarded; and it was obvious that forces which had been off Scarborough and Hartlepool, in the strip of clear water inside their own mine-fields, could only emerge from it by this gap in the middle, which lay exactly between those two places, and that we had only to make for this gap in order to catch them on their way out. A glance at the accompanying chart will show that the south-west patch of the Dogger Bank was a governing element in the operations of this day. The water over this patch is too shallow for big ships; and when we divided at 9 A.M. the battle cruisers went to the north of it and the battleships to the south. Similarly the German forces, when they divided, passed half to the north and half to the south.

A few minutes before 10.80 Sir George Warrender, acting on a signal received from the Commander-in-Chief, ordered the battle cruisers to pass through the gap, and our light cruisers were at the same time ordered to "penetrate the mine-fields and locate the enemy." This order caused some little excitement on board the *Southampton*, as paravanes had not then been invented,

The Raid on Hartlepool and Scarborough

and penetrating mine-fields was likely to be an operation not without incident.[1] At this point (10.40) the Admiralty took a hand in the direction of the operation, informing Sir George Warrender that the enemy was probably returning to Heligoland, and that he should keep clear of the mine-fields and steer a course to cut the enemy off. The battle cruisers were ordered by Sir George Warrender to obey this order.[2] It was met with a very slight alteration of course, and as a matter of fact we continued to go for the gap.

Things were much too exciting for me to leave the signal bridge. When we were in action the deciphering department was transferred to the Admiral's chart-room on the signal bridge, and as anything might happen at any moment, and as the ship was at action stations, no one thought of going below. And just now, while we were all on the tip-toe of expectation, Destiny made a move. At about 11.80 a sudden and most unwelcome change came over the weather. Heavy squalls, with thick mists and driving rain, came down from the north-west, whipping up the sea into white foam and sometimes blotting out the light cruisers where they drove into it five miles away ahead and on our port beam. And as they disappeared in the swirling welter a great flash of gunfire lit up the murk, and the deep note of the report was carried to us upon the wind.

Here was the real thing at last, the long expected, long hoped-for collision with the enemy; and with it, punctual to the moment, the weather that seemed always designed to favour the Germans. But they were making

[1] Etienne, "A Naval Lieutenant, 1914-1918," page 64.
[2] Jellicoe, "The Grand Fleet," page 178.

Rear-Admiral Von Hipper.
(In command of German Battle Cruiser Force 1914-1918.)

A Slip

for home, and we were to the eastward of them : that was the main point. The firing continued, although the *Southampton* was all but invisible to us, and in a few minutes a signal came through from Commodore Goodenough, "Engaged with enemy cruisers," and a further signal to say that he had altered course to the southward. He had, in fact, seen the shapes of ships driving through the mists, and had flashed our recognition signal at them ; and as they failed to make the reply, he opened fire.

Admiral Beatty, with characteristic quickness in adapting his plans to turn a disadvantage into an advantage, did not, in view of the thick weather, immediately turn to the south to support the light cruisers. It was impossible for *Lion* and our battle cruisers to have been sighted by the enemy, as the flash of their guns was all that was visible to us. The *Southampton's* signal, "Engaged with enemy cruisers," implied that they were engaged with the German light forces screening the retirement of the enemy battle cruisers, and that by holding on our westerly course for a few minutes longer we should run into the heavy ships themselves and take them, as we hoped, by surprise. It was the soundest deduction, but it was based, alas! on insufficient reports. Commodore Goodenough, engaged in fighting his ship on a bridge that was constantly being swept, was not in a position to make careful writing on signal-pads a very easy matter; probably his signal was transmitted to the signalman verbally, and as received by us it omitted the information that in fact there were two groups of Germans, one consisting of destroyers and light cruisers, and the other of light cruisers and an armoured cruiser, the *Prince Adalbert*. At that moment this whole force was flying homeward through the driving mists to the south of us.

In Admiral Beatty's mind, however, Commodore Goodenough was engaged only with the advanced force; and on the assumption that the battle cruisers were close behind them, his tactics were calculated to bring them to action with the greatest possible advantage to us. Having stood on to the westward until about 11.50, he altered course to the southward to keep within touch of the light cruisers. And then occurred the second of the two minute but fatal mistakes which, in the writer's opinion, had a profound effect, not only on the fortunes of that day, but of the whole war. The second of our light cruisers, the *Birmingham*, was about two miles astern of *Southampton*, and if we were about to engage the battle cruisers it was important that, having no destroyers, the light cruisers not actually engaged should be in a position from which they could repel any attack that might be made upon us by light enemy craft. Turning to the Flag-Lieutenant, the Admiral said, "Tell that light cruiser to resume station; she's too far astern." The Flag-Lieutenant, who was seldom at a loss for any knowledge or quality pertaining to his duties, and could recognize any ship in the battle cruiser force when she was only a smudge on the horizon, had a moment's doubt whether the shadow amid the driving mists on our beam was the *Nottingham* or *Birmingham*. To name her wrongly in signalling to her would cause confusion and delay, and he therefore told the signalman operating the searchlight to call her up simply as "light cruiser." The arc light was steadied upon her, and the signal made, "Light cruiser close," or "Light cruiser resume station"

A Narrow Escape

—I do not remember which. Although the beams of the lamp bore on this ship, they had a wide enough radius to be read also by *Southampton;* and the signal reached Commodore Goodenough, still heavily engaged with the enemy, as "Light cruisers resume station." He at once assumed, not unnaturally, that he was being recalled from his unequal combat in order that he should not hamper our battle cruisers in engaging the enemy. He altered course to the westward again; and in three minutes had lost touch. We drove on for half an hour, when we heard that the Second Battle Squadron and Third Cruiser Squadron had sighted the enemy in latitude 54.28 N., longitude 2.14 E., steering to the eastward. This again was a miss by the narrowest margin. When the commander of the German light cruisers saw the giant forms of our battleships looming up through the mist, he, with great presence of mind, made the recognition signal which Commodore Goodenough had made to him half an hour before, and was in consequence taken at first to be a British squadron. The deception could only be kept up for a minute or two, but it was long enough for him to turn again into the mist and thus make his escape from the 13.5 guns, a salvo or two from which at that range would have blown him out of the water.

Here was another moment in which rapid decision was essential. Wherever the German battle cruisers were, they were evidently not in company with the force which had been engaged, or we should have encountered them during the last half-hour, in which they and we, steaming on opposite courses, had between us covered a distance of 25 miles. On the other hand, the forces astern were definitely located. Beatty accordingly turned 16 points and

The Raid on Hartlepool and Scarborough

chased to the eastward. The Battle Squadron signalled that on their attempting to engage the enemy he had turned north at full speed and disappeared in the mist. Beatty then (1.15 P.M.) turned northward again for about 10 miles; but, hearing nothing more, resumed the chase to the eastward at full speed until dusk, when we were recalled to the Battle Squadron; but neither by us nor by any other of the forces present was touch with the Germans regained. Their battle cruisers, keeping to the north of the shallow patch, were never sighted.

Such is a brief outline of the facts as they appeared to one taking part, and in so far as they are ascertained by fixed positions and recorded movements. But a little analysis, even of these meagre facts, will show that the situation suggested by them is even more complex than one would at first sight suppose. The theory, the only one with which the public has hitherto been furnished, that we met the enemy's raiding force on its way home from Scarborough and missed contact with it in the mist, and so by a hair's breadth were deprived of an important victory, will not do. There were five points when British forces made contact with German forces on this day. To avoid confusing the reader we will not trouble about the latitude, but merely note these positions in terms of longitude east of Greenwich.

(1) The position of the engagement before dawn, when, it will be remembered, our destroyers were in action with two groups—a strong force of enemy destroyers and, later, one enemy cruiser and three light cruisers—was roughly about 2.50 E.

(2) The position of Scarborough is about 0.15 W.

Elements of the Puzzle

Hartlepool is, of course, much further west still, and enemy forces had been bombarding these places at 8 A.M.

(3) At 7.5 *Shark* signalled that she was chasing the cruiser *Roon* and five destroyers to the eastward in longitude 8.20 E. Further news of the same forces was that at 8.15 *Shark* reported that she was being chased to the westward and gave her position as 8.48 E.

(4) At 11.80 *Southampton* was in contact with other light forces in longitude about 1.55 E.

(5) At 12.16 P.M. German cruisers and destroyers were sighted by the Second Battle Squadron in longitude 2.14 E.

In the first of these positions, that in which our destroyers were engaged, the enemy were retiring to the eastward, in which direction they were chased. In the second of these positions the *Roon* was located in 8.20 E. In the third, at 8.80, the enemy was located at Scarborough. At 11.80 we were in contact with him in longitude 2.50 E., when he was on a south-easterly course, and at 12.16 the enemy cruisers and destroyers were in 2.14 E., proceeding eastwards. The greatest distance between any two of these positions is about 220 miles. Assuming that the bombarding squadron left Scarborough at 8.80, and was steaming at 24 knots, it could not have been in the nearest of the positions where Germans were sighted (our 11.80 position) before 1.80 P.M.; nor could the force observed on a westerly course in 8.48 E. at 8.15 A.M. have been at Hartlepool earlier than 5.80 the same evening. What, then, is the explanation?

Like most puzzles when you know the answer, this one, insoluble in the absence of information as to the

The Raid on Hartlepool and Scarborough

German movements, becomes fairly simple in the light
of that information.

To begin with, the German Battle Fleet had followed
the battle cruisers and light forces to sea. This we knew
that afternoon, but we did not then know that they had
turned back early in the morning. The German explanation of this is that they were too far astern of their
own battle cruisers to be of any use in supporting them
if they should become engaged.[1] This is a curious explanation. Von Ingenohl's destroyers had already been
engaged with ours; his cruisers, after their bombardment,
would be falling back on him; and by holding on he
stood a very good chance of catching the British battle-
cruisers between his Battle Fleet and the German battle-
cruisers. A more likely explanation is that his destroyers
found the seas too heavy for them to proceed at the
requisite speed, or else that the short visibility and
ignorance of our movements made discretion appear to
be the better part of valour.

Another point which throws light on the apparent
puzzle is that the Germans were in three separate groups
—the First Scouting Division, consisting of the battle
cruisers *Seydlitz, Moltke, Derfflinger, Von der Tann* and
Blücher; the Second Scouting Division, composed of
light cruisers and two torpedo boat flotillas; and the main
Fleet, consisting of battleships, with light cruisers, three
flotillas and two armoured cruisers *Prinz Heinrich* and
Roon. Considered as a raid, it was well planned and well
carried out by the Germans; considered as a means of
drawing us into action, it showed little enterprise, as the
Germans avoided the chance of contact. Rear-Admiral

[1] Scheer, "Germany's High Sea Fleet in the World War," page 71

102

The Explanation

Von Hipper sailed from the Jade River at 8.20 A.M. on the 15th. With him were the First and Second Scouting groups. The Battle Fleet sailed late in the afternoon of the same day. When the position marked 6 A.M. in the plan had been reached, however, the light cruisers and torpedo boats found the sea, as they approached the coast, so heavy that they could not maintain their speed nor be of any practical use. They were therefore detached with orders to fall back in the direction of the Battle Fleet. Von Hipper, with his five battle cruisers, went on to the coast, performed his bombardment and retired at full speed on a line to the east-north-east. He was therefore to the northward of us when our light cruisers became engaged with Scouting Group No. 2 to the southward; but we cannot have been far away from one another at two o'clock, and our tracks must have come very close again some time between three and four in the afternoon. The two forces on this day may have been likened to two men fumbling for each other in a dark room and occasionally even brushing together in their search; or we may say that one of the men was searching and the other was trying to avoid the search, as an analysis of the sketch chart of the German movements does not suggest any great desire on their part to become engaged with us.

It was a day of great excitement and nervous tension (which would have been greater had we known the truth) and was followed by a great reaction of disappointment. We continued our eastward chase until dusk, or nearly four o'clock. I shall not easily forget those four hours of rush through the mist and storm on that grey December day; nor the strange, deserted aspect of the ship cleared for action, and all its domestic life suspended. I went round the ship in the course of the afternoon; the men were busy with the eternal drill of guns and ranges in their turrets and at their gun-stations. Down in the fore transmitting-station, that telephone exchange where the mathematics of fire control are worked out by men and machines, I found the officer in charge of it and his assistants anxiously waiting for news of the world above decks, sceptical yet very hopeful that things might still happen. Parts of the ship generally swarming with life were blank and deserted; and clusters of men were grouped about—fire parties and such-like—in unaccustomed places. The wardroom flat was dark and deserted, as were all our cabins; and on this as on other days (the galleys being out of action when the ship was at battle stations) our servants took care of us by bringing up relays of strange meats and improvised snacks on which we subsisted through the day.

But after three o'clock we knew the chase to be useless and were recalled to the northward by Sir George Warrender. At this time, or an hour later, the German battle cruisers must have been near us to the southward, and an encounter would at that hour have astonished us both. The day was a complete failure—in one sense, that is; for had it had the kind of success for which we were trying, possibly very few of us would have been here to tell the tale. But the whole operation, even as viewed in the light of our partial and imperfect knowledge on that evening, was full of lessons. The uselessness of sending destroyers out without a leader was fully demonstrated. These gallant craft, which can and do render such invaluable service to a force of heavy ships, must always have a mother with them—a leader for

Defective Dispositions

The Raid on Hartlepool and Scarborough

Defective Dispositions

signalling and protection. We did not then know, of course, of the conditions in the Pentland Firth that had put the light cruisers out of action and made the sailing of the flotillas from Scapa impossible. This, however, was one of the lesser of the unsatisfactory features of the day. To the Admiral, the meagre and confusing information furnished caused very real anxiety. I have never known him to take a useless risk; and no strategist likes to risk his squadron in thick weather, in waters which he knows to be infested by the enemy, without either being furnished with information, or the means of scouting and obtaining it for himself. The Admiral of Patrols furnished not one scrap of information throughout the day; the Admiralty information was good, but consistently too late to be effectively acted upon. The whole operation afforded a striking example of the consequences of a complete lack of a system of Fleet Intelligence, as distinct from the always excellent Admiralty Intelligence —which was, however, only doled out to us in very small doses, and often too late to be of use.

And the events of this day finally demonstrated the folly of sending out any part of the fleet without reinforcements and support being within reach. The Third Battle Squadron were somewhere to the north of us, and Commodore (T) was coming up from the south, but both were too far away. If Ingenohl had held on to the westward we might quite easily have lost our Battle Cruiser Squadron, and possibly the greater part of the Battle Squadron as well. The lesson was learned at headquarters, however; and we never put to sea again, at any rate in my time, without the Grand Fleet being at sea and in a position in which contact with the enemy could have been

The Raid on Hartlepool and Scarborough

developed into a fleet action if he were willing, or could be forced, to fight.

Admiral Beatty had consistently proclaimed, hitherto to deaf ears, the uselessness of having the fast scouting forces of the Fleet based so far from the scene of operations as Cromarty. Confusion of mind on this subject before the war was astounding, but I am afraid that Lord Fisher must be held responsible. As far back as 1910 he wrote quite proudly : " I got Rosyth delayed four years as not being the right thing or the right place "[1]; and again in 1912 : " At the Defence Committee yesterday we had a regular set-to with Lloyd George (supported by Harcourt and Morley chiefly) against the provision of defence for Cromarty as a shelter anchorage for the Fleet. . . . As you know, I have always been ' dead on ' for Cromarty and hated Rosyth, which is an unsafe anchorage —the whole Fleet in jeopardy the other day—and there's that beastly bridge which, if blown up, makes the egress very risky without examination. . . . Also Cromarty is strategically better than Rosyth. . . . I still hate Rosyth and fortifications and East Coast Docks and said so the other day ! "[2]

It might seem unfair to quote these remarks if they had not been rescued from oblivion and published by Lord Fisher himself in the year 1919, when he apparently ignored the fact that Rosyth and East Coast Docks, once we did get them, proved our salvation. Lord Fisher had a clearer grasp of the truth when he wrote in the same book, page 182 : " But perhaps the most sickening of all the events of the war was the neglect of the Humber as

[1] Fisher, "Memories," page 194.
[2] Ibid., page 216.

"Keep Nearer to the Enemy"

the jumping-off place for our great fast Battle Cruiser
force, with all its attendant vessels, for offensive action
at any desired moment, and as a mighty and absolute
deterrent to the humiliating bombardment of our coasts
by that same fast German Battle Cruiser force. The
Humber is the nearest spot to Heligoland; and at
enormous cost and greatly redounding to the credit of
the present Hydrographer of the Navy, Admiral Lear-
mouth (then Director of Fixed Defences), the Humber
was made submarine-proof, and batteries were placed in
the sea protecting the obstructions, and moorings laid
down behind triple lines of defence against all possibility
of hostile successful attack. However, I had to leave the
Admiralty before it was completed and the ships sent
there; and then the *mot d'ordre* was Passivity; and when
the Germans bombarded Scarborough and Yarmouth and
so on, we said to them *à la Chinois*, making great grimaces
and beating tom-toms : ' If you come again, look out! '
But the Germans weren't Chinese and they came; and
the soothing words spoken to the Mayors of the bombarded
East Coast towns were what Mark Twain specified as
being ' spoke ironical.' "

If the last signal that was flying on the *Lion* when she
dropped out of the battle of the Dogger Bank had been
the last signal ever made by Beatty it could not more
simply have expressed his conception of war : " Keep
nearer to the enemy." It would indeed make a very
sound motto for a man's life in the everyday affairs
of the world, although there are people who think you
can best defeat your enemy by turning your back on
him and keeping out of his way. While another school
of opinion had been considering the advisability of

The Raid on Hartlepool and Scarborough

removing the Fleet bases westward to Loch Ewe and Lough Swilly, he had been agitating that the Humber, properly protected, should be made available as an advance base for the heavy ships, or at least that the battle cruisers might be moved south to the Firth of Forth. This action proved him right, and by Admiralty orders the battle cruisers changed their base on December 20 to Rosyth, where they remained throughout the war. To that extent, and it was a very important one, we were nearer to the enemy. The principle, in so far as it applied to a strategical base, had been grasped as a result of these operations of December 16, although whether the infection of the sane spirit that inspired it had been caught, is by no means certain.

The Commander-in-Chief, on hearing of the shelling of Scarborough on the morning of the 16th, had ordered steam to be raised in the Battle Fleet, and put to sea at noon on that day, at the same time ordering the Third Battle Squadron to leave Rosyth at 10 A.M. It is difficult to imagine what possible use these belated movements could have been, as Sir John Jellicoe knew 20 hours before that the Germans were out. His ships all met us on our way north on the morning of the 17th, and the day was spent by the whole Fleet in battle exercises. We in the battle cruisers did target practice with our 13.5 and 4-inch guns. At this period the routine of such practice was to launch a target, steam away from it for the requisite number of miles, and then steam past it at full speed, each gun being allowed so many rounds of ammunition to be expended during the run. The target was practically stationary and did not

Picking up Targets

really represent the conditions which we should have to encounter in an action, in which the enemy would be constantly altering course; but it was the best form of practice devised at that time. I do not know what the percentage of hits ought to have been, but it never satisfied Captain Chatfield or his gunnery officers. This day is memorable for the fact that it was probably the last time during the war when capital ships were stopped at sea, in waters infested by enemy submarines, in order to pick up the target. I watched the operation from the bridge. We slowed down, and the ship was steered with great skill to come up with the target practically at the moment when she lost way, and the whole of the watch, under the orders of the Commander, were stationed along the ship's side with slings and hooks in order to secure the great structure of wood and canvas as it came alongside. The business occupied a considerable time, and I could not help thinking how much more quickly it would have been performed by the mate of a merchant service tramp with half a dozen hands. It was one of the fetishes of the Navy to employ as many hands as possible, instead of as few, on any given job, with the result that jobs sometimes took a good deal longer than was necessary.

It was a very nervous moment when we were stopped; everyone was on the *qui vive* for submarines; and if a "U" boat had happened to come along at the time it would have had a sitting shot at us. I remember asking the Admiral what were the respective values of the *Lion* and of the target; and if it was really considered worth while to risk four million pounds for the sake of four pounds. He had asked the same question often before;

and this time he said he would decline to stop ships at sea again for any such purpose. Naturally the target, a structure sufficiently heavy and cumbersome to damage a light ship that should run into it, and bearing its tell-tale of the results of our battle practice, could not be left floating about in the sea; but after this day targets were no more picked up by us, but at the conclusion of battle practice were rammed and destroyed. Ramming targets was great fun; the ships formed into line ahead and made for the target; if No. 1 missed it, No. 2 had a chance, and if both missed it, Nos. 8 and 4 had an opportunity of covering themselves with glory. The success or failure of each ship depended very much on who the officer of the watch happened to be; for it was no easy matter to steer a battle cruiser going between 15 and 20 knots so as to hit a fifty-feet target fairly in the middle. If the blow was at all a glancing one, the target would slide off to one side and pass astern. I have often known the *Lion* miss, and the *Tiger*, a much more difficult ship to steer owing to her taking large sheers when given much helm, very seldom succeeded; but the *Princess Royal* rather fancied herself, while *Queen Mary* was a model target destroyer, and could generally be safely entrusted to hit the target in the middle, upon which it would disintegrate it to its component parts and be no more seen except in the form of bits of floating timber.

There is always a large amount of work consequent upon any operations in the presence of the enemy, whether they have been successful or not. The collection and co-ordination of signals received and sent, the collation of wireless reports from other ships, and the general attempt to find out what had really happened, kept us

Photo: Cribb, Southsea.

H.M.S. *Princess Royal.*

Photo: Cribb, Southsea.

H.M.S. *Queen Mary.*

Photo: Cribb, Southsea.

H.M.S. *Tiger.*

A Bitter Disappointment

busy all day. In the evening we were turned north again and sent back to Cromarty, where we arrived on the morning of the 18th. That day was a nightmare of coaling, with all its attendant confusion and filth, and of complicated activities. The Admiral had to write his despatch to the Commander-in-Chief; and before that could be done all the written despatches which came in from light cruisers and destroyers had to be analysed and digested by him.

The more we heard the more bitter was our disappointment at the failure of the previous day. The accounts of the horrible casualties to women and children in the bombarded towns were particularly affecting; the shelling of defenceless towns was something new in naval warfare, and the Admiral's mortification at having been so narrowly thwarted in inflicting punishment on the raiders was intense. He was at the time very angry with Commodore Goodenough for committing, what was in his eyes the unpardonable sin of letting go a hold of the enemy which had once been established—and I have no doubt told him so when he came on board that day to make his explanation. But Admiral Beatty's anger never lasted long, and he was the last man in the world to look for a scapegoat on such an occasion. Deeply disappointed as he was, he well knew the difference between the mistakes of a sound man and the mistakes of a duffer. To the duffer he would never give a second chance; but he knew very well that a mistake on the part of a first-rate man was, at any rate, a security that that particular mistake would never happen again; and his judgment of Commodore Goodenough was accurate. That gallant officer made no more mistakes, and in the

The Raid on Hartlepool and Scarborough

battle of Jutland (and I imagine on many other occasions) furnished an almost classic example of the way in which scouting by light cruisers ahead of a fast Fleet encountering the enemy ought to be done; and the combination of daring coolness and independent judgment which he showed on that and other occasions endowed him and his ship, the *Southampton*, with honourable fame.

That evening the Admiral, more affected and perturbed than I ever saw him before or since, wrote a brief manifesto or message to his Fleet, expressing his deep sympathy with them in their disappointment and inspiring them with his hope of an early retribution. The sheet of letter-paper on which the draft of this Order is pencilled in his strong, nervous handwriting lies before me as I write; and no simpler or truer evidence of the spirit of those days could be imagined. It was a personal and private message from the Admiral to his Fleet, and is not for the public, although I think they would endorse every word of it. The next day it was read by the captains to the assembled ships' companies at a general muster in every ship, and it awoke its due, although silent, response.

CHAPTER VII

THE FIRTH OF FORTH

THE arrival of the Battle Cruiser Squadron at Rosyth on Tuesday, December 22, began a second chapter in the existence of that force during the war. At Invergordon and Scapa one had an acute sense of detachment from everything but the sea and the Navy. Here we were at once nearer the world and nearer the enemy. The London papers reached us quite early on the day of their issue; and when ships were at four hours' notice (they were never at less) there was time for officers to go ashore, lunch in Edinburgh, go to a cinema or walk down Princes Street looking at the shop windows, and still be off at nightfall into the great unknown of the dark seas. This, although it had some disadvantages, was on the whole a welcome relief to men who had been cut off from the world since the beginning of the war, and to whom human faces and human voices other than those of their own shipmates meant a great deal. Personally, having had quite enough of the world for the time being, and finding naval society much more congenial than that of London, or even Edinburgh, I preferred the sombre and isolated life of Invergordon. So long as I was at sea, or isolated with the Navy in its majestic activities, I was happy and serene; but the presence of civilization in the form of shops, tram cars, luncheon-parties, cinemato-

I   113

graphs and people engaged in ordinary life, I found upsetting and disturbing. It made the war seem too unreal, an impossible nightmare out of which one would awake; and the contrast between the extraordinary business on which we were engaged and the daily life of the Scottish capital, spoiled one for both. Much as I like and admire Edinburgh, the possibilities of recreation afforded by that capital in a daily visit of two and a half hours are limited, and I was always glad to get back to the ship. Once or twice it was possible, by careful forethought, to arrange a game of golf, but the necessity of always being back by a certain time, the haunting fear that something might happen and the squadron go to sea without you, was incompatible with that leisurely frame of mind in which alone golf can be enjoyed. It was far pleasanter to go for a walk with the Admiral, but these occasions were rarer now than before; indeed we were all glad that he should have as much variety of company as possible, and the fact that Lady Beatty was living at Aberdour and that her yacht the *Sheelah*, fitted as a hospital carrier, was moored half a mile from Hawes Pier, made him the less dependent on his staff during his brief hours of recreation. On the whole the change was welcome to almost everyone, and the fact that we were eight hours nearer the enemy more than compensated for the dangers likely to attend the navigating of the narrow twenty-mile channel from the Forth Bridge to May Island on our way in and out. So we settled down to wait.

The fact that thousands of letters were written every day from the Fleet to the people ashore, and that prac-

The Anchorage.

The Second Battle Cruiser Squadron.

The Lion's Lair

tically no one outside it knew anything of its daily life, was one of the most remarkable conditions incidental to that remarkable war. The art of writing letters without saying anything had been brought to a fine perfection in the Fleet; and so steady and firm was this reticence that

The Firth of Forth

it had wellnigh broken down public curiosity. People had almost given up wondering and speculating about conditions of life that were so completely hidden from them, and were content to regard the Navy as a mysterious machine which produced perfection and efficiency without being watched or tended.

That was a fine tribute—justifiable, if not quite accurate. But, after all, it was human life and energy which were the motive power of the machine; and although on the technical side its doings had, and have still, perforce to remain a mystery, there was a human side to it which there is no need to hide. There is, indeed, no more human type of creature than your sailor, be he admiral or side-boy; and life in isolated communities afloat tends to develop these humanities in both big and little affairs. Of course the average sailor did not write home about the human aspects of his daily life. They were commonplace to him, he was too near them, he was even bored with them; and since his two great ambitions were to smash the enemy and have a long spell of leave, and as he was obliged to wait patiently for both, he was not exactly obsessed by the human interest or picturesqueness of his immediate environment. Yet it is worth making the attempt to convey something of it to the nation in whose heart, although it knew so little of him, he so securely holds a place.

Looking back on that winter of 1914-15, one had two paramount impressions—first, how long and dark it was; and, second, how easily we got through it. In this retrospect it seems like a long tunnel; the absence of the sun and the pervading presence of electric light are persistent in the memory, like the odours arising from the mess decks after a sixteen-hour night. And yet the bitter cold which so devastated the trenches in Flanders was never a really serious element in the life of big ships in the North Sea. For one thing, on the principle that if you take an umbrella out with you it won't rain, we had such a terrific provision of knitted and woollen protections against cold as must wellnigh have stupefied the elements and succeeded in producing a fairly mild winter. For another, there is hardly ever in our seas that strictness of cold which is produced by a wind that blows over miles of frozen land. Still further, large modern ships are very well heated and ventilated, and of their companies it is only a very small proportion which are exposed to the weather at one time. In the destroyers and patrol craft it is quite another matter; and they who, plunging day and night through those cold waters, swept by grey seas, whipped by half-frozen spray, and numbed from head to foot, yet kept their faculties alert, and their vigilance strung to an eternal concert pitch, knew what cold is, what winter is, and knew, too, the joy of that first spring day when one could stand still in the sunshine without having to walk briskly about in order to keep warm. It was to such as these that the thick woollen garments brought something of the warmth of the quiet firesides beside which they were knitted, and of the thoughts and prayers that so often must have been woven with the wool into the fabric.

Whether in harbour or at sea, winter life in the Fleet fell into a very ordered routine. At sea there was, of course, one constant preoccupation—the enemy. In this war the Navy was for the first time fighting with the invisible; and from the moment a ship left a defended harbour until she returned the assumption was that at any moment a blow might be dealt or received. For the individual officer this meant that he could never relax; for although he continued to do the ordinary things of his life—divisions, defaulters, turret drill, gunnery exercises, sitting down to meals, keeping watch on the bridge, sleeping, reading—he knew that there was no moment, no fraction of a second, in which these things might not suddenly go into silence and darkness for him, or in which he might not be called upon to put into practice all the science and efficiency which he had been building up through the years of peace. That was at sea. But in harbour there was, of course, a certain relaxation. Everything was always ready: that was the first condition of life; but once it had been got ready there was little to do but wait for the next call. And there were many officers in the Fleet who spent more hours in the wardroom during these winter months than they had put in during the whole of their naval career. Different ships had different fashions; but on the whole it was a winter of games. Every kind of game and puzzle would be produced, from jig-saws to attaque; and often the long wardroom table after tea would look like nothing so much as a kindergarten, littered with the apparatus of recreation; while gunnery " nuts," torpedo experts, the choicest blooms of Whale Island, and the most finished products of H.M.S. *Vernon* would vie with each other in laboriously compiling pictures of old women gathering sticks, or pore for an hour over the problem of a missing piece of a horse's nose.

What else we did depended on where we were. The deep-water harbours of these islands, for example, are rich in scenery, but rather poor in any of the amusements

Walking the Deck

which appeal to the naval officer with a few hours' leave. Most of them are remote from large towns; and in the short space available between lunch and dark (by which time everyone had to be on board) it required some enthusiasm to go ashore and tramp through the bleak landscape that became so familiar, and often, in its dead winter aspect, so distasteful. In harbours like Scapa even this austere recreation would not be worth while, owing to the distance of the ship from a landing-place; and the regulation tramp of deck with a companion would take its place. Walking the deck of the ship is an art; there are niceties to be observed, especially where many are walking at once. Different parts of the deck are tacitly left to different pairs or groups; the sensitiveness developed in people who live at very close quarters demands that you should not continually pass and repass another; two stripes will not brush against three stripes, nor three stripes (except by invitation) walk the same part of the deck as four stripes; and if by any chance a greater than four stripes should come up to take the air, there will be a gradual melting away of pedestrians from the quarter-deck until the great man has it to himself—which is one reason, possibly, why considerate admirals get less than enough exercise.

In the battle cruisers no leave in the ordinary sense could be given to the men; but they were sent ashore in parties of a hundred or so at a time, to play football, where that was possible, to have a brisk march where it was not. Even that mild recreation came but rarely to the individual seaman; and it is amazing to consider how happy and how healthy they had kept in the trying conditions of ship life. No praise, indeed, can be too high for the spirit they showed throughout the long and trying winter. They worked and slept and (when possible) fought and ate (especially ate) with unfailing appetite and punctuality; they grumbled hardly at all, and never, it can be literally said, when any call, however trying, was made on them in the execution of duty at sea. Because to be at sea was to be nearer that long-desired moment when the enemy would be discovered, and it would be possible to get a "biff" at him.

The stokers—who saw nothing, had the hardest work, and were in the greatest peril if the fabric of the ship was damaged—were the most enthusiastic of all. In the *Lion* the least informed could always tell when we were going to sea by the songs that used to rise from the mess decks as soon as the orders to the engine-room department to raise steam had been given; the whole ship began to murmur with strange music, like a hive. It was on the morning after the Dogger Bank action, which involved prolonged and superhuman effort from the stokehold crews, that a stoker petty officer fell in before the senior engineer lieutenant and asked him if he would "Please make an order that the men at the furnaces were not to sing in action, as he found it impossible to make himself heard in D boiler room." Mighty workers, indeed, and mighty eaters too. With no opportunities for spending money in drink, food remained the only indulgence; and the trade in extra delicacies done by the canteen was enormous. In the *Princess Royal* two thousand eggs were cooked for breakfast every morning and about one thousand in the evening; a hearty stoker or seaman would think nothing of eating six eggs for breakfast. His whole scheme of diet would make a food reformer turn pale. But his stomach was as stout as his heart; and the long

The Navy always at War

winter in the North Sea without change of scene or companionship, without a moment's relaxation of the strain of watching and waiting for an unseen enemy, came and went without finding a weak spot in either.

It is not necessary, when you think of your friends in the Fleet, to picture them as continually staring with strained vision into the mists of the North Sea. True there was always someone doing it, but no one was doing it always. The Fleet was so large, its distribution was so ingeniously arranged, that a murmur of the wireless could bring it together within a few hours at a given rendezvous, disperse it, concentrate it, and move it with ease and certainty at a touch of the master's hand which controlled it. In the intervals of movement its life was often a very quiet one, strangely like the routine of peace. For one of the profound differences between the Navy and the Army was the extent to which each was affected by a state of war. When war broke out the life of the Army was revolutionized; it was bodily transferred to a different country, its whole organization and environment were profoundly changed. But the Navy continued to move in its familiar element; its peace routine was so entirely designed for war conditions that the imminence of tremendous issues hardly affected its daily life and routine; instead of having been ready to fight at twelve hours' notice, it was ready at a moment's notice—that was all. There was no leave, there were no guests, there was less gold lace to be seen, but otherwise the daily round of life was very much the same as might have been witnessed in the North Sea harbours on any day during the previous five years of peace. There were little differences, infinitely affecting the situation; but for the most part they were

The Firth of Forth

invisible differences, and only the trained eye would mark them or realize their great significance.

The Edinburgh citizen whose windows gave him a view of the Firth might have seen, in the pale sunshine of one of these December mornings, a scene of great, but to him incomprehensible activity. Perhaps the day before the harbour had been almost empty; that morning it was populous with craft of every kind. The Fleet lay, squadron by squadron, in its ordered lines. How it managed to arrive in the dark, showing no lights, guided by no beacons, and to anchor itself with mathematical precision, was a mystery which resided in the keeping of that officer in each ship after whose name a large "N" appeared in the Navy List, and who was familiarly spoken of as "the Pilot." But there it lay, battleships, cruisers, destroyers, colliers, store-ships, oil-ships, ammunition carriers, hospital ships, and a dozen other types of vessel included in the designation of "Fleet auxiliaries," apparently dreaming in the stillness of a winter calm. Strange local craft—drifters, barges, and the like—plied among the immobile hulls of the warships, supplying their various needs; steam picket-boats were darting about over the glassy surface of the harbour—it might be glassy that day, but often they were buried in sheets of spray as they went about their duties. Colliers were casting off, having already, early as it was, poured their thousands of tons of coal down the iron throats of the monsters. Everything was moving except the ships themselves, which lay solidly planted like rocks, as though they were part of the earth which nothing but a cataclysm could move.

They were ceaselessly talking in their own strange silent language. Hoists of bunting broke out at yard-

Physical Drill at Sea.

Turning Together.

The Talking Ships

arms, ascended to mast heads, hovered a minute or two, and came down in rainbow curves where flagship talked to flagship. A shore signal station was speaking in white flashes that dazzled you even in the strong sunshine; and between ship and ship of the same squadron minute conversations, visible only through a strong glass, were being carried ceaselessly on by the busy tossing arms of semaphores and by the small flags that a signalman, perched on the rail of a bridge like a fly, was waving to his opposite number in the next ship astern.

What were they all saying? The onlooker, of course, longed to know; but really it was not so interesting as he thought, nor so exciting as it looked. Someone wanted two engine-room ratings to be transferred from one ship to another; that glorious burst of colour against the sky referred to boiler tubes; that violent whirling of wooden semaphore arms only meant that some thousands of stones of potatoes were adrift. That variegated strip of bunting that drooped from a yard-arm near by was a Church Pendant, and signified that the ship's company were still at morning prayers. If you listened, you could just hear the harmonies of the band and the sound of a familiar hymn. Apparently unnoticed, a single flag was flying from the triatic stay of an auxiliary. It was as though you should put a Carter Paterson's card up in your window; sooner or later some craft would thread her way out in response to this dumb request, and deliver the fresh water that was being asked for. Up went a hoist in a near-by battleship; it was a signal for the duty steamboat; and all it meant was that in another ship some way down the line (whose turn it was to supply the boat on that particular day) a bosun's mate, after a preliminary blast on his pipe, would put his head down a hatch and shout, "Away second picket boat!" that half a dozen men, cheerfully but with murmured oaths, would hurry from the mess decks and crawl out along the boom, and drop into this boat; and a midshipman would be summoned from writing a letter home to take command of her and conduct her wherever she might be required. All routine, all commonplace. The really interesting things were not being said by flags or flashes or semaphores. They came viewlessly through the ether, in a voice like the buzzing of a fly, to the ear of a wireless operator sitting in a steel box below the water-line, and came to him only in uncomprehended groups of letters or figures, which were deciphered by an officer in a locked office, sent as a sealed signal to the Flag-Lieutenant, and by him delivered personally to the Admiral. That, and what might happen because of it, were almost the only difference that an outsider would notice between peace and war conditions in many a big ship in the Fleet.

So the daylight hours passed on. The ships had been washed down after coaling; the men had washed themselves, their clothes, and the mess-decks all together; all the other things that had to be eternally washed and cleaned and polished and tested and oiled had been attended to; dinner had been piped and eaten, the officers had lunched, some of them had gone ashore, and the ship settled down to the comparative peace of the afternoon. There was a cessation of trampling feet; and all about the mess-decks, and in certain of the officers' cabins (for the ship only came into harbour in the small hours and had coaled since), men were deeply asleep. There was little left below decks to remind you of the

Going out Again

sea. The eternal click of typewriters sounded from the engineer's office, the armament office, the secretary's office; but the rest, for an hour or two, was silence; you might have been in a factory where the hands were all on strike, or in a city from which the inhabitants had fled. And the immobility, the everlasting fixedness of the Fleet, seemed greater than ever.

But that insect voice had been buzzing on in the wireless office of every ship, and in every ship an order of half a dozen words had been given to the senior engineer officer. Not six people in the whole ship knew anything, and they said nothing. The officers came off from the shore, the ship woke up again, the familiar bugles sounded for evening quarters, searchlights, and a dozen other routine functions or exercises. Sunset sounded, the ensigns came slowly down, the boats were hoisted in, men gathered in the wardroom and discussed the latest printed matter and resumed their mild convivialities. A gin and bitters, a game of bridge, and— what was that?

Cable officers! The throaty voice of the bugle crashed down the enamelled steel passage-ways. We were going out again.

No one knew, but it didn't matter, because everything (except one's private arrangements, which were of no importance) was ready. As darkness fell little groups of officers and men assembled on the fo'c'sles, and the titanic business of unmooring and weighing was commenced. No lights, no sound, no signals—it was perfectly automatic. And presently, as you stood there in the peaceful darkness and silence, you heard a sound like the tearing of silk, and a destroyer slid past, black and secret as the night. Another and another and another, each tearing the silk of the waters, each keeping her perfect station, until a whole division had passed you and vanished. A pause, and then a deeper sound, like the murmur of a weir, heralded the passage of a longer and larger ghost—the flagship of the light cruiser squadron, which followed in her swirling wake, each ship as stealthy and intent as her leader, out into the, night.

And then at the exact moment, not sooner or later, a quiet order of two words was given from the bridge, and your turn had come. There was a little clanking of metal from the fo'c'sle as the last links of the cable were coaxed in over its steel bed, a voice or two, a sound of hammering, and then silence again. There was nothing in the action of modern turbine engines to tell you when the ship was under way. All you knew was that your position in relation to the dark masses around you was slightly altering, that there was a ripple beginning to set outwards from the ship's shoulder, and that a breeze was stirring against your face. As suddenly, as silently, as secretly as the rest, the great ship was again setting about her fell business. There was no sound but the steady surge of the waters where the sixty-foot steel stem tore them. The dark shapes round you melted into the surrounding void, the loom of the land faded into the universal blackness, and there set in that blowing which was the wind of destiny, which would not cease until you touched the shores of death or of home again. Before you and on either hand was absolute blackness; behind you one shadow of grosser blackness, which was the ship astern; and from blackness into blackness, nose to tail, thirty thousand tons apiece, we were rushing at twenty miles an hour. And that also was routine.

Something should here be said as to the system of Intelligence which gave us such accurate information of the German movements. Captain Hall,[1] who had commissioned the *Queen Mary*, and until after the action in the Heligoland Bight had been captain of her, was then appointed Director of the Intelligence Division at the Admiralty. He had shown imagination as a captain; his organization of the *Queen Mary* was unique in the Navy. He had abolished ship's police, and thereby reduced crime on board his ship to an unheard-of minimum. He had a strong and most interesting personality, and he brought to the Admiralty the same imagination as had distinguished him as a captain. A real account of the doings of his department during the war would be a most fascinating book, but it will never be written. Its activities were world-wide, and the department which concerned the Fleet, and of which alone I propose to say something here, was only a small part of these activities. Its main task was, of course, to procure information as to the enemy's doings in so far as they concerned the Navy. It must be understood that, so far as Fleet movements were concerned, the old system of spies during war is practically obsolete. Spies can do a great deal before war, but once war has started the difficulties of communication render information obtained in this way almost useless, either because of the danger or the delay in communicating. We had people in German ports, but they were of little use as regards

[1] Now Rear-Admiral Sir Reginald Hall, K.C.M.G., C.B., M.P.

information concerning movements of the German Fleet. What distinguished our Naval Intelligence, and was indeed one of our great triumphs of the war, was the establishment of a system of Directional Wireless, by which the position—as well often as the course and speed —of German craft were made known to us. The Germans discovered this later, but at first we had the field entirely to ourselves.

In the use of Directional Wireless we were greatly favoured by the position and formation of our coast-line. Along that coast-line, from the Orkneys to Kent, was established a string of directional stations—I do not know how many, but let us say thirty or forty at least—engaged in nothing else but taking in German wireless. There were enough of them to ensure that any wireless signal sent out from German naval sources, on whatever wavelength, would find at least two of these stations tuned to receive it; an achievement founded on the fact that the compass bearing of a wireless signal received from any point in space can be located. After that the system is simplicity itself. Let us suppose that a German submarine at the point " B " makes a signal. That signal is heard by directional stations at " A " and " S."

The signal bears E.S.E. from " A " and N.N.E. from " S." " A " and " S " both immediately communicate this to the Admiralty, giving the call sign of the submarine heard. These bearings are laid off on a large chart in the recording room, and where the two lines of bearing intersect is the position of the submarine at sea at that time. Another reference establishes where the same submarine was last heard, and therefore gives its course, or at any rate gives an idea as to whether it is coming home or going out. So perfect did this organization finally become that from the time of the submarine being heard by stations, let us say, at Aberdeen and Scarborough, the particulars being sent to the Admiralty, the bearings laid off on the chart and checked with previous information of the same submarine, and the reception by ships in the Grand Fleet of the informa-

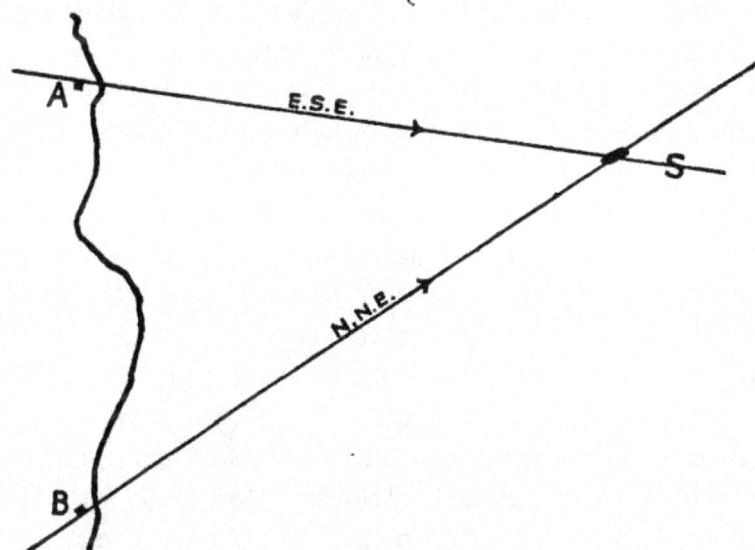

tion that that particular submarine was then in such and such a position, was eight minutes.

The material to be taken in and to be sorted was vast, for the unimportant as well as the important had all to come into the net. Our own call signs, of course, were known and disregarded, and the German call signs soon came to be known and attended to. The amount of material to be dealt with may be guessed from the fact that the signals published in the Parliamentary Paper on the Battle of Jutland, emanating from only a portion of

The Firth of Forth

our own ships actually at sea, and covering the period noon of May 80 to noon of June 2, occupy 166 pages of close type. Practically all this vast drift of wireless matter into our nets was in code or cipher, utterly unintelligible until decoded and translated, and then only in a condition of raw material from which information of value might be sorted out and deduced. How it came to be decoded and deciphered is a matter that it is, I am informed, even now undesirable to explain, although it seems to me likely that the German Intelligence Department is equal to solving the riddle. The great point was that we read clearly all they said, whether it was in code or cipher. To deduce from the mass of material thus obtained an intelligent knowledge of the doings of the German Fleet required another staff of experts to co-ordinate, study and digest—and this is where we lost some of the great advantages which this system should have given us. Obviously it should have been entirely in naval control; and it was not. It was the old story of personal jealousy interfering with the public interest. A piece of grit got into the machine here, with sad consequences. The result of an analysis of the material by non-naval minds, and not the material itself, was given to the Intelligence Division, which again dealt with it and handed it on to the Operations, who again digested it 'and passed on the result in the form of orders to the Fleet.

It was thus always known to us when the Germans were going to sea and generally where they were going; but often the information did not reach the Fleet until it was too late to act upon it effectively.[1] Hence in the

[1] See Chapter VI. Operation of December 16, 1914.

130

Poor Use of Good Material

early part of the war so many chances were lost, while the enemy were still unaware of the fact that his movements were known to us beforehand. Later, of course, he discovered this; and it became much more difficult to take him unaware. The Dogger Bank battle affords a brilliant example of the perfect working of this system up to a point. Everything was known to the Intelligence Division: the number and organization of the German Fleet, the time it was to sail, and its course and speed through the night. Instead of being instantly communicated to the Fleet, however, this information was communicated to the Operations Division, who fixed what they thought a suitable rendezvous, and merely informed Sir David Beatty to be there the next morning, when, so to speak, he would see what he would see. If, instead of that, he had been given the facts as they were given to the Operations Division, he would have gone to a position farther south and east, so as to get between Admiral Von Hipper and his base, as his principle always was. Instead of this, the given position put him twenty miles to the east-north-east of the Germans when they were sighted—which made all the difference. If the Admiralty had fixed a position even ten miles to the south of the rendezvous they gave, it is practically certain that the Germans could never have escaped.

The days before Christmas were very raw and foggy and we were not able to see much of our new surroundings. The 23rd was in violent contrast to our recent sombre doings at sea and at Invergordon. The huge scale on which things were done on board a large ship struck me anew. I remember that I watched the arrival of 250 turkeys on board, accompanied by tons of other festive material, and realized that the same thing was happening on every ship in the Fleet. The Flag-Lieutenant and I lunched that day on board the *Sheelah*, and afterwards we walked in the fog half-way to Aberdour and motored back to the Hawes Pier. I never embarked there without thinking of David Balfour and Hoseason and the brig *Covenant;* and from the *Lion's* anchorage (as shown in the chart on page 115) one could survey much of the ground of Stevenson's exciting romance, from Limekilns to the Pentland Hills. We were not to have a Christmas in harbour, however. Orders came from the Commander-in-Chief that we were to sail at 7 P.M. on Christmas Eve; and as I was not likely to get much exercise for the next few days I took a solitary walk as far as Davidson's Mains and back. It was a day of clear, hard frost and full of the atmosphere of Christmas; and it was strange to leave the lights and the holly and the Christmas preparations of the shore and go out in the cold darkness of the night to spend our Christmas at sea.

I remember that the chief Christmas present which I found waiting for me from home when I came on board was a swimming waistcoat; and my servant thoughtfully laid it out on my bed that night when, during the small hours of the festive day, linked for me with the legend of the angels' song of peace, we passed through a minefield.

CHAPTER VIII

CHRISTMAS AT SEA

CHRISTMAS, 1914, found the Grand Fleet at sea; temptingly, and indeed almost appealingly, disposed. No enemy with even the faintest love of a fight for its own sake could have resisted coming out to meet us. Our attitude and intention could hardly have been made plainer if we had made a wireless signal *en clair* to the Germans, "It's a lovely day; come out and have a scrap." Light cruisers, battle cruisers, destroyers, battleships—they could have had their choice and taken on any group they liked, and the rest would have stood by to see fair play. It was indeed a lovely day at sea, cloudless, with conditions of what gunnery people call "extreme visibility"; one of the best of those many days when watch-keepers, almost reluctantly leaving the bridge on the arrival of their relief, would say with a sigh, "What a day for a fight!"—the kind of day that gunnery lieutenants dreamed of, with a sparkling atmosphere very different from the soup of fog, spray and driving rain in which most important operations in winter had had to be conducted.

We had come out the night before from Rosyth, where the snow lay on the surrounding hills and a curtain of fog had shrouded our formidable but stealthy exit. We had indulged in more than the usual speculations as to what the morrow would bring forth and what the first Christmas Day of the war would be like. At that time we still had the feeling that one particular date was more lucky than another, more likely to bring about the long-expected fight; and high hopes were entertained of so august a day as December 25. But, like so many other things—like almost everything else—in the war, the reality was entirely different from what most of us expected. Christmas Day at sea suggested all kinds of rigours—icicles hanging from the yards, frozen blocks, decks covered with snow, and so forth. But none of these picturesque visions was realized. On the contrary, I woke up on Christmas morning to find the ship steaming towards a sunrise of liquid amber. The air was delicious, without a trace of that shrewish bite which the hills ashore had imparted to it, and the sea, after the sun had climbed up into a cloudless sky, was of an almost Mediterranean blue. What a day for a fight indeed! But failing that, a very good day on which to be alive at all, a very good day to be at sea, and a very good day indeed on which to keep (failing a fight) the feast of peace and good will.

The only thing lacking to our comfort on this delicious day was the enemy. There was not a sign of him. We met the Commander-in-Chief and the whole of the Grand Fleet in the familiar waters of 55.45 N., 1.25 E., and solemnly paraded and swept the blue-grey waters and danced stately *pavanes* and set to partners in all the ceremonial magnificence of fleet exercises; but, although our light cruisers searched far and wide, the enemy did not appear. I do not know if he was even expected; but it was probably far safer to have the Fleet at sea, lest

Round the Mess Decks

there should be an attempt to celebrate the day in some more than usually frightful fashion; and our being at sea did not prevent the observance of the day in the timely fashion of a man-o'-war. The great event was, of course, the going the round of the mess decks. After church, at which the usual Christmas hymns were sung to the dire accompaniment of a harmonium and the more piercing of the band instruments, there was a short interval filled in by the usual duties of the morning. We had all been at action stations at daybreak, but when the mockery of the bright sunshine and the negative nature of reports from the scouting squadrons had caused the guns' crews reluctantly to abandon hope for another day the ordinary routine was resumed, and the majority of the men were free to make their preparations below decks. And at eight bells the customary procession began. It was the simplest possible ceremony. The Admiral, accompanied by all the officers of the ship who were not on duty elsewhere, made the round of the mess decks, where the men were sitting at their dinner, and personally wished them a happy Christmas. It is practically the only occasion on which the men are visited by officers in the dinner hour, otherwise sacred to the nearest approach to privacy obtainable for the ship's company of a modern super-dreadnought. But the function, although simple, was certainly impressive. From the familiar and businesslike order of the main deck we passed down a steel ladder into what at first looked like a kind of underground toy fair. The numbers of the messes varied, but let us say they averaged twenty men each. To these twenty men was apportioned a certain space in the long, low vista of the mess deck; and the space which

135

was theirs was roughly that occupied by the mess table, the forms or stools on either side of it, and a little space at either end where mess gear and utensils are stowed. And, of course, one mess is just as close to another as space permits.

Now it is the custom on Christmas Day to decorate the ends of the tables facing the gangway along which the various visitors pass with trophies, consisting of all the most decorative objects on which the mess can lay hands. Naturally there was great variety in these trophies, as the resources and the artistic tastes of the messes were various. Anything was pressed into service, from real or manufactured holly to family photographs, and from pictures out of illustrated papers to puddings and cakes. Some produced elaborate structures covered with frost and snow, in which seasonable mottoes were embedded, or the words, " God bless our Admiral," in green icing would surmount a perfectly villainous portrait done in oil paint abstracted from the paint locker. The ship herself figured ubiquitously, either in photographs, paintings, or models; and of course the picture postcard did duty in many ways.

What chiefly impressed one during the walk along the packed area was the way in which so much had been made out of so very little. That these same mess decks, which earlier in the morning had been lying all stark and orderly under the ruthless eye of inspection, every dish and fork in its place, and no extraneous scrap of colour or ornament visible, should then be transformed into the likeness of the bargain basement of a dry goods store was remarkable enough ; yet that, after all, was only such a feat of transformation as was a daily common-

Much out of Little

place in the organized life of ships. What was more remarkable, and not a little touching, was that men living such a life of unchanging routine and toil, cramped and crowded, poised insecurely between life and death, should think it worth while to add to their labours by building up for such a brief moment these childish structures of decorative rubbish. It was eloquent of the need there is in every heart to make festival at some time or other, and surely eloquent also of that enviable gift, one of the best which the bluejacket possesses, of making something out of nothing, of being happy with little, and of constructing out of the material of daily toil a bright-hued fabric of pleasure.

As the line of officers struggled past the apparently endless succession of decorated tables, exchanging the compliments of the season with their occupants, and here and there being obliged to taste some deadly dainty, words of critical appreciation of this or that effect became inevitable; and with them just a little delicate badinage, of a kind inconceivable at any other moment, but which never by a hair's breadth went beyond what the relaxations of the hour and the " matelot's " inner sense of the fitness of things dictated. And, as in all human displays, the element of rivalry and competition was not absent, nor the pathos inseparable from the juxtaposition of some vast structure of ice and snow enshrining various objects of high value and ingenuity, the effort of a prosperous and rather swanking mess; and the feeble little collection of Christmas cards, home photographs, pencil cases, packets of sweets and more or less decorative articles of diet momentarily diverted from their destiny on the dinner-table itself, which represented the effort of some

Christmas at Sea

small and poor mess whose members were often in trouble with the master-at-arms, and whose joint exchequer had been heavily depleted by "stoppages." But on Christmas Day the defaulters' bugle did not sound; there was respite for those who had trouble hanging over them; and a joke could even be cracked with the stern Rhadamanthus who would on the morrow whack out the due doses of 10A without turning a hair.

And that day, just on that one day, there was handshaking accompanying the good wishes. People who work together, month in, month out, in the combined intimacy and austerity of ship routine, whose lives depend on one another and the degree of whose mutual goodwill is measured to a hair's-breadth, could on this day touch hands and give outward expression to that sense of brotherhood which is very real in the Navy but which is seldom openly expressed. And when the procession of blue and gold (inclined to tail off into rowdiness where the gun-room brought up the rear) had struggled and cloven its way through the packed masses of blue and white, the mess decks were left to themselves, and the true festival begun. To describe it as an orgy of eating would be mild. The celebrants steadily ate their way through tons of the most solid viands. The rum ration, diluted into grog by Act of Parliament, was served out on each table by the cook of the mess, from the "Fanny" or basin; and what is always the best hour of the bluejacket's day was passed with yarns and songs, until the fortunate ones who had a watch below subsided into stillness or snores, extended on any area of mess stool or steel deck which happened to be free from the boots or heads of their messmates.

The Unchanging Routine

But through it all the unvarying routine of the ship at sea in war time went on. The bells were struck, the watches were changed, the Pilot and his "Tanky" paid their periodical visits to the chart-house and made minute marks on the chart. Warm signalmen went up to the lofty, windy signal-bridge, and cold signalmen came down. Cool, clean stokers went down to the boiler-rooms, hot and dirty ones came up. Nothing was permitted or tolerated on that day that would not have been tolerated on any other day; but there are methods of keeping out of the way at the right moment, and of being oblivious to non-essentials in which people who have to administer discipline at such close quarters are adept. And when the Commander went his rounds at night the Toy Fair or Wonderland had all vanished, and the mess decks had resumed their normal aspect. Perhaps the snores or sighs that came from the clustered hammocks hanging in the mess spaces were a little more stertorous or disturbed than usual; perhaps the doctors were a little busier the next morning; but that was all the trace left of our first Christmas Day at sea.

It blew up from the south during the night, and by lunch time on the 26th it developed into a gale with a strong, heavy sea, in which the gun-room and the ward-room were both washed out, but we escaped. The squadrons were safely tucked up above the Forth Bridge again soon after midnight.

CHAPTER IX

THE New Year found the *Lion* at the latter end of a dinner-party given by the Admiral to all the officers, including warrant officers, in the ship. Sixty-three of us sat down in the dining cabin, and the gaiety was in proportion to the numbers. There were about twenty speeches, some of which would make very amusing reading if one could recall them; but there is only one that I can remember in full. It was that of the Boatswain. Reduced to a truly unwonted shyness, he spoke as follows:

"Admiral and gentlemen" (long pause). "I mean to say" (long pause punctuated by "Hear! hear!"). "What I mean to say is" (loud and prolonged applause). "Well, all I say is, I hope we don't go to sea to-night!"

It was quite the best speech of the evening and was received with terrific acclamation. I remember at a late hour risking the perils of the many ladders up to the bridge, conveying a bottle of champagne and other dainties to the officer of the watch, who was keeping his solitary and uneventful harbour duties on the bridge, where only rumours of the gaiety below reached him. I remember also that there was a heavy scrap in the ward-room afterwards, in which the evolution "out staff" was performed with some difficulty, after a prolonged and

Lessons Unlearned

stubborn resistance at the cost of a good deal of broken furniture.

The first weeks of the year were marked by a kind of reaction, subtle but inevitable, from the high and continuous hopes of the first months of the war. With the coming of a new year it began to be realized that the war might last, not only through that, but conceivably through another and another year. After the victory of the Falkland Islands and the raid on Hartlepool and Scarborough, naval activity seemed to have fizzled out, so far as the big ships were concerned; the enemy submarines were extending their operations, and the Admiralty seemed to have no policy for dealing with them. The loss of the *Formidable*, of which we heard on New Year's Day, was another sign that the obvious lessons of the war were not being learned, and added, with the *Hogue*, *Aboukir*, *Cressy*, *Audacious* and *Bulwark*, another to the record of ships lost without any advantage in return. And it was characteristic that the Admiralty, even in the little parish magazine of "Secret Intelligence" that was served out to Commanding Officers afloat, continued to report the *Audacious* as being with the Second Battle Squadron, although everyone in the fleet knew she had been sunk in November, and the fact had been published in the American Press. It was a good example of the somewhat childish point of view of Intelligence, in which it seemed to be held a clever thing to tell a lie, in the general hope that someone might be deceived. It was one of the more innocent of the ways in which we tried to imitate the Germans. When they told lies it was with a definite purpose: we told them without any purpose at all.

A New Year

In the small hours of a day early in the year a series of ciphers came in conveying various alarms, and there seemed to be a general stir of enemy activity. Heavy firing was reported from Hartlepool (afterwards found to be blasting); then enemy cruisers were reported to be at sea; and later in the day Zeppelins were sighted over Crowborough and at sea farther north. We made various signals to the Commander-in-Chief asking if we should prepare to go to sea, but could get no definite orders or information. The various reports seemed to indicate that something was happening; and the Admiral, alive to the risk of a mining operation at the entrances to our bases, preparatory to some general enemy movement either in the Channel or on the East Coast, decided to raise steam. In spite of various discouragements he went out after dusk, having, of course, reported his intentions and movements to the Commander-in-Chief. But no reply, either approving or forbidding, came until we were well out at sea, and then only a signal asking, "What is your position?" We took the light cruisers out with us and we were very glad to be clear of the Firth of Forth.

Once at sea, however, even the alarming signals ceased. We were left severely alone, without any information whatever, and felt that we were being treated like naughty boys for having gone out without leave. There was no sign of the enemy the next day, and in a rather crestfallen manner we did four-inch gun practice, in the midst of which came a cipher ordering us to return. We got back to May Island just after dark that evening and performed our dangerous twenty-mile gallop. It was always an exhilarating hour, and I loved to be on the bridge

A Rap on the Knuckles

with the group of silhouettes that moved about in the wind and darkness. The signalmen on the bridge, when not busily engaged (as was the case at night), suffered from attacks of acute self-consciousness, being thrust into close quarters with all the great people of their world, some of whom were mere myths to their messmates, and if things did not go absolutely smoothly the suppressed and *sotto voce* wrath of the Signal Bosun was fearsome to behold. On this particular evening, as we approached the war defence station at Inch Keith, we made the usual challenge on the shaded lamp, which throws a very small and dim beam, but is clearly visible on the proper bearing to anyone who is keeping a bright lookout. Again and again the brief challenge was made, and without response from the darkness ahead. The Admiral grew impatient. We were rushing along towards a station which had orders to fire on anything that approached without due recognition signals having been made and answered; and we could get no answer. At last, in desperation, a signal was made by searchlight, and a white and most unseemly glare lit up the night, and even this had to be repeated twice before the answering wink came from the station. This station was not then under naval control but was manned by the Garrison Artillery; and the opinion of the Navy at such a moment on soldiers in general, and the Garrison Artillery in particular, was terrible to hear. And tempers were not improved when after dinner a general signal from the Admiralty was taken in, beginning " As large ships have been taken out without orders," etc., etc. It was not a pleasant evening.

One morning soon afterwards the Admiral sent for me and said, " I am sick of the ship: if you are free, let us go for a walk." I hastily turned over to the ever-obliging junior flag-lieutenant and joined the Admiral, and we were soon skimming ashore in the barge like truant schoolboys. It was a delightful change, for the Admiral's mornings were invariably devoted to work; but on this occasion, the need for doing something energetic being paramount, he wisely yielded to it and worked it off in a brisk walk through Dalmeny Park. It was a blowing day, wintry and sad, but in a way invigorating; and as we walked beside the chasing leaves through the deserted park, we discussed the difficulties of the situation and speculated as to what, if anything, could be at the back of the collective Admiralty mind. Their last action, apart from the affairs of the day before, had been to issue an order dividing the Battle Cruiser Squadron into two, and appointing a Rear-Admiral.[1] The Second Squadron was to consist of the *Invincible* (Flag), *New Zealand* and *Indomitable;* but as the *Invincible* had not yet returned from abroad there were only two, and the electric gear of one of them was threatening to give trouble and to require a long overhaul. The *Queen Mary* was away refitting and the *Tiger* was a constant source of anxiety and trouble (she had got herself aground a week before on the bank inshore of our anchorage, and it had been a strenuous business getting her off); so at the moment there was not sufficient material for two squadrons. The Second-in-Command had been appointed without any reference whatever to Admiral Beatty, so that between him and the captains of this carefully trained unit, in the command of which no other experience could provide the necessary knowledge, was to be interposed an officer who had no

---

[1] Rear-Admiral Sir Archibald Gordon Moore, K.C.B.

experience of battle cruisers, and for whom, although he was highly esteemed by both Mr. Churchill and Lord Fisher, there appeared to be difficulty in finding a suitable command.

The reader has already grasped the principles on which the battle cruiser force was trained, and will readily see how incompatible with the efficient carrying out of those principles was the advent of a second-in-command who possibly knew nothing about them. It was all very puzzling and rather depressing, but I managed to raise a somewhat grim smile on my chief's face by reminding him of Lord Fisher's aphorism : " Some day we shall lose the Empire because it is Buggins's turn." And we very nearly did. The Admiral, as always, was philosophic and bracing ; and on our return to the *Lion* we found an order that we were to go to sea that night after German battle cruisers, which cheered us greatly ; but unfortunately the order was cancelled later. There was another alarm of the same kind the next day. An Admiralty signal ordering us to sea, on which we should have had to act at 7.80, arrived at seven, having taken six hours to come because ceremonial procedure decreed that it should be transmitted through the Vice-Admiral commanding the Third Battle Squadron, he being senior to Sir David, although the signal did not concern him at all. Another example of " Buggins's turn." Fortunately it had been intercepted and taken in by another route, and subsequently cancelled, before its official arrival.

Things, however, seemed to be working up again. On January 16 and 17 orders came about going to sea, those of the 16th being cancelled, but those of the 17th confirmed, our objective being a force of German

A New Year

destroyers that were patrolling between the mouth of the Ems and Horns Reef. We had one of our rare luncheon parties on one of those days, in which we were visited by the world in the persons of Lord and Lady Linlithgow, Lady Mar, Lady Beatty and Sir F. Milner; and at ten that night were gliding out again, through a wonderful soft starlight, in which the lights of shore, reflected in the smooth water, made us feel as we passed them as though we were leaving a Venetian festival. It became rough off May Island and continued so throughout the next day. This was the first time the squadron had been split into two, and on this and the following two days the new Rear-Admiral was exercised in his Command. On the morning of the 10th we went to action stations at daybreak. It was a lovely morning, with a red sunrise and clear sky. Contact was duly made with the light cruisers and Commodore (T), but the enemy was not visible. We saw a Zeppelin shadowing us twenty miles away to the south-east, and undoubtedly as a result of this the intended destroyer patrol did not take place. A seaplane also came towards us from the direction of Heligoland; we fired at it with our twelve-pounder pop-gun, with no result whatever, but a shrapnel was fired from one of the forward 13.5 guns, a terrific affair which went whanging away into the silence and burst like a firework about a quarter of a mile away from the seaplane —on which the latter was seen to bump heavily, turn round and make for home. We had reluctantly to part with Commodore (T) and his fine Harwich Flotillas, there being nothing for him to do. Squadron exercises, four-inch gun practice and range-finding exercises filled up the two blank days through which we came home again.

Dark Suspicions

On the 21st, the morning after our arrival, a "buzz" began to develop.[1] While we were at sea an important signal had been taken in on board the *New Zealand* (Admiral Moore's flagship) from the Admiralty to Commodore (T), giving the position of the German force. Admiral Beatty first heard of it from Captain Halsey when he came on board the morning after our arrival, and naturally he wanted to know how it was that it had not been received in the *Lion*. The log of the Intelligence Office, where all ciphers were entered, had no trace of it. The "buzz" developed into a "flap." It was discovered that it must have been taken in during the afternoon of the 18th, and reference to the log showed that I had had the afternoon watch. I began to feel extremely perturbed. Was it possible that, in spite of conscientious vigilance, I had been caught napping, and committed the unpardonable sin? I am old enough to know that nothing is impossible, and yet, search my memory and conscience as I might, I could not think of a single moment in which I had been on duty when I had not been fully alive to the responsibility of every action taken; and I remembered, not so much that I had never shirked that duty, as that I had been always much too interested in it to want to shirk it. And yet things looked black. I was not made more comfortable when the duty of searching for the missing signal was entrusted, not to me, but to another. Indeed, the whole staff took a hand since the credit of all was at stake. The "flap" developed into a "panic."

"Here it is," said someone, picking off from the file a

---

[1] There are three degrees of sensation or commotion in naval slang: "buzz," "flap," and "panic."

cipher which was ticked across, showing that it had been dealt with, and entered in the log as "undecipherable." It happens sometimes, though rarely, that signals are taken in in a cipher which the ship does not possess, or—much more rarely—that they are so full of mistakes in the coding as to be unreadable. In such a case, if the signal had been addressed to the Vice-Admiral one would have had it repeated; but as this signal was addressed to Commodore (T) that request would not be made. I firmly asserted that I had tried this signal in every cipher and that it would not come out in any. Supposing I had stopped trying too soon? Suppose I had not been patient enough in trying several variations of a number of groups in order that something could be discovered? I was pretty sure that I had not given it up without reasonable attempt to elucidate it; but if indeed I had been at fault; if by bad luck I had only chosen as a test groups that were incorrect; if, by failure in efficiency I had let the flagship down with a cipher that was taken in by the new Rear-Admiral and lost one of the rare chances of coming to blows with the enemy—then indeed there would be nothing for it but to slip over the side in the dark hours. I looked on with a slight air of injury, while the rest, tried group after group, in one cipher after another, without success, although there were sickening moments when they seemed to be on a hot scent. But at last the constellation of intellects at work arrived at the same conclusion as my poor mind had reached in the course of its duty, and after being like a schoolboy in coventry, I was spoken to and smiled at again. The explanation was that the signal was in a new cipher, his copy of which Admiral Moore had brought with him upon his arrival

A Bad Hour

from London, while ours, having been sent by messenger, arrived an hour or two after the " panic " had subsided. All the same, it was the most uncomfortable hour I spent during the whole war. Which shows that a clear conscience is no insurance against misery.

CHAPTER X

DAYS WITH THE FLEET

1. AN ADMIRAL'S DAY

TO some careful and anxious administrator, doing his war work amid office files and the click of typewriters and the electric lights of winter in some crowded and littered town office, and trying to keep his vision of efficiency clear in the fog of figures and words and forms through which he had to work, the mental picture of an Admiral in a sea command must often have seemed brightly lit by everything that was enviable and desirable. Many a General even, whose dream of service in the field had come down to the reality of sitting all day and half the night in an uncomfortable room in a farmhouse or a village inn, and dealing with stacks of Army forms, must have thought enviously of his brother over whom the Cross of St. George was blowing in the breezes somewhere at sea.

That is human nature, which sees things partially instead of wholly, and is prone to dwell on what is unfamiliar and enviable in the lot of others. And of all the stars in the firmament of war the Admiral commanding a fleet at sea appeared in war time to the imagination as the most remote and picturesque. His business was farther removed from the life and experience and knowledge of ordinary men than was the business of anyone else about whom they read. He was a monarch and lived in something of a monarch's state; and he was in many respects not merely a constitutional, but an absolute monarch, wielding powers even of life and death over his subjects.

Yet he lived not remotely, but among them, like a queen bee in the heart of a hive; they were packed about him in close ranks, and every citizen was a soldier. He had his capital, which was the flagship; his royal palace, guarded by sentries, was the Admiral's quarters. He had his territories strictly defined; his provinces were the squadrons and flotillas under his rule; and each was commanded by a lesser monarch who had to render account to him. He had also his allied sovereigns, rulers of equal degree, from whom (let us breathe it gently) he might have sometimes to defend his own borders if, in that natural ambition from which even the naval officer was not always free, they ventured to encroach. Over him, an elder brother and fellow sovereign, although a greater, was his Commander-in-Chief. But above and around them all was a strange and inscrutable providence, called the Admiralty, possessed of a high-power wireless apparatus, which directed all their doings and watched and listened to them night and day; from whom they could not be hid; who led them often by ways that they knew not and from which their hearts sometimes rebelled. For all their rank and state they were prisoners to their duty. Their daily lives, noble and splendid in circumstance, were often monotonous to a degree almost incredible to the average civilian, who perhaps thinks his own life is monotonous enough. Their familiar or domestic intercourse was restricted to half a dozen or a dozen officers; day in and day out, they saw the same faces and listened to the same conversation; for people who have lived together, cut off from the world for even six months, can have little that is new to say to one another.

The Admiral's life in war varied between two conditions: life in harbour and life at sea. One might imagine that his most arduous time was spent at sea and that he went into harbour for rest and recreation: but it was the other way about. Going to sea, where there was at any rate the chance of a fight, was his delight; and when the smoke began to billow from the funnels and the motor of the gyro compass began to hum, the lines disappeared from his face and his spirits began to rise. It was on his return to harbour, when the anchor was down and the picket boats came alongside, and heavy parcels of paper and bundles of big envelopes and bags of typewritten matter began to come on board; when the navigating officer was departing from his last interview, and the secretary came in with his first basket of urgent papers, that the real anxieties of the Admiral's life began again. At sea there was only the enemy; in harbour there was—well, there was the Admiralty for one thing.

In harbour the Admiral was lucky if he was not wakened in the small hours by the unwelcome apparition of his flag-lieutenant holding a signal in his hand. If his command was a very high one this would not happen to him unless the signal was very urgent; but if he was only a Rear-Admiral, new to his work and fearful lest things were being kept from him, it very likely would happen. With the great men the Admiralty and the Commander-in-Chief communicated direct, and they were not active without due cause in the small hours; but the lesser

Rear·Admiral F. W. Kennedy.
(Captain of H.M.S. *Indomitable.*)

A Quiet Moment

light had to receive his signals filtered through the Admiral senior to him, and perhaps a still more senior Admiral ashore; and his communications might be sent at any time most convenient to the various staffs which had to deal with them. And he might thus be wakened from a sweet sleep to learn that the effects of Able Seaman Smith, O.N.000876128, were to be forwarded to the senior naval officer, say, at Leamington, for disposal. It was not a good beginning for the day. Even in the case of Admirals in high command there were constantly signals arriving in cipher which the deciphering officer on the morning watch would not risk withholding from the flag-lieutenant until breakfast-time, and on receipt of which the flag-lieutenant, hesitating between the wrath of the Admiral at being awakened and his wrath at not being awakened, decided that the latter would be more formidable.

The Admiral of whom the writer has most knowledge, being wise, breakfasted alone in his own pleasant day-cabin with a few favourite pictures and books about him, and where above the mahogany mantelpiece some little group of photographs reminded him of people belonging to the far-away time before the war. It was often his only moment of comfortable solitude throughout the day. To have sat down to breakfast in the dining-cabin with his staff would have been asking a little too much of him, for sociability at breakfast is not one of the virtues—if, indeed, it be ever a virtue—of the naval officer.

And after breakfast came the secretary. The ordinary secretary is a being who has been trained from infancy in the strange arts of service correspondence; who can tell you at a glance the certain effect upon circumstances and upon your career of beginning a document " Submit that " or " Submitted " ; who knows that vital secret of existence in the Navy, what you " can " do and what you " cannot " do. " You can't say that, sir," our secretary (who was not ordinary) would murmur over the Admiral's shoulder, when that forthright man was about to state that two and two made four. He would cogitate for a moment, considering the possibilities of documents beginning variously, " With regard to your memorandum as to the composition of four, I have the honour to submit the following considerations " ; " In regard to their Lordships' request for information as to the effect upon the efficiency of this squadron likely to be produced by the addition of two and two " ; or " It having been submitted to me by the commanding officers of ships in this squadron, whose reports are appended, that considerable economy both of time and material would be effected if two and two could be officially known in future as four." Finally, with a happy smile, he exclaimed, " I tell you what we *can* do, sir ; we can make a signal and say, ' Your 2080 not understood ; submit should be addressed to R.A.' " Through mazes of which problems like these were mere shadows the secretary had to support and guide the Admiral through all the hours of the forenoon.

The Admiral's day in harbour was never quiet. The wind and sea might be calm outside, but within those white enamelled walls there raged a tempest of paper. Sometimes it blew reports and despatches ; sometimes a strong breeze of memoranda and reference sheets set in ; always there was a gale of letters—official letters, service letters, personal letters. The relation between an Admiral and his secretary is stereotyped. The typical secretary,

Table Talk

while regarding the Admiral with the devotion and veneration due to his unrivalled qualities as a commander and fighting man, deplores his ignorance of official jargon, and his persistence in attempting to say for himself that which a trained and qualified man can say much better. The facts are probably more often on the secretary's side than on the Admiral's, secretaries being better versed in the strange warfare of official forms; and for days after one of them has scored off some other Admiral's secretary in a heavy engagement of paper his face will be irradiated with a kind of unearthly joy.

At luncheon the Admiral would meet his staff collectively—half a dozen officers at the outside, all of whom had seen him in the course of the morning, individually, on some point or other connected with the great machine. Our talk was always interesting to us because we were always concerned with subjects vital to what we were doing; but I dare say it would seem dull to readers accustomed to the artificial spice of most recorded conversations. After luncheon might come a brief excursion ashore, or a walk perhaps, or even (rarely) a short game of golf. But at tea-time the Admiral was back again, the secretary waiting for him with more baskets of paper. The same routine as that of the morning went on until dinner-time; and the same party assembled, with much the same conversation. After dinner there might be a game of bridge, and then more secretary and more paper work until bedtime. In addition to all this the day was shot through with various interviews with captains, junior Admirals, gunnery officers—all and every kind of expert whose affairs and activities needed some direction or sanction; and probably in the midst of it the barge would

Days with the Fleet

be called away and the Admiral would set forth to pay a
visit of inspection to one of his outlying provinces.

The Admiral's day at sea lasted for twenty-four hours ;
but it was a happier day for him than the shorter day in
harbour. He deserted his warm and roomy sleeping-cabin
in the after quarters, and his bed was made for him in
the Admiral's sea cabin, high up on the superstructure
that clustered round the foremast. Here he retired for
brief and intermittent periods of rest when the unlighted
shores had been left behind, and the course and speed
had been decided for the night, and the Fleet had settled
into its stride and was standing stiffly into a hardening
easterly gale. True, the flag-lieutenant might often
during those brief periods put his head in at the door and
deliver various items of information ; but he had no wrath
to fear on these occasions, nor were there any unnecessary
communications to be delivered. For although down in
the wireless room the ebony dial of the high-power
wireless was tuned to the Admiralty wave-length, nothing
merely vexatious was likely to be received in the small
hours.

And when the Admiral came out on to his bridge
at daylight and saw that the order and disposal of his
Fleet was as he wished it to be, he could feel, as he
watched day warming over the wrinkled billows of the
North Sea, that he was back in his true element again,
and that his day contained all the possibilities that he
had dreamed of. Although the business at sea was almost
as monotonous as the business in harbour, there was a
refreshed and stimulated feeling in the mental and social
atmosphere, just because being at sea contained great
possibilities which being in harbour did not.

"5 Blue."
(H.M.S. *Queen Mary*.)

The Good Hours

And all day, except perhaps for an hour or two in the evening, the Admiral was on his bridge, tuning and tempering the mighty instrument which had been entrusted to him; disposing it to fight if that boon were to be vouchsafed; if not, exercising it in all its magnificent functions. It was in these hours, full of realization and possibility, that the Admiral could forget the weight of paper that was accumulating for him at his base; when, I think, he envied no man, and was to be envied by most.

2. THE ELUSIVE ENEMY

From the point of view of the ordinary naval officer the real trouble about the war, the thing that robbed it of joy and excitement, was the continued absence of the enemy. Hardly anyone in the Fleet had seen a German since war had been declared, and only a few had seen a German ship. It was even characteristic that the enemy was but rarely referred to by that name—only, in fact, in action and in manœuvring exercises. He was at other times alluded to as the Germans, the Huns, or, more colloquially, the Sausages, in obedience to an essentially British tradition of describing nations which were distasteful to us by some characteristic article of their diet. The practice has never been reciprocated, and is abandoned when friendliness and understanding take the place of mistrust and enmity; and the terms Frog, Macaroni, or Hokey-Pokey were no longer heard in this connexion. But "Sausages" seemed to have come to stay. There is something tight and apposite in the word; it suggested skins filled to bursting, and ripe for puncture by the fork or bayonet.

Days with the Fleet

The attitude of mind in the Fleet towards the German Navy definitely changed within a year from August, 1914. Our people had seen far more of the German Navy in peace than they had seen in war; they probably had seen more of it than of any other navy, and perhaps even liked it better. Both had been building and preparing for the same great conflict. Both had been drawing nearer, step by step, and almost in step, to the great day that should decide their destinies and scatter them, from friendly neighbourly converse in Portsmouth and Kiel, into the invisible out of which the pounce should be made. And the German seriousness, thoroughness, and enthusiasm for efficiency had awakened a response in the heart of the British naval officer; what either did not know of his profession, he felt could be learned from the other. Thus when the war was declared, the naval combatants went into it as into an interesting duel between rival scientific experts who respected each other's powers and attainments. But that was all changed by the conduct of the Germans themselves. Even the outrages in Belgium did not affect the Navy's point of view as to its opposite number. What drunken soldiers might do did not impugn the honour of a great sea service. But when time and again the German Navy broke one after another of the vital rules in which the honour of sea-fighting is enshrined, then, indeed, reluctantly but finally, the mind of the Fleet changed. It was not only the German Navy—it was naval traditions generally that had been smirched. The idea of our "honourable foe" had reluctantly to be abandoned, the Germans became Huns, the enemy became "the Sausages," and the Navy's attitude was thereby greatly

Fighting the Absent

simplified. It was tiresome to have a respect for people whose ships you were trying to sink, and disagreeable to blow up those whose bravery you admired and whose traditions had been founded on your own. But after certain incidents it became much simpler. As "the enemy"—our enemy—we had a certain perfunctory respect for them. As Germans, we had much less.

But the continued absence of the enemy constituted a very real difficulty. Fighting an individual or absent enemy requires a double set of qualities—one of imagination and one of action. You had constantly to visualize your enemy, imagine where he was or what he was doing (for you would not be told), and in addition, actively prevent him from doing it. It was a tall order. The Admiralty had a great deal of information about the enemy, but do you think they told the Fleet everything? In certain printed and numbered reports, gingerly distributed in the ratio of one to a Vice-Admiral, they condescended to impart certain facts; but by no means for general information among the Fleet. The eager expert on whose state of mind the result of an action might conceivably depend had to get his information from the daily papers. In the strange, and (to an outsider) almost incredible, relationship that existed between the Admiralty and the naval officer it was not considered necessary to take a general professional interest in the doings of another navy with whom you happened to be at war. Either a particular thing concerned you personally, in which case you were expected to know all there was to be known about it, not by being told, but by inspiration; or it did not concern you personally, in which case it was no business of yours. Yet I have heard

Days with the Fleet

officers say that if the Admiralty had taken more care
to hide some of their own vital doings from the enemy,
and less to prevent our own people from knowing something about the operations they were engaged in, it
would have been well.

The worst of that distance and absence was that the
enemy began to grow unreal, chimerical. Was there
an enemy after all? We read about him every morning
when we were in harbour; we conversed with lucky
fellows who had really seen him as with explorers from
the Pole, or hunters of an almost mythical prey. We
quarrelled among ourselves as to the relative importance
of his doings in this place or that. We thought about
him, wondered about him; and the sentence most fre-
quently heard in the ante-room of a big ship was: "Do
you think they'll ever come out?" We lived our whole
lives, like those blessed servants whom their lord found
watching, on the *qui vive* for the enemy's appearance;
there was no hour of the twenty-four when we were not
prepared to receive him; we waited for him, although
not patiently; we "looked for" his coming, and the
word "*Expecto*" might have been engraved on every
pair of binoculars that swept the misty horizons of the
North Sea. But we did not see him. He was not
coming, and our real difficulty was sometimes to believe
that there was any such person, and that we were at war
at all. Routine is so hypnotizing; there were so many
enemies about us more active than the German Navy.
There was the enemy of boredom—the same faces, the
same food, the same scenes, the same conversation, the
same routine, day in day out. There was the enemy of
red-tape, a spider's web of which was quickly woven

What Really Happened

round anyone who had the temerity to be young and to have an idea. There was the sense of individual helplessness to drive on the war or improve conditions; nay, there was the healthy appetite of the North Sea, at the bidding of which our winter circumference slowly but surely made headway against Müller and Commander Coote. There was the eternal question of leave, the absurd unreasonableness of the commander, the direct villainy of the captain, the criminal malice of the Admiral—in a word, the poor N.O. had himself to fight as well as the German Navy and the Admiralty. No wonder actual contest with the enemies was longed for to the point of sickness. No wonder, when it did come, that it was hailed as high privilege and fortune.

And yet the reality, when it did come, was somehow different. The sausage took strange forms. I had seen the enemy at sea in the form of a Zeppelin on the horizon, a seaplane or two, a periscope at the apex of a great triangle on the smooth sea; flashes and puffs of smoke in a December haze; weed-covered mines drifting and bobbing past in the trough of the waves, and presently going up in a Struwwelpeter-like mushroom of smoke and flame. And once he appeared as four tiny wedges of smoke, like hurrying hedgehogs visible on the far horizon of a cold grey sea—wedges of which there were presently visible only three. This meant that a great ship, with the population of a large village, after being seared and pounded into a shambles, had quenched itself, a whitehot hell of agony, in the pale winter sea. And when, later, the small tale of rescued Germans came to be provided for, one saw the typical British attitude. Into the wardroom, where reprisals the thought

L 161

of which would turn your blood cold had been advocated in matter-of-fact detail, came battered Carl and Friedrich, still wet from the hungry sea, still shaking and twitching from the searing blast of the lyddite, still uncertain of their fate. Where were the reprisals now? The torturer-in-chief went off to get a dry sweater; cigarettes, drinks, offers of clothing, food, and services were heaped on the astonished enemy. Here he was, an actual, living German: an enemy in the flesh at last, but still, as an enemy, elusive. The poor Sausage, damn him, had had a hell of a time—you couldn't strafe him any more. Nothing for it but to shrug one's shoulders, give up one's bed to him, and carry on. He was not like a fighting enemy; he was like a sailor whom you had fished up from drowning in the nick of time. Many things changed during the course of the war; but it would have taken more than the war to make the Naval Officer on board his own ship forget that his enemy was also his guest.

8. CLOSING THE LAND

The night is dark and stormy; in the wardroom, where at sea electric radiators are substituted for the coal fire of harbour days, it is rather cold and rather stuffy. A few officers are reading in armchairs, or, in the case of those who will be on watch again in a few hours, enjoying a short pipe before turning in. The doctors and the paymasters, who have little to do at sea, have finished their game of bridge and are pessimistically turning over the pile of periodical literature in the hope of finding something they have not read. The cornices strain and creak; the great ship begins to feel the shorter and more troubled motion of the waves as the water

shoals, for we are closing the land. And above the drone
of the dynamos and the roar of the fans you can hear
the slobber and gulp of the waves as they clamber up the
ship's smooth side, or the thunder of the blow as she
takes a sea full on her shoulder. Outside, in the wardroom lobby, the spaces of white enamel are brightly lit.
In the direction of the stern there are crowded the
banana-like shapes of the suspended hammocks; a grove
or forest of them, packed just as tightly as they can be,
and swinging low enough to make it necessary to stoop
almost double as you pass in the alley-way beneath. It
is a point of honour, but one hard always to observe,
not to brush against them as one passes, for in this light
and publicity, amid the noises of the ship, hundreds of
men are forced to take their nightly rest; and if every
one who passed brushed against them they would have
hardly a moment without disturbance. Therefore you
stoop very low and, as the tunnel continues, pray for the
gap which will enable you to stretch up again for a
moment and take the kink out of your backbone.

But forward, between the wardroom and the
Admiral's quarters, the spaces are empty and look more
like the corridor of a hotel. The numbered cabin door-
ways on each side are screened by red curtains; and as
the ship rolls to starboard with a slow and steady rhythm,
the curtains of the inboard cabins swing slowly out into
the alley-way, while those on the opposite side swing
inwards, withdrawn into the cabins; and as the ship rises
again on her slow roll to port, the curtains of the inward
doors retire into their cabins, and those of the outward
doors swing into the alley-way. You pass more cabins,
the Captain's dining-room and sleeping-cabin, the Com-

mander's cabin, and farther on you come to the Admiral's quarters, where are the cabins and the offices of the staff, and at the end, where the marine sentry eternally mounts guard over the glass case wherein all the keys of the ship are kept, you come to the apartments of the great man himself. But he is not there; he is up on deck, and buttoning yourself into a greatcoat and white neckcloth, you prepare to follow.

Up the spiral staircase you pass from light into darkness, from peace into storm. Through the steel doorway, lighted only by one dim blue glow screened from outside view, you emerge into utter blackness with the wind and the night roaring about you. The gale is north-east and the course is very nearly north-west, and the great ship is driving stiffly into it at 16 knots. Struggling round the corner, where the wind snatches you and shakes you so that you can hardly make way against it, you are in the sudden lee of the superstructure, and feel for the first of three steel ladders which lead up past the upper 4-inch gun deck, past the recording office and the captain's and admiral's sea cabins to the searchlight platform. The marine orderly standing by the cabin door as you pass it is an indication that the Admiral is snatching one of his brief intervals of rest at sea. Another clap of wind, another respite, and you are at the foot of the next ladder leading to the signal bridge. Fortunately you hear the clatter of feet above you just as you begin the ascent. It is a messenger coming down out of the blackness above, who would have descended on your head if you had not heard him. Up on the signal bridge there are places of shelter in the lee of the two chart-rooms; out at each end you are open to the wind, the sky above and the sea

below, and the cold is searching. You can see nothing
at first but a few dim silhouettes against a background
of sky only less dark than the figures themselves. The
signalmen stand at their posts by the dark lamps. The
Flag-Lieutenant is keeping himself warm by walking
up and down the little clear space on one side, and the
signal bo'sun moves up and down on the other. There
are no stars, no moon, no lights of any kind, but
the position of every ship in the surrounding blackness
is known, and in case of absolute necessity she can be
called up at a moment's notice by the training of the
shaded lamps on to the point of darkness where she is
holding her station.

You go into the Admiral's chart-room. An interesting place at night this, because it is lit by switches
operated by the opening and closing of the door. When
the door is shut, the light is on. The moment the handle
is turned to open it, the light is off; therefore (the
scuttles being obscured) no light can ever be shown from
it. You feel for the handle, open the door, step into
the dark room and close the door behind you, and the
whole springs into light, dazzling after the blackness
outside. And as you bend over the chart the room is
once more plunged into darkness, as you hear the door
open behind you; and as it closes and the light comes on
again, you see that the Flag-Lieutenant has come in to
look something up in one of his many codes. Sometimes
amusing things occur; as when, going in on just such a
night to look at the chart, one finds difficulty in closing
the door, without which, of course, there is no light to
see by; and as one heaves and struggles with the handle
on the inside, another is pushing and struggling on the

outside to get in, both being strong men; both, of course, in complete darkness, both cursing loudly, and each ignorant that there are any forces arrayed against him other than those of the wind or some stubborn messenger. There was an awful night too, when the switches went wrong and, on someone emerging from the chart-room, a great oblong ray of light showed forth into the night. The effect may be imagined in circumstances where the instinct against showing the smallest light at night had become as firmly rooted as any other of the instincts of self-preservation. It is in such moments that one realizes how many things you have to know at sea. To put that switch right there was only one man to be invoked. Of all the people standing near each had his own proper duty, from which he could not be withdrawn. The ship was full of artificers, electricians, mechanics, plumbers, carpenters—hundreds of men, all of whom could repair this damage, but you might not send the messenger to them; and your purpose would not be accomplished unless you knew that the right and only person to deal with such an emergency is known by the mysterious title of "L.T.O. of the watch."

Up above you is the compass platform, open to the windy sky, with a clear view all round to the horizon except immediately aft, where the great fore-funnel pours its billows of sooty velvet behind you into the night. Here are more figures silhouetted against the dim sky—the Officer of the Watch, aged twenty-six, to whose charge the whole ship is committed for four hours; beside him (since we are closing the land) is the Navigating Commander leaning upon his familiar, the compass, watching over those high mysteries by means

Compass Platform, Signal Bridge, and Searchlight
Platform of *Lion*.

Working Cables.

Harmonies of the Night

of which the whole fleet has been guided towards the pin point of light that will presently, at the appointed moment, be sighted on the appointed bearing. Standing in the background are the sub-lieutenant or midshipman of the watch, the starboard and port look-outs, the signalman, the bridge messenger, all standing ready, throughout a watch in which perhaps nothing happens, for everything that might happen. You are far above the rage and trouble of the water here; only the wind pours past you, changing its note according to the angle at which your head is turned to it, and singing in harmonies as of a gigantic harp through the bar-tight steel stays and the straining arcs of the signal halliards. There are no telegraphs here, as on the bridge of an ordinary ship, only the gaping voice pipe beside the compass, and the navyphones which communicate with every essential part of the ship and are arrayed round the inside of the wind screens. But below in the dark conning tower the brass mouths of the voice-pipes open wide beside the quarter-masters at the steering wheel, telegraphs, revolution indicators and tell-tales—the nerve centres from which the whole system of the ship's movement is controlled.

Well forward where the compass is, there is shelter from the wind, and there you exchange a friendly word or two with the Navigator and the Officer of the Watch, relative to the time of getting in. "Alter course at 1 A.M., anchor at 2.45, coal at 6," is the programme; it has all been arranged, and the colliers for every ship allotted and ordered by wireless, although in this raging darkness there is nothing to suggest that such a thing as land exists.

Days with the Fleet

But the Navigator has looked at his watch. "We ought to pick up May Island about now," he says, and almost on the instant comes the gruff voice of the lookout—"Light two points on the starboard bow, sir." And there, in the expected quarter, in answer to our wireless signal of eight hours ago, "Request that May Island be lighted from midnight to 1.80 A.M." shines, not the glorious star of peace time, but the dim yellow glow that is all we ask or need to guide us in. The Navigator notes the time and, well pleased with his landfall, retires with his satellite to the chart-room, to add the tiny delicate circle with the figures "12.45" to the long line ruled in pencil that represents our magnificent night march across the thundering seas. Messengers are sent to call the Captain, and the Flag-Lieutenant goes to call the Admiral; for altering the course of a fleet at night, especially when approaching a coast haunted by submarines, is an affair in which responsibility is not delegated.

But there is another side to the picture. Come down from the windy bridges, past the deck where the sprays crash and rattle on the gun casings; down into the light and warmth again, along the quiet hotel-like corridors where the curtains still keep up their grave and steady pendulum swinging, and the only sign of the ship's thrusting progress is in the hollow and muffled roar of the sea's assault. Down again, through the brass-bound hatchway, to the mess decks, crowded with hammocks, where a breath of the gale above would be a godsend; and still down, through a rising temperature, until you find yourself in a tropical cathedral of lights and

Who Sings in his Sleep

polished metals, adorned with dials and clocks and gauges, festooned with monstrous padded pipes that lead to vast and uncouth cylindrical shapes; its lofty spaces filled with a mist of oil and an uncanny atmosphere of tremendous forces lurking within lagged cauldrons and casings. Nothing seems to be moving; only a profound murmur, a tremor as of a bass organ pipe, tells you of the turbines with their thousands of blades whirling to the thrust of the invisible steam. Up above, when the great guns are firing, you can hear the Lion roar; here his voice is attuned to a gigantic purring, as of one well pleased with his strength, who breathes and sings in his sleep.

Here at a little library desk, like a professor in a vast laboratory of power, sits the Engineer officer of the watch, and rules in his kingdom. Ministers represent him in different parts of it, couriers go to and fro on its business; on the dials about him he can read its state and condition at any moment, and periodical reports are brought to him from outlying provinces, so that the amount of coal in any bunker, the steam pressure in any boiler, the behaviour and temperature of those sensitive bearings on which the power of the ship depends are known to him at any moment. Far from him here, surely, that little world we left peering into the night ten minutes ago, high up in the wind and storm. Far from here the shouldering seas, the stiff driving of the ship against them, the doings of Admiral, Captain, Navigator. . . .

Far? The clash of the gongs awoke the drowsy air, and giant fingers moved on the dials. Someone gave a great shining wheel half a turn and the purring rose a semi-tone in pitch, as though the Lion were dreaming of the chase.

"Eighteen knots," said the Engineer officer, looking at the revolution indicator, while certain of his coadjutors were busy with subsidiary indicators and telephones. "We're passing May Island: it will be twenty in a minute." Again the gongs clashed, the giant fingers moved round the dials; and the note of the turbines rose in pitch—"Nineteen knots." Once more another rise in pitch, and the pace, after a little more clashing conversation from the gongs as to revolutions, steadied to 20 knots. We had entered on the long straight gallop home from May Island to Inchkeith, where the waters were narrow and the submarines were waiting and the goal was in sight. "Tattenham Corner," the Admiral called it, and he never failed to be on the bridge during that twenty-mile rush in or out. Our passages were always timed for the dark hours of the night—except once, I remember, when the necessity of being at a certain place at a certain time required us to pass down the Firth of Forth in bright moonlight, in which every line of every ship stood out like ink on silver, and the sense of naked exposure, compared with our habitual stealth and concealment, was like that of the familiar nightmare in which one is entering a crowded ballroom clad only in a shirt.

The temperature in the engine-room rose with the speed, and the oily mists thickened. "Come along to X boiler-room," said my friend; intelligence having reached him that X's contribution to the national treasury of steam pressure was falling off. Through more steel passages, which began to be like ovens, we suddenly entered what was apparently the mouth of hell. Demons with rolling white eyes and armed with monstrous long rakes and prickers sliced and tore at the molten fuel in the furnaces. Red-hot doors slammed, white-hot caverns yawned, trolleys bearing coals shot past, a gale of coal-dust blew from the bunker doors, and one's flesh was scorched by the heat. "Pretty warm," I said to one of the demons while my friend was making investigations. "Oh, this isn't a bad stokehold," said my demon. "It's a bit of all right, this is; now ' Y ' does get a bit warm not half, when we're going all out. Any chance of a Scrap, sir?"—for that was the demon's sole interest. Not to get out of this oven for ever and go and live in Greenland; but to have a Scrap, in which his only participation might be that, after being half roasted for four or five hours, he would be suddenly blown up or boiled. Great heroes were these men of the stokeholds. The Engineer with his brain and his skill made a war-horse of steam that carried you into battle. The gun crews might perform miracles of attack upon the enemy; the Admiral might combine all the courage with all the skill of the world; but the primitive source of the power of the whole gigantic weapon was in the sinews and the will of these grand fellows, whose work was done in red-hot prisons, and for whom battle afforded only the alternative of doubled work or death. A Navy stoker is a tough nut in many ways, and is not included in the ornamental part of his Service; but he and his mates did a mighty part in the winning of the war.

CHAPTER XI

SATURDAY, January 28, found us with the impression that nothing would ever happen again and that we were fixed in the Firth of Forth for ever. The morning being fairly fine, however, I persuaded the Secretary, who could never be induced to leave his work and go ashore (I think he had landed about twice since the war began) to come and spend an afternoon in Edinburgh. So after an early lunch we made the usual trip ashore in the picket boat and walked up to the train at Dalmeny, and were duly unloaded amid a crowd of other naval officers at the Caledonian station. The day was not a success. I had already plumbed the depths of boredom latent in two and a half hours of an Edinburgh Saturday afternoon with an east wind blowing, although I hoped that the novelty of seeing streets and houses and people in everyday clothes might cheer up the Secretary. I led him up and down Princes Street, and we pressed our noses against the shop windows; and underwent as many operations as possible at the hairdressers; we climbed to the castle ramparts, where we shivered in the east wind and looked down under a black sky on the celebrated view of the Forth. But all my companion noticed was that there seemed to be an undue amount of smoke coming from the funnels of the battle cruisers.

On |Board in a Hurry

" There, I knew what it would be," he said; " ,we have probably been ordered to sea, ciphers are pouring in, the Admiral has probably come on board, and here are you and I shivering on this," etc., etc. We descended and while waiting for the train had tea at Mackie's, but the Secretary would not be comforted. " This is what comes of going ashore," he said, and muttered strange objurgations. After we got to the station the " buzz " had already developed; in fact, the hall porter at the Caledonian Hotel always knew when the squadron ,was going to sea long before a feather of smoke had shown from the funnels, and certain great and high officials used to wonder how the news, so jealously guarded from the wise and prudent executive officer, was revealed to the very babes ashore. The fact that a mess caterer would suddenly inform his contractor on the Hawes Pier that instead of requiring certain eggs, milk, and fresh provisions on the morrow, he ,would require . nothing at all, did not seem to strike them as a possible basis from ,which inferences might be drawn.

But there was no doubt about it this time. There was a frantic commotion at the slipway where the steam boats were waiting, and much panic on the part of individual officers lest their respective boats should depart without them. In half an hour the pier was empty and the boats were being hoisted in aboard the battle cruisers. We came on board at half-past five and found that all had happened as foreseen by the Secretary. There was an orgy of ciphering and deciphering going on in the Intelligence Office, and the orders which had been received really seemed to mean business. We were to sail almost at once, for the rendezvous appointed by the

Battle of the Dogger Bank: Prelude

Admiralty was some 220 miles away and we had to be there by daybreak on the morrow. The following was the signal which set all these activities in motion, and inaugurated the first historic encounter between super-Dreadnought ships.

Admiralty to C.-in-C.; V.A. *Lion*; Commodore (T); V.A. 3rd B.S.

" Four German battle cruisers, six light cruisers and 22 destroyers will sail this evening to scout on Dogger Bank, probably returning to-morrow evening. All available battle cruisers, light cruisers, and destroyers from Rosyth should proceed to a rendezvous in 55.18 N., 8.12 E., arriving at 7.0 A.M. to-morrow. Commodore (T) is to proceed with all available destroyers and light cruisers from Harwich to join V.A. *Lion*, at 7.0 A.M. at above rendezvous. If enemy is sighted by Commodore (T) while crossing their line of advance, they should be attacked. W.T. is not to be used unless absolutely necessary. Telegram has been sent to C. in-C. Home Fleet; V.A. *Lion*; V.A. 3rd Battle Squadron; and Commodore (T)."

We sailed at 6 P.M., the Third Battle Squadron following us at 8.30 towards a point well to the northward of our rendezvous, where they would be in a position to intercept any forces which might break away to the northward from an encounter with us. Everything was " out " that night, but everything near us was to be under the Admiral's orders, and the dispositions had been admirably made. The only difficulty was that in order to reach our rendezvous at the proper time we should have to cut off a corner, and pass through the edge of a suspected mine-

Possibilities of the Morrow

field. Usually we stood out to the eastward a good distance after passing May Island, as the belt of mines laid by the enemy off the East Coast extended eastward for a considerable, although uncertain, distance off St. Abb's Head. The time at which we should pass through this suspect region was about 2 A.M., and my own determined intention was to be fast asleep at that moment. We dined at 8.45, when we were well past May Island. I had the first watch; very quiet, as wireless was practically unused while we were at sea on an operation of this kind, and nothing was likely to come in. As his custom was, the Admiral looked in upon his way to his windy sea cabin, and we talked over the chart and the possibilities of to-morrow. For some curious reason we were confident on this occasion, in a way we had never been before, that we should meet the enemy on the morrow. No one had any doubts about it and there was an air of suppressed excitement which was very exhilarating.

Just before I turned in I had another visitor, in the person of an officer who has since risen to high rank and honour. He was a man of few and strange words, who by virtue of his character had probably more personal influence on the general tone of the *Lion* than any other of the ship's officers. When on board he spoke, in a jargon of his own, words of brevity, wisdom and humour. On this occasion he only made two remarks, which would be inexplicable to anyone unacquainted with the argot of the *Lion's* wardroom. "Jimmy Hush," he observed, putting his head in at the door, bending round in an endeavour to see the chart. On being invited in (strictly against rules) he stood in front of it, observing the rendezvous and the course of the various forces of the fleet on their way towards it. Looking at the track of one such portion, and observing that it was somewhat widely deflected in order to avoid a spot where floating mines had been sighted, he laid his finger on the spot, uttered the mysterious words, " Jimmy Funkoins," and departed into the night.

The ship drove on calmly and stiffly through the dark surges. Midnight came, and with it the brief commotion incident on the changes of the watch; a slight aroma of cocoa was added to the other perfumes below deck, and I departed to turn in. In my cabin I stowed away everything movable and breakable, saw that the door was hooked back, that my swimming waistcoat was on the bed, looked at my watch, realized that we were still an hour and a half off the mine-field, and fell asleep.

CHAPTER XII

FROM the signal bridge of the *Lion*, when I went up at 6.80 A.M. on January 24, the eastern horizon showed light and the sea was beginning to grey over, but it was still dark night about us. The Admiral was already there, and at 6.45 signals were beginning to come in from the Harwich Flotillas indicating that the rendezvous chosen by the Admiralty had been hit off exactly. Too exactly, in fact, for we and the light cruisers arrived at the appointed spot in more or less of a bunch, and our scouting forces were not spread enough to give us the advantage of an ideal position in the expected contact with the enemy. At ten minutes to seven I went down to breakfast; and when I returned fifteen minutes later the daylight was beginning to spread and the cloud-banks to roll away. It promised to be an ideal morning, with a light breeze from the N.N.E. and a slight swell on the sea. At seven the bugles sounded off Action, and a few minutes later came, with a thrill to all of us, the flash of gunfire and a signal from *Aurora* that she was in action with enemy forces. The fact that she described herself as engaged with the whole maritime strength of Germany gave a laughing start to the grim business of the day.

Battle of the Dogger Bank : The Chase

7.20 a.m.

The first contact with the enemy was signalled by *Aurora*, from whom at this hour came a message :

" Am in action with High Seas Fleet."

7.21 a.m.

Lion to Light Cruisers :

" Chase S. 10 E."

7.27 a.m.

To Destroyers :

" Take station ahead 8 miles."

7.30 a.m.

By this time the battle cruisers had advanced about ten miles to the south of the rendezvous, and the Admiral had held this course a little longer as his desire was to get to the southward of the enemy and cut him off from his base. The light cruisers at the first moment of the enemy being located had been chasing to the E. of S. and were now visible about five miles on our port bow. Commodore (T), with the fast destroyers of the " M " class, was on our starboard bow, converging on the enemy to the S. of E. *Aurora*, with the first flotilla, had come up from farther off and was also making for the enemy, slightly on our port bow, and *Undaunted*, with the third flotilla, was some ten miles away to the S.E. At about 7.45 the enemy, whose course was N.N.W., turned 16 points and at a speed of 24 knots made E.S.E. At the same time Admiral Beatty altered course from W. of S. to S.S.E.

7.47 a.m.

Southampton to *Lion* :

" Enemy sighted are 4 battle cruisers, speed 24 knots."

The Leeward Position

7.50 a.m.

The *Lion* altered course more to the eastward.

7.59 a.m.

Southampton to *Lion*:

"Enemy in sight are battle cruisers and light cruisers, steering between S.E. and S."

8.10 a.m.

The battle cruisers increased speed to 24 knots and five minutes later to 25.

8.12 a.m.

Southampton to *Lion*:

"Enemy altering course to N.E."

This brief alteration of course by the enemy battle cruisers was probably necessitated by the disposal of Von Hipper's light forces; but brief as it was it helped Admiral Beatty in getting to the southward of the enemy's course. This he desired to do, not only so as to get if possible between him and his base, but also so that he could secure the leeward position and prevent the smoke from our own guns from obscuring the sights. The alteration of course did not last long, however, and in ten minutes the enemy was reported to have resumed his south-easterly course, which he maintained practically without a break for the next three hours.

8.23 a.m.

Lion to Battle Cruisers:

"Speed 26 knots."

8.24 a.m.

Southampton to *Lion*:

"My position 54.58 N., 4.5 E. Enemy in sight consists of 4 battle cruisers and 4 light cruisers, steering between E. and S.E."

Battle of the Dogger Bank: The Chase

The *Southampton* had taken up an excellent position on the enemy's port quarter, from which she was able to keep good observation, not only of his movements, but also later of the effect of our fire.

8.25 a.m.

Battle cruisers were ordered to fall out of line one point to receive signals.

8.28 a.m.

Arethusa to *Lion*:

"German destroyers to southward of their fleet; enemy battle cruiser course S.E."

Owing to the superior speed of the "M" class destroyers, they were able to get into a position within four miles of the *Blücher* and on the starboard bow of our battle cruisers, from which position the *Meteor* was fired at by *Blücher*. Captain Meade from this position was able to obtain exact particulars as to the composition of the enemy's force. Having done so, he fell back on the *Arethusa* and the slower destroyers, which were not able, owing to their situation when the enemy began his retreat, to take up positions advantageous for attack. In order not to obscure the range from our battle cruisers they took station far enough astern of the enemy to be clear.

8.29 a.m.

Meteor to *Lion*:

"Enemy altered course E. to S.E."

8.30 a.m.

Lion to Battle Cruisers:

"S. 40 E."

8.34 a.m.

Lion to Battle Cruisers:

"Speed 27 knots."

Working up Speed

This was increased at 8.48 to 28 knots and at 8.54 to 29 knots. During the last hour the battle cruisers had been steadily working up speed; and although it is not likely that the actual speeds ordered by signals were attained, there was no harm, from the point of view, of encouraging the engine-rooms, in giving them something big to aim at. So well did they respond that the sensation of speed was now becoming remarkable. We were all in high spirits. As usual when the ship was in action, the decks were deserted, and although during action the navigating staff of the ship, as well as the Admiral and his staff, are supposed to retire to the conning tower, no one had thought of going as yet. The signal staff were still on the signal bridge, and the rest of us including the Navigating Commander, Captain Chatfield, the Admiral, the Flag-Commander, the Secretary, two Flag-Lieutenants and myself, were all on the compass platform, enjoying the sensation and prospects of the chase in that clear North Sea air. There was immense exhilaration in the feeling, whenever another hoist indicating a speed signal was hauled down, of the splendid ship's jump forward through the seas. Through the whole of that long and magnificent chase there was never any sensation of the ship being urged forward, but rather of her being held back as though by a bit, which she was striving to get between her teeth.

8.35 a.m.

Lion to Commander-in-Chief :

" Enemy sighted consists of 4 battle cruisers, 4 light cruisers and destroyers, bearing S. 61 E. eleven miles. My position 54.44 N. 3.44 E., course S. 40 E. Speed 24 knots."

Battle of the Dogger Bank: The Chase

8.38 a.m.

Lion to Battle Cruisers:
" S. 50 E."

8.43 a.m.

Lion to Battle Cruisers:
" Speed 28 knots."

8.44 a.m.

From the *Lion's* bridge the enemy appeared on the eastern horizon in the form of four separate wedges or triangles of smoke, with another mass of smoke ahead of them, coming from their destroyers. Suddenly from the rearmost of these wedges came a stab of white flame.

" He's opened fire," said Captain Chatfield, and we waited for what seemed a long time, probably about twenty-five seconds, until a great column of water and spray arose in the sea at a distance of more than a mile on our port bow. The first shot in the first battle between super-dreadnoughts had been fired, and another epoch in the history of war begun. All this time the Gunnery Officer had been getting the ranges at intervals from the range-finder on the bridge, and we were approaching the limit of 22,000 yards at which target might be reached. Minute by minute the ranges came down; and during each interval further flashes were observed from the enemy, and further fountains of water rose between us—always creeping a little nearer, but still short. One looked on in a curiously detached way, as though the performance could be no particular concern of ours.

8.52 a.m.

As soon as the range, as reported, had come down to 22,000 yards, Captain Chatfield told the Gunnery Lieu-

Rear-Admiral Sir Alfred E. M. Chatfield,
K.C.M.G., C.B., C.V.O.
(Captain of H.M.S. _Lion_ 1913–17.)

tenant to try a sighting shot. Almost on the instant one of our 13.5's in " B " turret roared out, and the cordite smoke blew back in our faces. Again there came the interval of waiting; and far away, between us and the nearest of the smoke wedges, one could see through one's glasses the tiny fountain of water that told us that the shot was short.

8.54 a.m.

Lion to Battle Cruisers :

" Speed 29 knots. Keep on line of bearing so that X guns will bear."

8.55 a.m.

Lion to *Indomitable* :

" Well done, *Indomitable*."

The Admiral's signals were now asking for a speed which none of the ships, except possibly the *Tiger*, was supposed to possess and which none of them was quite attaining; but there is nothing like asking the impossible, and although the first three ships were drawing away from the Second Battle Cruiser Squadron, it was still keeping gamely up, a performance especially creditable to the *Indomitable*, slowest of the five. Hence this signal, which would not be long in being transmitted to the *Indomitable's* boiler rooms.

9.5 a.m.

Lion to Battle Cruisers :

" Open fire and engage the enemy."

By this time others of the German ships had opened fire; the sea between the two forces was becoming alive with spouting columns which were now coming very near, and as the *Lion* had apparently straddled her target, the duel would at any moment develop into a general action.

Battle of the Dogger Bank : The Chase

9.9 a.m.

After what seemed an interminable interval, although in fact it was only seventeen minutes after the first ranging shot, *Lion* registered her first hit on the *Blücher*.

9.20 a.m.

" Destroyers take station ahead and proceed at your utmost speed."

At this moment some commotion and change in formation in the mass representing the enemy's flotillas seemed to indicate the threat of a destroyer attack, so this signal was made; although it was soon seen that at the speed at which we were going only the " M " division would be able to get ahead of us. The slower boats, therefore, resumed their stations on our beam. At 9.20 A.M. exactly the *Tiger*, just astern of us, opened fire on the *Blücher*, and there was a momentary lull in our firing while the *Lion* shifted to the third ship in the line, the *Derfflinger*, the range being now 18,000 yards.

9.21 a.m.

Up to now there had been very little sound but the rush through the wind and water, with the occasional roar of our guns; but now the noise of firing was becoming louder and louder; the enemy's shots were falling on both sides of us and quite close, so that the spray from them drenched our decks. The moment had come for an adjournment to the conning tower—that small armoured citadel, the mechanical brain of the ship, whence she could be steered and manœuvred and her gun-fire controlled by means of the complicated mass of voice pipes, telephones and electric and hydraulic gear. As it was already overcrowded with the units indispensable for all these purposes, the Admiral's staff divided, the

In the Foretop

2nd Flag-Lieutenant and I repairing to our windy eyrie in the foretop. As we were climbing up to it a terrific blow and a shake proclaimed the fact that the *Lion* had been hit. The climb had been bad enough in ordinary circumstances. It was perfectly horrible now. We were already pretty cold from standing in the wind, we were encumbered with thick clothing, swimming waistcoat, oilskins, etc.; and the wind on the mast, as we got out of shelter of the compass platform, was terrific. It shook and tore at us until I really wondered whether my hands would be able to keep their grip on the steel rungs, and my one supreme apprehension was that I should disgrace myself by falling off the mast before the battle had properly begun, and so miss all the fun. I felt sure the end had come when, having dragged myself step by step to where the floor of the foretop overshadowed us, I found that the steel covering of the manhole, giving entrance to it, was shut. This was serious. It would be impossible to make the man inside it hear, and my companion immediately below me on the ladder was hailing me vehemently to hurry up, as he could not hold on much longer. Fortunately, the Navigating Commander, who was just leaving the bridge, saw our dilemma and hailed the foretop, with the result that the manhole was opened just in time. It was impossible to endure the wind standing up in this square box; so we knelt on the steel floor and could just rest our elbows on the rim and keep our eyes and glasses over the edge.

9.25 a.m.

We had just settled down on our very uncomfortable perch when a glare amid the smoke of the *Lion's* target advertised a hit. There was no mistaking the difference between the bright, sharp stab of white flame that marked the firing of the enemy's guns, and this dull, glowing and fading glare which signified the bursting of one of our own shells.

9.35 a.m.

Lion to Battle Cruisers :
" Engage corresponding ship in line."

On this signal being made and hauled down, the *Lion's* guns were trained on the enemy's leading ship, leaving the second ship, the *Moltke*, to the *Tiger*, while the *Princess Royal* and *New Zealand* had the *Derfflinger* and *Blücher* respectively as targets. It was not until afterwards that we discovered that the *Tiger* had not obeyed this order, but had continued to fire on the *Blücher*, thus leaving the *Moltke* to uninterrupted target practice on the *Lion;* for the German battle cruisers were concentrating their fire on the head of our line, in the hope of the advantage to them which might (and later did) arise from the flagship being put out of action.

9.43 a.m.

The movements which had been observed among the enemy's destroyers now seemed to be developing into an attack; and although they could not come down on our engaged bow without masking the fire of the German guns and coming under fire from ours, their situation was such as to make a long-range torpedo attack on our line worth attempting.

9.45 a.m.

The *Lion* came very near her end at this moment. An 11-inch shell from the *Seydlitz* or *Moltke* hit her

A Terrible Effect

and penetrated the 4-inch magazine trunk—and did not explode.

9.50 a.m.

A great glowing mass of fire appeared on the after part of the *Seydlitz*. What had happened may best be described in Admiral Scheer's words : " The first shell that hit her had a terrible effect. It pierced right through the upper deck in the ship's stern and through the barbette-armour of the near turret, where it exploded. All parts of the stern, the officers' quarters, mess, etc., that were near where the explosion took place were totally wrecked. In the reloading chamber, where the shell penetrated, part of the charge in readiness for loading was set on fire. The flames rose high up into the turret and down into the munition chamber, and thence through a connecting door usually kept shut, by which the men from the munition chamber tried to escape into the fore turret. The flames thus made their way through to the other munition chamber, and thence again up to the second turret, and from this cause the entire gun crews of both turrets perished almost instantly. The flames rose as high as a house above the turrets." [1] Well do I remember seeing those flames and wondering what kind of horrors they signified.

9.53 a.m.

Lion to Battle Cruisers :

" Speed 24 knots."

Owing to the extreme speed at which we were steaming, the battle cruisers were beginning to straggle out. The *Tiger* was close astern of the *Lion*, but there was an interval between her and *Princess Royal*, and

[1] "Germany's High Sea Fleet in the World War," Scheer, p. 84.

Battle of the Dogger Bank : The Chase

a much greater one between *Princess Royal* and *New Zealand*. This reduction in speed gave the slower ships an opportunity to close up. At this time an enemy shot put *Lion's* "A" turret temporarily out of action, but it was soon repaired.

10 a.m.

Just as the *Lion* received a severe hit a vast cloud appeared from the enemy destroyers, who were sending up a smoke screen with the intention of masking some manœuvre which they intended and of obscuring our view. Under cover of this screen the enemy battle cruisers opened the range by turning for a short time to the northward; and this, coinciding with the slackening of speed on our part for the purpose of closing up the line, undoubtedly served to increase the range and to make the fire on both sides for a time ineffective. For about a quarter of an hour we practically lost the range, as did the enemy, for although at this time the sea was covered with splashes from his shot, nothing came very near us for about ten minutes.

10.4 a.m.

Lion to Battle Cruisers :

"Speed 26 knots."

10.5 a.m.

Lion to *Arethusa* :

"Destroyers attack enemy destroyers."

The threatened attack on the part of the enemy destroyers now developed, and at about 12,000 yards *Lion* and *Tiger* opened fire with their secondary armament; and so effective, even at this long range, were the 4-inch and 6-inch guns, that the enemy destroyers quickly resumed their station at the head of his line and

A Violent Blow

did not repeat their threat of attack. At 10.7 A.M. the right gun on the *Lion's* " B " turret was out of action for about fifteen minutes.

10.14 a.m.

Owing to the causes already mentioned the range had momentarily been completely lost. At 10.14 the *Lion's* guns were firing at extreme elevation a long way off the target, and the range came down 2,000 yards in one step. After this, however, the range was recovered and held until the end of the action. At this time it was observed that the after turrets of the *Seydlitz* were silenced.

10.18 a.m.

The *Lion* here received a blow so violent that we thought she had been torpedoed. The ship seemed to stop, and the mast, to which the foretop was secured, rocked and waved like a tree in a storm, and the ship seemed to be shaking herself to bits. We looked at one another and prepared to alight from our small cage into whatever part of the sea destiny might send us; but nothing happened, and the old *Lion* seemed to pick herself up and go on again.

The enemy's salvoes were seen to be falling in pairs and in groups of threes and even in fives, and it is quite possible that this blow was a result of this extremely close calibration. It drove in an armour plate, as shown in the accompanying photograph. The feed-water tank of the port condenser was pierced, and although the engine-room staff did everything that was possible, this ultimately caused the stoppage of the port engine. But this result was not to develop fatally for half an hour yet. This was one of the shots which in published accounts of the action has always been referred to as a

Battle of the Dogger Bank: The Chase

"lucky shot"—although why a shot that did what it
was intended to do should be described as "lucky" I
do not know. It is an amusing instance of the persistence
of an error. Admiral Beatty in his original report
described it as an "unlucky" shot, which for us it
certainly was. The word was misprinted as "lucky,"
and every subsequent writer has accounted for the
breaking off of the battle by saying it was due to a
"lucky shot." So history is written.

10.27 a.m.

The *Blücher* now seemed to be well on fire, and the
interval between her and the other battle cruisers was
increasing. Admiral Von Hipper had definitely decided
to leave her to her fate and push on for safety. She was
the weakest of his ships and had been in the most
exposed position the whole time. If he had put the
Blücher in front of him on the way home she would have
been better protected and might have kept up her speed,
while he himself would have had the post of honour in
the rearmost ship. In speaking of posts of honour I
had forgotten to say that the Admiral and his staff did
not remain long in the conning tower. The only view
from that protected place is through a very narrow slit
at the height of the eye which, although it gives a view
of a kind around three-quarters of the horizon, was of
little use to the Admiral. He was thoroughly enjoying
himself, and did not like to waste his day in the cramped
and crowded security of the conning tower; and he and
the Flag-Lieutenant, the Flag-Commander, and Secretary were soon up on the compass platform again, where
the view was perfect, although the danger from splinters
was considerable. They were flying about us all the

Armour Plate on *Lion's* Port Side, driven in by Shell Fire.

Flying Splinters

time in the foretop; often we could see them, and one had the feeling that if one put a finger out beyond the shelter of the thin steel screen, it would be shot off. During a lull between salvoes the Admiral hailed us to ask how we were enjoying ourselves. If I had told the truth I should have answered that I was miserably cold and rather frightened, but deeply interested; and if I had not been so stiff and cold I would have dared the horrors of the descent and joined them on the compass platform. But as a matter of fact we were so cramped from kneeling on this steel floor that our chief physical preoccupation was that of trying to find an attitude which would not bring our kneecaps directly on to rivet heads. I had one really unpleasant experience. Very soon after the Admiral had hailed us, and following the tremendous blow and shake which I have described, I put my head out to look down and see what had happened. There was a great drift of cordite smoke all round the compass platform, and to my horror, instead of the four figures I had last seen standing there there were only four tumbled smudges of blue on the deck. After the smoke cleared away I saw that they were greatcoats, and presently, to my inexpressible relief, my four friends reappeared, eating sandwiches. What had happened was that, having been very hot in the conning tower, they had taken off their greatcoats when they came up, and there being at the moment an unusual lot of splinters flying about, the Admiral, much against his will, had been persuaded to return to the conning tower. But after five minutes he broke out again and came on to the compass platform, which always thereafter he occupied in action.

Battle of the Dogger Bank: The Chase

10.28 a.m.

Lion to Battle Cruisers:

"Form a line of bearing N.N.W. and proceed at your utmost speed."

It was absolutely necessary now to press the chase as hard as possible, and the definite speeds signals were abandoned, especially as full speed had now been worked up to in every ship, and it was a case of getting in as close as possible to the enemy and pressing the advantage of our gun-fire, which was beginning to punish him severely.

10.35 a.m.

Lion to Battle Cruisers.

"Turn together one point to port."

10.45 a.m.

Lion to Battle Cruisers:

"Turn together one point to port."

These two alterations were made with the same end in view—that of closing the range. The Lion was at this time being heavily battered by the constant fire of the *Seydlitz* and *Moltke;* it was marvellous how she stood the pounding of their formidable 11-inch shells which, although they had neither the weight nor the bursting power of our 18.5's, had been able, as we have seen, to stave in the armoured side of the ship. But it was obvious that the *Lion* could not keep up her speed much longer. At 10.35 she was hit, and again a minute later, and at 10.41 we thought her last moment had surely come, when we got a message up the voice pipe from the lower conning tower saying that " A " turret magazine was on fire. We sat amid that terrible din waiting for the last gorgeous explosion and the eternal silence that

The *Lion* Disabled

would follow it, but it did not come; and after four minutes of suspense our sentence of death was reprieved in a welcome message that the fire was out, the magazine flooded, and we were proceeding at 20 knots.

10.47 a.m.

Lion to Battle Cruisers:

"Close enemy as rapidly as possible, consistent with keeping all guns bearing."

It was now clear that the *Lion* could not maintain her position at the head of the Squadron, and the Admiral, in this and the following signals, endeavoured to make it clear to the others that they should continue to press the attack.

10.48 a.m.

Lion to *Indomitable*:

"Attack enemy making to the northward."

The *Blücher* had hauled out of the enemy's line to the northward on fire, with a heavy list, and as *Indomitable* was too far astern to be able to engage the three other ships, she was detailed to finish off the *Blücher*.

10.49 a.m.

Lion hit by salvoes twice.

10.51 a.m.

Lion hit by salvoes twice.

10.52 a.m.

Lion listing ten degrees to port. Port engine stopped. All lights out and wireless out of action.

10.58 a.m.

Lion to Battle Cruisers:

"Turn together eight points to port."

Battle of the Dogger Bank: The Chase

This signal was made in consequence of the sighting of enemy submarines on the starboard bow. It was necessary to make a sharp turn so as to get clear of the track of the destroyers ahead of us.[1]

11.2 a.m.

Lion to Battle Cruisers:

"Course N.E."

This was made to modify the eight-point turn ordered a few minutes before which, while it was necessary in order to clear the squadron of the track of the destroyers, would, if persisted in, cause it to lose ground in the chase. The "Course N.E." signal, if obeyed, would take the Squadron between the sinking *Blücher* and the other enemy battle cruisers, in case they should attempt to close round her; while if they continued their flight it would bring at any rate the two fastest of our battle cruisers closer on their track.

11.5 a.m.

Lion to Battle Cruisers:

"Attack the rear of the enemy."

All the signal halliards had now been shot away except two, and on these the two separate signals before described were blowing out in the wind, each consisting of two flags, "Compass B" and "A.F." (Attack rear of enemy).

11.7 a.m.

Lion to Battle Cruisers:

"Keep nearer to the enemy."

The *Lion* had now hauled out and the remainder of the Squadron was about to pass her, heading to the N.N.E. in a somewhat straggling line of bearing. To

[1] See Appendix A. Vice-Admiral Beatty's Despatch, para. 18.

"Keep Nearer to the Enemy"

make his intentions finally clear as they passed the *Lion*, the Admiral made one more signal. The compass signal was hauled down and the signal "74" made—"Keep nearer to the enemy." This signal, with "A.F." and another hoisted on a tack line, "Repeat the signal the Admiral is now making," was flying as the Squadron passed, and remained flying until it had gone out of sight, and indeed for some time afterwards.

It is necessary now to leave the *Lion* and follow the other battle cruisers into the mysterious hour as to which the official account is completely silent, and Admiral Beatty's original despatch very nearly so. The *Tiger* and the *Princess Royal* apparently did not alter course in answer to either of the Admiral's two signals; it seems possible that, in the somewhat dramatic circumstances, there was a slight failure of observation on the part of the signalmen concerned, or that the signals were actually obscured by smoke. What these two ships did was practically to maintain the course on to which the eight-point (or right-angle) turn had put them, and they neither altered to a north-easterly course nor "kept nearer to the enemy" unless indeed the enemy were to be regarded as consisting of *Blücher*. Possibly the signal, "Attack the rear of the enemy," if it was taken in, was interpreted as applying to the *Blücher*. One can only say, from the absence of actual knowledge as to what actually took place in the minds of Captain Pelly and Captain Brock, either that they interpreted the Admiral's signals in a spirit entirely contrary to the whole of his character and training, or else—what is more likely—that for some reason or another they were not aware of them. Captain

Battle of the Dogger Bank : The Chase

Brock, although the senior officer of the two, and intimately acquainted with Admiral Beatty's mind, was in the position of being the rear ship of the two, and therefore obliged to follow *Tiger*, or else add to the ambiguities of the moment by assuming the leadership on his own account. Consider the situation. Admiral Beatty's flag was still flying in the *Lion*, so he was not killed, although the flagship was apparently out of action. Captain Pelly was leading the line of remaining ships. Rear-Admiral Moore was the senior officer present, so presumably in command. For Captain Brock to have taken the lead and, forsaking the *Tiger*, gone after the enemy on his own account and so added a fourth to the existing possible elements of leadership, would have caused indescribable confusion and would be an action impossible in an officer of his experience. There was nothing for it, apparently, but to follow the *Tiger's* course in the direction of the unfortunate *Blücher*. The eight-point turn to port had enabled the *New Zealand* and *Indomitable* to cut off a corner and to fall in astern, although a long way astern, of the *Princess Royal*. She and the *Tiger* now proceeded to circle round the *Blücher*, firing all the time, and the other two ships fell into line astern of them. The doomed *Blücher*, already shot to pieces and in the act of dissolution, might well have been left to the squadron of light cruisers and flotillas of destroyers which were rapidly closing her; but her actual destruction seems to have been a kind of obsession with the captains of the two British battle cruisers. The psychological effects attendant upon the "blooding of the pack" must not be ignored. Yet Admiral Beatty's idea had been so very simple. The "cats" were to con-

Photo: Russell

Vice-Admiral Sir O. de B. Brock,
K.C.B., K.C.M.G., K.C.V.O.
(Captain of *Princess Royal* 1912-1915.)

tinue the chase of their living prey, while to the gallant but slower *Indomitable* was to be allotted a fine fat mouse in the shape of the *Blücher*, which could not get away. Instead of which, as we have seen, the main enemy force was making good its escape, while the British battle cruisers, hypnotized by the presence of the still fighting, though mortally wounded, *Blücher*, lost the vital half hour which, in a chase, could never be made up on that winter day. In the great game of war " the cards never forgive," and there is no cure for a lost opportunity.

What was the frame of mind of Rear-Admiral Sir Archibald Moore during this time I have no means of knowing. The facts as I understand them, however, are simply that he made no signal whatever during the whole fifty minutes in which the fortunes of the day were decided. It was impossible for him not to have known that the command had devolved upon him as the senior officer present; the *Lion* was out of sight twenty minutes after the turn to port, and it must have occurred to him that someone was in command. He appears not to have liked the situation and to have been preoccupied with thoughts of risk and danger from mines, and it is hard, reading such signals as he did make, not to believe that his conception of his duty as a commander was to get his squadron away from the track of the enemy (which it had already crossed) as quickly as possible. The following are the only signals known to me made by the Rear-Admiral; the times are approximate.

11.52 a.m.

Flag *New Zealand* to Battle Cruisers :
" Form single line ahead, course W."

Battle of the Dogger Bank: The Chase

11.56 a.m.

Flag to Battle Cruisers:
" Cease fire."

12.2 p.m.

Flag to *Southampton*:
" Retire north-west."

12.40 p.m.

Second Battle Cruiser Squadron to Commander-in-Chief:

" My position 54.18 N., 5.22 E., course N.N.W., speed 20 knots. Commodore (T) reports High Sea Fleet coming out.[1] I am retiring."

In criticizing the conduct of this action after the withdrawal of the flagship, one or two considerations should be borne in mind. It was the first occasion in which the new weapons, new organizations for fire control, and new fighting equipment were tried on a grand scale; in fact, it may be said that the whole of the conditions were entirely new in naval warfare. Theories that had been arrived at through years of laborious study and training had to be put to the test; and it has always been found that after a long period of peace those exercising command are inclined, and rightly, to exercise a degree of caution which later experience may prove to be excessive. Two of the unknown elements in this case were, of course, mines and submarines, and undoubtedly in the mind of Admiral Moore they exercised an influence which was

---

[1] A rather amusing incident occurred in this connexion. The High Sea Fleet was taken by surprise, and was not in the least ready to come out, but in the middle of the confusion, in order to scare the English forces away, a signal from the Commander-in-chief was sent to Von Hipper *en clair:* "High Sea Fleet coming out;" and then was added in cipher, "as soon as possible."

determining. His position at the rear of the Fleet, practically out of sight of what was going on, and with the slowest ship but one of the Squadron, may have made it difficult for him to have grasped the essential elements of the situation. The idea that he was being led into a trap in the neighbourhood of Heligoland was probably present to his mind, and overrode his natural desire to pursue the action to a finish.

But although the weapons and methods by which warfare is made are constantly changing, the basic principles of war do not change; and it was the misfortune of some of our commanders that they had a less firm grasp of these basic principles than of the circumstances which might modify the application of them. It was precisely in this respect that Admiral Beatty was unique. He never lost sight of the main principles of warfare, nor of the first and supreme importance of annihilating his adversary, even if in so doing he were to bring about a proportionate annihilation of his own force. His own force being superior to that of his enemy, he could afford to do so. He knew that where the enemy could go he could go. But there was no blindness on his part as to the danger of mines and submarines, and in his conduct of the chase he had throughout, with the greatest skill, so manœuvred as to reduce the risk from torpedo attack, and from the mines laid by the fleeing enemy, to a practically negligible quantity. Unfortunately the combination of coolness and restraint with his natural daring was not common. There were other leaders who had daring as great as his, and others who had caution equal to his; but there were none, among those who had the opportunity of proving their qualities, that had both in anything like the degree that he had. What might have been foolhardy in others was perfectly safe with him, because he knew and calculated all the risks and either took them or refused them. There is something tragic in the thought that here, as on a later and even greater occasion, we were robbed of the fruits of this steel-bright, steel-hard genius for battle. In each case everything was done, and rightly done, to lead up to the climax of annihilation— and there was no climax. On January 24 there was no reason whatever why the chase should not have been prolonged for at least another hour, or for an hour and a half, in which case the destruction of the enemy ships, which were beginning to suffer severely, would probably have been completed. But he was not there; and the diagram on the track chart, following that of his long and skilful pursuit, indicates only too eloquently the result of loss of a leader at a vital moment, and of his replacement by a substitute not trained in his clear ways, and preoccupied by the risks rather than by the favourable possibilities of the situation.

OGGER BANK

1915

30 P.M.

15   20

in Red

30'   40'   50'   6°

10'

55°

54°

30'   40'   50'   6°

CHAPTER XIII

BATTLE OF THE DOGGER BANK : THE RETURN

WE may now return to the *Lion*, which had turned out of the line at eleven o'clock in a disabled and, as we thought, quite sinking condition. The list to port was increasing steadily, and as we came down from the foretop we left our oilskins and other gear there, in order to be more free in the water, as it seemed possible that the end might come at any moment. The decks presented an extraordinary spectacle, battered and littered with fragments of smashed and twisted steel, with here and there yawning gashes where heavy shell had burst or fragments penetrated. The men came up from below and swarmed over them, picking up souvenirs in the shape of splinters and fragments of shell. A signal was made to the destroyers present to close round the ship, and one of them, the *Attack*, was after about a quarter of an hour manœuvred alongside so that the Admiral might follow the other ships and resume his command. The stokers, who had come up from below, pressed around him, cheering, and in the enthusiasm of the moment one of them clapped him on the back as he stepped on to the destroyer's fo'c'sle and shouted, " Well done, David ! " The flag-lieutenant, carrying an armful of flags and signal books, followed him on board and in a few minutes the *Attack*, proudly flying his flag from her little foremast, swept off after the others and disappeared in the haze.

Battle of the Dogger Bank: The Return

Meanwhile, Commander Fountaine had been working hard in the damaged part of the ship, shoreing up bulkheads, getting out collision mats, and doing what he could to see that the damage inflicted did not go any farther. It was found that the water was not increasing, although the feed supply of fresh water to the boilers was so interfered with that steaming was impossible with the port engine, and presently also with the starboard. These investigations and the means employed to preserve the ship from further damage took a good while and meantime we were able to take stock of the damage below decks. No one had been killed and only about fourteen were wounded; almost all by a shell which had burst in the confined space of " A " turret lobby and had, amongst other things, wrecked all the cabins there and reduced their contents to unrecognizable litter. Further aft, the Admiral's quarters had received considerable damage, particularly his dining cabin, the steel walls of which were riddled with splinter holes. My greatcoat, which I had left behind me on a chair when I came down to breakfast, was torn into rags and ribbons and looked as though a pack of hounds had been worrying it. All this damage, however, was superficial. The serious wound was below the waterline. The engineer officers told me that when the blow was received the whole side of the port engine room, on which were fixed most of the gauges and dials and instruments, had seemed to come bodily at them across the ship, and it is a wonder that no one was killed from the flying instruments and pieces of heavy metal which were sent hurtling across the engine room with the blow.

The dynamos being out of action, the ship was in dark-

Admiral Beatty's Dining Cabin after the Dogger Bank Battle.

We Start Homeward

ness except for the feeble light of candles and lanterns. The continuous firing of our own guns had shaken from its place everything that was not firmly secured; in my own cabin I found the contents of a chest of drawers sliding about the deck in six inches of water. There were, of course, no fires, and it was very difficult to get anything to eat; but the Admiral's steward (and peace-time valet) Woodley, who never failed to rise to an occasion, managed to get a case of champagne up from the flooded store-room, and with that and some *foie gras* sandwiches, which happened to be the only things in the pantry, we made a strange picnic lunch in the secretary's cabin. Our faces were blackened with cordite smoke, our nerves jangling with the relaxation of the tension, our ears were bleeding, but our hearts rejoicing, as we believed that the others who had gone on would complete the good work of the day. It was not until Admiral Beatty came back at about three o'clock that we heard of the destruction of the *Blücher* and of the breaking off of the fight, although even then it was thought doubtful whether the three re-maining German battle cruisers would manage to reach their harbour safely. Fortunately we did not know that one of them, the *Moltke*, was practically untouched, or our enthusiasm over the great events of the day might have been less unclouded than it was.

Both the *Lion's* engines by this time having been stopped, and there being no sign of her making any more water, the *Indomitable* proceeded to take her in tow, but it was two hours before the necessary hawsers, which several times broke, could be passed between the two ships, and it was after five before we began our slow progress homeward, along the road over which we had

Battle of the Dogger Bank: The Return

made such an exhilarating chase in the morning. It was a strange journey, lasting all that night, and all the next day, and through the night following. The wounded *Lion*, in tow of her consort, was surrounded by a cloud of destroyers, and from her bridge that evening I watched in the calm twilight the beautiful evolutions of these craft as, weaving in and out in ever changing formation, they formed a submarine screen round the ship. All about us, as far as we could see, the divisions were zigzagging, weaving their web of safety for us, and very comforting indeed was the presence of these glorious little ships with their trembling bodies and furious hearts. As night fell the Commodore (T) made a general signal to them: "Keep a good look-out for submarines at dawn; if seen, shoot and ram them regardless of your neighbours."

It was indeed a strange evening and night. Perhaps the silence of the ship was the strangest element of all—the absence of those buzzings and whinings that come from the innumerable dynamos, ventilating fans, refrigerating machines and motors that are never silent while there is mechanical life in the ship, and the sound of which one hardly notices until its cessation makes audible other and fainter sounds—the echo of voices through the long steel alleyways, the strange gurgling of water where no water should be. Most of us had headaches; all of us had black faces, torn clothes and jangled nerves. The ship was as cold as ice, all the electric radiators by which the cabins were warmed being out of action. Blows and hammerings echoed on the decks down below where the carpenters were at work. The sick bay, into which I looked before turning in, was a

German Gunnery

mess of blood and dirt, feebly lighted by oil lamps, from whence moans proceeded. The Admiral had gone back to the *Princess Royal*, but the remaining staff managed, nevertheless, to have quite a cheery little dinner with Captain Chatfield, whose galley and pantry were fortunately in commission. But there is nothing so cold as an unwarmed steel warship in the winter seas; the only place to get warm was in bed, and I turned in after dinner and slept like the dead.

During the journey home there was only one topic of conversation in the ship, and the chief matter of discussion was concerning the effects of our own and the German gun-fire respectively. This discussion lasted for a long time afterwards, and indeed is still going on; and on the net result of it many questions of future construction will have to be decided. It is a matter as to which impressions are valueless; it can only be decided by elaborate analysis of recorded facts. My impression was that the German gun-fire was better than ours initially, and that they got sooner on to the target, but that ours improved whilst theirs deteriorated. To anyone sitting, as I was, on the target, surrounded by the enemy's shells, his shooting appeared to be painfully accurate; and, indeed, towards the end of the action, when two and possibly three ships were concentrating on the *Lion*, she was very nearly smothered by their fire. Sometimes from the foretop one could see the shell coming, a black speck in the smoky atmosphere, but gradually growing larger; in that case one knew that the direction of the shot was accurate, exactly between one's eyes, and the only possibility of escape from it was that it should be either short or over. The time of flight averaged about twenty-three seconds, which often seemed curiously long when viewed as the possible remainder of one's life.

We had no " Director" firing[1] fitted in any of the ships except *Tiger*, and her gunnery conditions were not such as to afford any evidence as to its value; some of the observers in our small craft on the port quarter of the enemy, who were in a good position to see, alleged that she never hit anything at all. That was no doubt an exaggeration, but it is probable that the effect of her gun-fire in the actual engagement was negligible, and apart from a certain moral value that her presence afforded she might as well not have been there. If the *Queen Mary* had been with us the story would have been a very different one. All this involves no reflection on the officers and crew of the *Tiger*. The ship had been hurried out of the builders' hands before she was completed. No adequate time or opportunity was given to her officers for tuning her up. I believe at the time of her action she still had some dockyard hands on board, engaged in completing her fittings. It was all the more unfortunate, therefore, that she was the only one of the battle cruisers who had men killed on board, a shell having exploded in her Intelligence office on the forward superstructure. This shell killed five men, and also Engineer-Captain Taylor, a much valued member of the Admiral's staff who had his quarters in the *Tiger*. Otherwise the *Lion* was the only ship of the squadron to suffer any serious damage. An incident occurred which proved the

---

[1] A device by which all the guns can be trained, laid, and fired simultaneously and accurately from one central position, generally on the foremast well above the smoke.

After the Battle.
(Unengaged side of *Lion's* upper deck, looking aft.)

Bombing the Survivors

uselessness of mere visual impressions as to the effect of gun-fire. As the *Tiger* passed us when we turned out of the action there was a great fire raging on her after deck. As a matter of fact all that was the matter with her was that some of her boats, which were collected in that position, had caught fire and were burning furiously —a fire which soon burnt itself out and had no importance whatever. Yet you may be quite sure that the effect was put down by the Germans to the destructive effect of gun-fire, and I have no doubt they counted her as practically disabled. A ship, therefore, which is being fired at may appear to be enveloped in flames and half disabled, while in fact she has received no essential damage at all.

As we turned out of the action we observed a Zeppelin approaching, apparently about eighteen or twenty miles away, and I confess that we felt rather helpless with both our engines stopped, and had no doubt that she was coming to finish us off. Apparently, however, she did not see the *Lion*, but headed instead for the *Blücher*, and hovered about her. When our light cruisers and destroyers closed the *Blücher* to give her the *coup de grâce*, she was in an appalling condition, almost on her beam-ends, glowing red-hot in many places with the furnaces that raged within her, and yet gallantly firing with two of her remaining 8-inch guns that were pointing up very nearly skywards. The *Arethusa* went in and put a couple of torpedoes into her, which mercifully brought her struggles to an end, although with one of her last shots she managed to kill and wound a number of men in the *Meteor*. It was when our destroyers were at work picking up the survivors who were struggling

Battle of the Dogger Bank : The Return

in the water that the Zeppelin began to drop bombs into the area where the rescues were taking place, and Commodore Goodenough was obliged to make a signal from *Southampton* that all ships were to leave the spot at once. But for this extraordinary action on the part of the Zeppelin many more of the survivors would undoubtedly have been saved. It was due to a mistake as to the identity of the *Blücher*. She had tripod masts, and was no doubt thought to be either the *Tiger* or *New Zealand*, because for some time afterwards the Germans believed that they had sunk one of these ships.

The experiences of those on board the *Blücher* were graphically described in a remarkable article which appeared some time afterwards in the *Times*, written by an officer who had talked with many of the survivors. The following is an extract from it :

The British guns were ranging. Those deadly water spouts crept nearer and nearer. The men on deck watched them with a strange fascination. Soon one pitched close to the ship and a vast watery pillar, a hundred metres high one of them affirmed, fell lashing on the deck. The range had been found. *Dann aber ging's los!*

Now the shells came thick and fast with a horrible droning hum. At once they did terrible execution. The electric plant was soon destroyed, and the ship plunged in a darkness that could be felt. "You could not see your hand before your nose," said one. Down below decks there was horror and confusion, mingled with gasping shouts and moans as the shells plunged through the decks. It was only later, when the range shortened, that their trajectory flattened, and they tore holes in the ship's sides and raked her decks. At first they came dropping from the sky. They penetrated the decks. They bored their way even to the stokehold. The coal in the bunkers was set on fire. Since the bunkers were half empty the fire burned merrily. In the engine-room a shell licked up the oil and sprayed it around in flames of blue and green, scarring its victims and blazing where it fell. Men huddled together in dark compartments, but the shells sought them out, and there death had a rich harvest.

The terrific air-pressure resulting from explosion in a confined space, left a deep impression on the minds of the men of the *Blücher*. The air, it would seem, roars through every opening and tears its way through every weak spot. All loose or insecure fittings are transformed into moving instruments of destruction. Open doors bang to, and jam—and closed iron doors bent outward like tinplates, and through it all the bodies of men are whirled about like dead leaves in a winter blast, to be battered to death against the iron walls.

There were shuddering horrors, intensified by the darkness or semi-gloom. As one poor wretch was passing through a trap-door a shell burst near him. He was exactly half-way through. The trap-door closed with a terrific snap. In one of the engine-rooms—it was the room where the high velocity engines for ventilation and forced draught were at work—men were picked up by that terrible *Luftdruck*, like the whirl-drift at a street corner, and tossed to a horrible death amidst the machinery. There were other horrors too fearful to recount.

If it was appalling below deck, it was more than appalling above. The *Blücher* was under the fire of so many ships. Even the little destroyers peppered her. " It was one continuous explosion," said a gunner. The ship heeled over as the broadsides struck her, then righted herself, rocking like a cradle. Gun crews were so destroyed that stokers had to be requisitioned to carry ammunition. Men lay flat for safety. The decks presented a tangled mass of scrap iron. In one casement, the only one, as they thought, undestroyed, two men continued to serve their gun. They fired it as the ship listed, adapting the elevation to the new situation. Yet through it all some never despaired of their lives. Others from the beginning gave themselves up as lost. The disaster came upon them so suddenly that few had time to anticipate their plight or to realize it when it came.

The kind of gallantry displayed in this ship is a gallantry of human nature and sea training, of which

Battle of the Dogger Bank: The Return

(one may say thankfully) no nationality has the exclusive monopoly. Her record was marred by her participation in the bombardment of Hartlepool, which was a murderous attack on civilians; but she went far to redeem it in this gallant fight against overwhelming forces. Her grave is to the south-east of the Dogger Bank in 54° 25′ N., 5° 25′ E. Her commander, Captain Erdmann, was rescued from the water, but died later of pneumonia following shock and exposure.

There was much discussion amongst us as to the object Admiral Von Hipper had in view in taking his force to sea. It could hardly have been a contemplated raid on our coast, otherwise he would have started much earlier than he did, and been much farther to the westward at dawn. It seems more likely that it was a movement based on the belief that we periodically swept that part of the North Sea with small craft, some of which might in that way be destroyed. Some kind of success was "very essential" to Germany at that moment. It must be remembered that there was never any reluctance to fight on the part of the German Navy, but the policy of those who controlled it was the perfectly sound one that a Fleet action should not be risked until, by mine laying and submarines, an equalization of the opposing forces in the North Sea had been brought about. But as action of some kind was necessary for the *moral* of the men, the prohibition was relaxed in so far as the big cruisers and scouting forces were concerned, and they were allowed to do what they could without, of course, suffering too much loss. We may be quite sure that the German Battle Cruiser forces were only too delighted to

The Sinking of the *Blücher.*

Object of the Expedition

go to sea on these or on any other terms; hence the raid of December 16 and this second attempt to account for such of our light forces as might be encountered. Moreover, the Germans were convinced (as we intended they should be) that we were about to attempt a blockade of the estuaries of the Ems, Jade and Elbe rivers, and as the island of Wangeroog had not at that time been fortified, the approach to the Jade was regarded as particularly vulnerable, and the Germans were anxious about it. Our expedition on the 19th (when the Zeppelin was sighted) had confirmed this suspicion, and may have been an additional reason for a demonstration in force.

It was very unfortunate for us that the *Queen Mary* was absent for re-fitting, for, as has been pointed out, during the greater part of the action we were fighting with two effective ships against the German four. In these circumstances the result of the action, from a gunnery point of view, may be considered satisfactory, as we inflicted far more damage than we received.[1]

During the 25th the following two signals were made to the Admiral :

12.10 P.M. *Admiralty to V.A., 1st B.C.S.*

" I most heartily congratulate you, the officers, and ships' companies of squadrons on your splendid success of yesterday.—GEORGE, R.I."

12.05 P.M. *C.-in-C. Home Fleet to V.A., 1st B.C.S.*

" I have waited to congratulate you on your fine achievement until I could do so by telegram. Please accept for yourself and all under your command my warmest thanks for all you have done and my most sincere appreciation of the result of your efforts. The successful

[1] See Appendix B

Battle of the Dogger Bank: The Return

return of the *Lion* is a fine feat, reflecting the greatest possible credit on all concerned. Please telegraph me a short account of the action and probable damage to enemy. I am deeply grieved to hear of the death of Engineer-Captain Taylor and the men named in your telegram, but the victory has been gained with the minimum loss of life.''

What may be called the moral effect of a modern sea battle on the people concerned in it is probably what interests the general reader most. It is extremely difficult to describe, partly because it is like nothing else in human experience and partly because that amazing adaptability and power of adjustment which enables mankind rapidly to alter its standard of what is possible or endurable causes men to pretend, even to themselves, that things are nothing which are, in fact, something very terrible; just because there may be even more terrible things waiting behind them, and it does not do to admit that the limits have been reached. As a matter of fact, in this battle they were not reached, on our side at any rate, although in the *Blücher* and the *Seydlitz* the most appalling limits were reached quickly. Moreover, I can only speak for myself, and my point of view must necessarily be different from that of the professional naval officer, whose hope and outlook it has always been to find himself in just such a position. As a spectator I was well placed, having practically nothing to do except general look-out duties. My position, one ideal for observation, was an entirely exposed one; and my point of view, having nothing to do but look at what was going on, as though at a panorama, and be aware of my own sensations, can have

nothing in common with that, say, of a gunnery officer
in his turret, who had his men round him to whom in
all ways he must set an example, and who is absorbed
in the performance of a highly technical and engrossing
duty. I can only say that, although I was in a sea battle
because I wished to be and because I would not willingly
have been anywhere else, I was very glad when it was
over; and, considered merely from the point of view of
spending a pleasant Sunday morning, I would not
willingly be in another. At least, I think so; and yet if
the opportunity came I would probably jump at it, and
curse myself for doing so when the horrid actuality blazed
up around me.

The modern naval battle is different from everything
else in the world in this: that nowhere else do men,
banded together in such numbers and wielding such
powers, contend with one another at so extreme a peril
to themselves. It is more ringed with terror than any
other human experience. Each man commits himself
with a thousand others to a vulnerable shell, and launches
it into an arena sheeted and bolted with flame and concussion. He can do nothing for his own safety, but only
for the common purpose. In addition to the ordinary
risk of destruction to the human unit, there is the almost
equal risk of destruction to the naval unit; and a single
stroke of a single weapon might wipe out a thousand
lives. This is warfare at the point to which Christian
civilization has so far succeeded in bringing it; and no
Pagan ingenuity has invented anything more hellish than
this—that man's floating home and citadel can in a second
be turned into a weapon to destroy him by the thousand.
For if his floating tabernacle be dissolved it is not to a

hospital or dressing-station that he passes, but into the cold sea; hospitals, patients, and surgeons in the very act of operating are tumbled into it too; the fight sweeps on; in ten minutes it is three miles away, and there are no stretcher-bearers in the sea. He may die by a blow, by asphyxiation, by flaying, by boiling, by mutilation, by drowning, or may be instantaneously consumed in a glory of mauve flame, accompanied by the thunder of a detonation which he never hears. With all these varieties of death in visible and audible demonstration around him, and instantly menacing himself, he has to continue quietly and coolly doing the exact work for which he has been trained—work, perhaps, with delicate and scientific instruments such as other men handle in the calm of a laboratory or observatory. And often he has to continue this work in what he knows is the last minute or two of earthly existence left to him, and to do it as carefully as if his career in the Navy depended on it. It is the supreme glory of the British Navy, and of the naval training which other nations have based on its traditions, that thousands and thousands of men are always ready to do this as a matter of course; do it easily, desire to do it. There is no one to whom life is sweeter than to the average sailor, whose mental habit it is always to be looking forward to pleasure; and there is no one who can so utterly put aside the preoccupation of safety and lose himself in his immediate duty. How else, indeed, would such events as the battle cruiser fight at Jutland, or the attack of our destroyers after it, be possible? If men thought of themselves in such a situation, their demoralization would be indescribable, and the names of *Queen Mary, Invincible* and *Indefatigable*

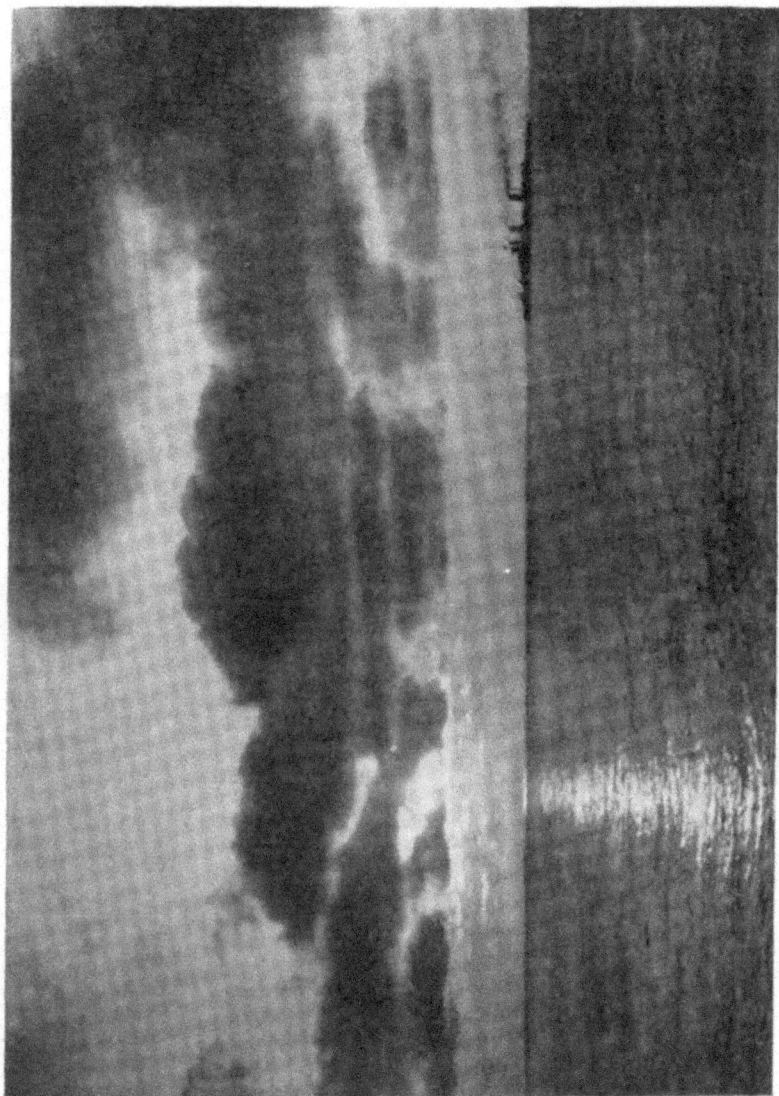

Sunset: H.M.S. *Queen Mary.*

A Scroll of Thunder

would be names of terror. Instead of which it is the high *moral* which is indescribable, and these names are names of glory.

One has some right to say this who for the whole of a grey January morning knelt in the *Lion's* top while the storm of that concentrated bombardment gradually enveloped her, and had nothing else to do but consider it and give myself to its sensational embrace. I remember that the increasing uproar and concussion came gradually to have a stupefying rather than an exciting effect; the mind became numb to mere terror, while it remained actively interested in what was going on. Many mere details are registered on my mind and memory : the smell and taste of cordite smoke, as the wind drove it back upon us from the mouths of our guns; the great sounds about us, which I must admit to be among the noblest sounds I have ever heard, so enormous were they, so deep and trembling. No sharp or musically distressing note had place in that orchestra; it was as if the whole heavens were rolling up in a scroll of thunder. I remember also the silences; lulls that came in the very heat of the battle, when sometimes for five or ten seconds there would be no sound but the soft brushing of the wind and its harp-like harmonies in the rigging, until a salvo from our guns would split the heavens again and, like its echo, the hollow growl of the enemy's guns would fill the gap between it and the next. One could clearly see the flashes of salvos from the *Seydlitz* and *Moltke*, both of which were firing at the *Lion,* and, timing their flight on a stop-watch, know to a second when their arrival would be signalled either by an explosion and a shake which rattled the teeth in one's

Battle of the Dogger Bank : The Return

mouth, or by the uprising of a group of lovely and enormous fountain blossoms; where the water slowly rose in columns two hundred feet high that mushroomed out at the top, stood for five or ten seconds, and then as gracefully subsided, deluging our decks with tons of water in their fall. And it was strange to think, observing those flashes and the little black second-hand ticking steadily round the dial of the watch: " I have perhaps twenty-three seconds longer to live; when the little hand reaches that mark, then—oblivion." Strange, but not terrible, although even then one was conscious of its being a very, very curious way for a sane human being to be spending a winter morning, with the world full of loveliness about him and all his faculties alert, yet all under sentence of death, with reprieve from minute to minute. This imminence of death, and the tremendous drum-rolls that gave it voice, did not distract one's attention. They became monotonous, at times almost narcotic in their effect. Certainly I could not discover that it had any effect whatever on the nerve of a highly trained ship's company. Many of them obviously enjoyed it; enjoyed it at the time, which is a very different thing from enjoying it afterwards, as I did. Sometimes the whole emotion of battle seems like a kind of insanity; and yet I remember observing in the Admiral and the Flag-Captain—who enjoyed this performance more than I have ever seen anything enjoyed by anyone —a child-like blandness of demeanour which I had at no other time observed in either of them, but which had nothing whatever of insanity in it. And so, in their degree, with other men cast in the same strange mould. The officer in charge of the fore-transmitting station,

The Old Red Duster

after the explosion of a shell in the lobby above, followed
by an outbreak of screams and cries, was heard to observe,
"That either means Kingdom Come or ten days' leave"
—the inference being that the damage was so serious
that it would mean the explosion of a magazine or a
long refit. There was no insanity there; and the mind
that could so think in such a moment must have been
functioning with a calmness that reduced everything to
the absolutely normal. He and his kind were not
terrified. On my part, I had spasms of terror which
passed off and left a calm and sometimes pleasant
reaction; enough to make me realize that, with a little
practice, terror and enjoyment can exist together. The
body may quake, and the belly fall, and the muscles
shrink from the screaming messengers of death; but the
fighting mind may and does rise above all that, sitting
enthroned above the terror and commotion in serene
vision and assurance that in the midst of death we may
be in life.

Of this assurance there was present with me then,
and remains vivid in memory, a curious symbol. To
the forestay, immediately where it passed down in front
of the foretop, was bent a red ensign—which in this
war was restored to the Navy as a battle-flag. Sometimes it was obscured for a moment, sometimes lit up
by the redder glare from the gun-flashes; other flags
were shot away, but not it; and from the cloud of smoke
it would always emerge, waving steadily and proudly
before me—the flag that had never been conquered at
sea! There were moments when its presence was
infinitely comforting, and seemed to signal the spiritual
presence of generations of the noble and the brave.

Battle of the Dogger Bank: The Return

On the pictorial side the chief impression of the
action was its remoteness. The *Lion* being our leading
ship, there was nothing before me but the horizon and
the four black smudges on the port bow that only through
binoculars were identifiable as big ships. If one looked
abeam, however, the whole pattern of the chase could
at times be observed as I have drawn it on the plan inset
on the chart of this action; and a curious effect of this
great outspread chase to the S.E. was that it seemed
motionless, like a problem spread out on a chess board.
The far line of enemy battle cruisers, the farther line
of our light cruisers on their quarter, our destroyers
astern and in the middle, and at the apex and head of
the whole the smoke from the German destroyers and
light cruisers—these for half an hour at a time would not
change in relation to one another, and so being the only
things visible on the circle of the sea, appeared to be
motionless. Once, far ahead, appeared more smudges,
a group of trawlers fishing quietly off the Bank, which
suddenly found themselves enveloped in the thunders of
a sea battle. The German battle cruisers passed to the
north-east, and we to the south-west of them, so
that our fire was passing far over their heads, but to
me it seemed as though they had been swept on to
the stationary chess board, swept down the centre of it,
and in twenty minutes swept out of sight off the northern
edge of it.

What I could not see, and never properly saw, was
the majestic aspect of our battle cruisers as they tore
through the seas enveloped in smoke and thunder.
Captain Von Hase, of the *Derfflinger*, wrote of us forming line of battle on another occasion: "They were still

Mists and Cheers

a long way off, but even at this great distance they looked powerful, massive. . . . It was a stimulating, majestic spectacle, as the dark-grey ships approached like Fate itself. The six ships, which had at first been proceeding in two columns, formed line ahead. Like a herd of prehistoric monsters they closed on one another in a slow movement, spectre-like, irresistible."[1] And herd-like we must have appeared in the eyes of the astonished Dutch fishermen, who saw us thunder past in the primitive herd formation; the bulls, or battle cruisers, bellowing in the van, followed by the females, the light cruisers, with the destroyers, like the young, bringing up the rear.

And majestic in a different way was the return of the wounded leader, surrounded by packs of fierce questing destroyers. We arrived off May Island early in the morning of the 26th. Tugs had been sent out to meet us from the Tyne, and to them the *Indomitable* surrendered her charge during the difficult passage from Inchkeith to the anchorage in the Forth Bridge. The Admiral had boarded us off May Island and was in his usual place on the bridge as we came in, accompanied by Commodore Tyrwhitt, whose responsible escort duties had been so successfully carried out. There was a thick fog that morning, but as we approached the little island on which the central pier of the Forth Bridge is founded we could hear the sounds of cheering coming faintly to us through the mist, which thinned just enough to show us the shore of the island thronged with people, cheering and waving. The *Lion's* band was formed up on the 4-inch gun deck, and played "Rule Britannia" and

[1] Von Hase: "Kiel and Jutland," p. 134.

other appropriate strains of music. As we came under the bridge we could see that the mighty span above us was also lined with diminutive human figures, waving and cheering. And so, amid mist and cheers, true symbols of our warfare, the *Lion* came home.

CHAPTER XIV

AFTERMATH

RIGHTLY considered, the battle of the Dogger Bank was by far the most important thing that had happened in the Navy for over one hundred years. Since Trafalgar the whole mechanism of sea gunnery (which is the ultimate essence of naval warfare) had been revolutionized, and in this battle the new conditions were for the first time tried out. One would have supposed, therefore, that its results, the innumerable lessons and new data to be gathered from it, would immediately have been fastened upon by the thinking department of the Navy and the Admiralty, in order that when the next battle came there would be a chance to put to the test the changes and revisions which the first action had shown to be necessary. That, at any rate, was the spirit animating the Battle Cruiser Force immediately following our return to the Firth of Forth. Reports on every subject were called for and furnished by the people concerned. Discussions and conferences were held among experts in the various technical branches involved, and a mass of very valuable material, which would have furnished food for a real staff for months, was collected and forwarded to the Admiralty. But it soon became apparent that technical interest in these matters was pretty well confined to our own force. The Admiralty having

Aftermath

acknowledged the receipt of the masses of material presented to it, made no further sign. Doubtless throughout the Fleet there were hundreds of officers who were keen to get all the information and technical data that they could, but there were no means of furnishing them even with the results arrived at in our own force. Every gunnery officer in the Fleet wanted to know exactly how the great ranges, and the high speeds of the ships engaged, affected the existing organization for fire control. Every one of them, you must remember, had been brought up on the theory of the big gun, the first blow, etc. We had the biggest guns and we got in the first blows, but none of the results that the gunnery expert of those days had been taught to believe as gospel had happened. It was true we inflicted far more damage than we received, but the idea that one blow from a 18.5 shell was going to do the business of any capital ship had to be abandoned. We had gone on hitting, and hitting, and hitting—and three out of four ships had got home. Why?

Again, the faultiness of our turret and magazine design was revealed by the fact that charges in " A " turret magazine had become ignited; and if that could happen it was a mere chance that the whole ship might be blown up at any moment. This was pointed out; but nothing was done towards remedying the defect until after Jutland, when three battle cruisers actually were blown up from the same cause. As to tactics, torpedoes had for the first time been employed defensively, with the object of making the attacking side turn away from its objective; there was a good deal to be considered with regard to that. Smoke screens had also been used for the first time. There were matters to be considered relating to deck

Safe in Port: H.M.S. *Lion* with repair ship *Assistance.*

The Battle Cruiser Fleet Formed

protection, having regard to the steep angle of descent of projectiles at long ranges. All these things were subjects as to which we were exercised, and as to which a mass of material was available among the forces under Sir David Beatty's command; but there was no Staff to take any interest in it, and the Board of Admiralty were too busy.

Following the usual British procedure, the real arduous headwork which should have followed the battle of the Dogger Bank was shirked, and such results as it had were expressed in changes of commands and shuffling of *personnel*. The battle cruisers were reorganized once more. Captain Brock was promoted to Commodore and a week or two afterwards to Rear-Admiral. Admiral Moore was relieved of his brief command and promoted or transferred to an even more important one elsewhere. A new force was created entitled the Battle Cruiser Fleet, with Sir David Beatty as Commander-in-Chief. The *Lion* was to be the Fleet flagship, and there were to be three squadrons commanded by Admirals Brock, Pakenham and Hood respectively, their flags to be flown in *Princess Royal*, *Australia* and *Invincible*. Two squadrons of light cruisers and a flotilla of destroyers made up the Fleet, which, with its ten battle cruisers was extremely formidable on paper, but was in fact an unnecessarily large concentration of ships of that class opposed to an enemy having only five. Still, one could always be sure that any force under Sir David Beatty's command was not likely to be wasted; although it would have been more to the point if the Admiralty had sat down and thought how the existing available battle cruisers could be improved.

It was a very busy and rather confused time for us on

Aftermath

the staff with the inevitably heavy work following the action. Personally I believe that I wrote replies to between two and three hundred letters and telegrams of congratulation addressed to the Admiral within forty-eight hours of our return. On Wednesday, January 27th, the staff was transferred bodily to the *Princess Royal*, an operation which meant the displacing of about half a dozen of her senior officers from the best cabins in the ship and otherwise thoroughly disturbing the serene calm which always reigned on board that charming and admirable ship. I was left behind in the *Lion* as there was no room for me. The Admiral offered to have part of his large dining-cabin cut off by a partition for a cabin for me, but Captain Brock was firm in his decision to have " no more," and to make no structural changes. I was the fifth wheel and the last straw, so for the moment I was left behind. It was decided that I should be sent up to the Admiralty to supplement orally the written dispatch concerning the battle. The Admiral had had a letter from Lord Fisher urgently inquiring how it was that the action had been broken off; and as the matter was extremely confidential it was decided that I should carry the reply to London the next day. But that night, while we were all at a somewhat hectic dinner given by the *Lion's* gun-room to the Admiral and his staff, orders came that the battle cruisers were to go to sea. There was only time for the Admiral to write to Lord Fisher, telling him that I knew his mind and could give the information he desired, and to give me verbally a brief outline of his views on the action, supplemented by a dozen lines scribbled in my notebook in his own hand, containing a succinct explanation of the occurrences between 11 A.M. and noon.

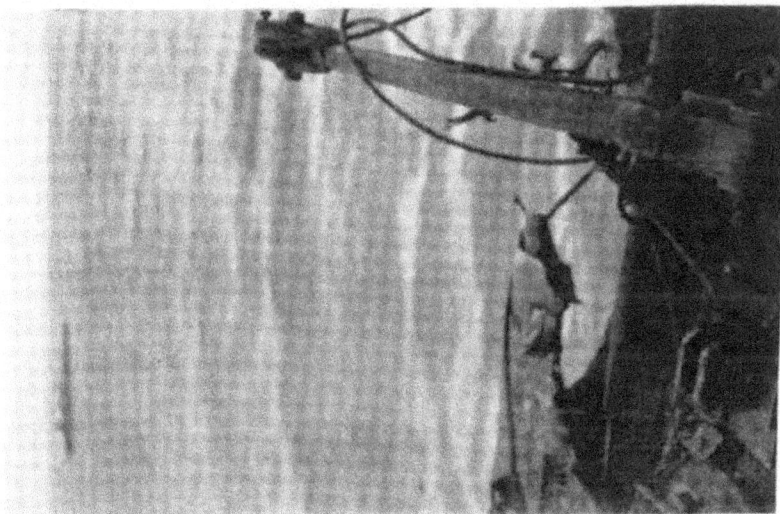

13.5 Guns.

Where an Unexploded Shell passed through *Lion's* Upper Deck, Starboard Side.

Lord Fisher's Questions

The dinner party broke up, and I saw the Admiral over the side on his way back to the *Princess Royal*, when I turned in in preparation for an early start the next morning.

I arrived in London at six on the evening of January 29th and went immediately to the Admiralty. I was taken to Lord Fisher at his room in the Mall House. I was immediately struck by his appearance. He had aged a great deal in three months, and the yellow face looked very old and worn, but grim as ever. I thought his manner curious when I came in. He merely said " Well? " and waited in a stern and expectant silence. I handed him the Admiral's note, and after he read it he looked at me: " Oh! it's you? " he said, " I didn't recognize you in the dim light; all they told me was ' an officer from Sir David Beatty.' "

He shook hands with me, but the countenance immediately became grim again, and turning his hard, wise old eye upon me he said, " Well, tell me about it. How was it they got away? What's the explanation? Why didn't you get the lot? And the *Derfflinger*—I counted on her being sunk, and we hear that she got back practically undamaged.[1] I don't understand it."

He looked at me as if I were personally responsible. I gave the explanation based on the Admiral's notes—purely technical, having to do with the alteration of course and signals made as the *Lion* was dropping out of the fight.

" Submarines? " he said. " There weren't any; we knew the position of every German submarine in the

---

[1] This was a mistake. It was the *Moltke* that escaped; the *Derfflinger* was badly damaged.

Aftermath

North Sea;[1] and there wasn't a mine within fifty miles."
He looked at me as though my explanation had been a
mere invention. "Come," he said, "you were there.
You saw it. What do you think? What is your own
opinion?"

I told him what I thought, which was very simple and
could be expressed in one sentence. Lord Fisher made
no reply except a brief "Oh!" and sat for perhaps a
minute staring hard at me, during which time I began to
wonder whether I had not perhaps been a little too frank.
When I got outside and told Captain Crease what I had
said, he replied, "Well, you have put your foot in it;
—— was one of his men." I was sorry, but Lord Fisher
had asked me what I thought, and I had told him. "As
it happens, you needn't worry," said Captain Tom.
"He's not so keen on him now." All of which was
extremely characteristic, and not very pleasant. In any
case, I was not proposing to "worry."

A great part of the next day was spent at the
Admiralty with various people who wanted to hear the
news, and that night I returned north with Winston
Churchill and Admirals Lambert and de Bartholomé
(Third and Fourth Sea Lords), who were making a personal visit to the Firth of Forth. They spent most of the
next day with the Admiral and went on to Scapa. I was
occupied all day on board *Princess Royal* working with the
others on the preparation of the many supplementary
documents accompanying the Admiral's formal despatch,
which was now approaching completion and which I was
to carry to London the next day. There had been urgent

[1] This seems unlikely, and in any case Lord Fisher was wrong. See
Appendix A, Vice-Admiral Beatty's despatch.

Rising to the Occasion

telegrams from the Admiralty asking that it should be hurried forward. Presumably the Government wanted something to publish; although, as will be seen, when they did get it they wanted it altered and trimmed in accordance with their own views. It was not ready until late on the evening of Thursday, February 4th. I had made my arrangements for catching the night train from Edinburgh. A motor-car was waiting for me on the Hawes Pier, and the barge had steam up all the evening.

I dined on board the *Princess Royal* with the gunnery officer, and during dinner received a charming note from Captain Brock saying that as the Admiral had definitely expressed a wish that I should be accommodated on board *Princess Royal*, a cabin would be ready for me on my return from London; that personally I was more than welcome, and that only the grave difficulties as to space, etc., etc. This sent me off in very good spirits, and I shoved off from *Princess Royal's* side at 10.50 with the precious despatch in my hands. There was a strong tide running in the Firth, and although I found the motor-car waiting for me on the Hawes Pier, the delay in finishing the despatch had run the time very close, and I thought it likely that we should miss the train. We did. Ten minutes before I arrived at Waverley Station it had departed south, and there was no other express until ten in the morning, which would not get me to London until half-past six. Here was a moment for initiative and presence of mind, and I decided to display both. Turning to the inspector on the empty platform I said, "I had better have a special train." He led me to the room of the night station-master, who never turned a hair, but immediately telephoned to the engine sheds and said,

Aftermath

" You're in luck, sir. The express was going south double-headed, but as the load was not so heavy the second engine was not used and she is in steam and all ready. Your train will be at platform five in fifteen minutes. All I have to do is to get a guard." This also having been arranged by telephone, he said, " And what about the payment for this train, sir? "

Things had gone so smoothly up till now I felt this was not the moment to lose hold.

" I will give you a chit for that," said I, and taking pen and paper wrote : " This will be your authority for providing a special train for me from Waverley Station to King's Cross, February 4th/5th, 1915. Proceeding to the Admiralty with urgent despatches," and signed it. To my surprise he took it and, locking the door behind him, led me out to the deserted station. Presently, to the accompaniment of a slight hissing, a huge sleek express locomotive, hauling a saloon carriage and brake-van, slid alongside the platform—my special train. The guard alighted and opened the door for me, touching his hat. With the station-master I graciously shook hands, stepped into the train and said, " Carry on—I mean, that's all right; we can start now." And with a very gentle whistle we pulled out under the bridges on the road to the south.

It was the first time in my life I had ever had a special train, and I dare say will be the last. I confess to a childish interest in such matters, and was only sorry that, being so sleepy, I could not keep awake to enjoy the sensation of travelling the length of England in my own train. Before I went to sleep, however, I asked the guard what was the first station we should pass after six o'clock

My Special Train

where there was a refreshment room, and on being told said, " Very well, we will stop there and you will get me a cup of tea." And on that I reluctantly fell asleep, feeling that on the whole I had risen to the historic occasion.

It used to be the custom that the bearer of a despatch from a sea battle was received by the King and knighted. This ceremony was omitted in my case. I delivered my despatch formally to Sir Graham Greene, and then informed the Accountant-General's office that I had taken a special train. Nothing much was said, but I was left with the impression that I should be expected to pay for it; I saw visions of myself serving for interminable years in the Navy, as Jacob served for Rachel, while the cost of the train was stopped out of my humble pay of eleven shillings per day. It was an unheard-of thing in the Navy for an officer to take a special train; and the department who knew to a penny every cab fare in London, Plymouth and Portsmouth was not very likely, I was informed, to pass an item of two or three hundred pounds without protest. And in fact, to finish this little story, three or four weeks afterwards, when the departmental wheels had ground their due course, came a formal letter to the Commander-in-Chief of the Battle Cruiser Fleet from the Accountant-General asking if he could furnish any reason why the cost of a special train taken by an officer on his staff should be " allowed " to that officer. The letter was minuted for reference to me, and I retired to my cabin and summoned my neglected literary faculty to the composition of a service letter to the Admiral. It had six paragraphs, and I dragged in all the phraseology of service correspondence that I knew,

Aftermath

with a great deal about "Their Lordships," "hastening," "submitting," "within my knowledge," "exhausted all measures," "Their Lordships' convenience," etc. The letter was forwarded, no more was heard about it, and I am now beyond the reach of the Accountant-General. I created more than one precedent in my short stay in the Navy, but this was by far the most successful, although I fear that my lead has not been followed by a generation that still goes in fear of the Accountant-General and other powers of darkness.

When I got back to the Fleet it was to a changed condition of things. The comparatively small and happy party in the *Lion* had been enlarged to an uncomfortable degree. Commodore Brock was promoted to Rear-Admiral, and *Princess Royal* flew both his flag and that of Sir David Beatty. He was unwilling to leave the ship which he had commanded so long and so happily, which made things rather awkward for his successor, Captain Cowan, for whom there was no room. Admiral Brock had his staff also, of course, and to our own number was added another officer in the person of Captain Rudolf Bentinck, who came as chief of staff to Sir David Beatty. With our dining table thus thronged with Admirals and Captains, those of us at the other end of the scale sank into greater obscurity, and I was now to see the working of that formidable atmosphere of seniority, and incidence of mere rank, which has embittered and belittled so many lives in the Navy in the past, and will doubtless do so in the future. In an Army mess the opinion of a Second Lieutenant is as good as that of a Colonel on unofficial matters; but in a

H.M.S. *Lion* at Sea.

H.M.S. *Princess Royal.*

A Way of the Navy

Naval mess, with the close juxtaposition, the isolation, and the sensitiveness which is developed in these conditions, the shipping of another stripe on one's arm is supposed to invest one automatically with authority on all subjects exceeding that of one's unfortunate junior. And I could not help being amused at the attitude adopted towards the new Captain of the ship when he joined. Naval men are very like schoolboys in many ways, but in nothing so much as in their treatment of the new boy, whatever his rank may be. If he is in the wardroom, and no one happens to have known him before, it is quite possible that no one will speak a word to him for two or three days. I met Captain Cowan wandering about the ship one day asking to be directed to his cabin, which happened to be next to mine in " A " turret lobby, his own quarters being, of course, still occupied by Admiral Brock. And at lunch, which was his first meal with us, I think no one spoke to him at all—the seniors because they did not appear to notice his existence, the juniors because they, who were only guests themselves, could hardly take the line of making him at home on board his own ship. But it is only to an onlooker that such things are astonishing. Captain Cowan took it all as a matter of course and, after wandering about the ship like a lost soul for a few days, gradually slipped into his place and won the warm regard of those who had cried anathema on him for coming there at all. Which also is a way of the Navy.

The *Lion*, after being patched up in the Firth of Forth, went round to Newcastle to be repaired, and while she was there I went down to Captain Chatfield with some papers. Her picket-boat met me near the station and buzzed me up the dark and hideous river. I could not bear to think of the noble and magnificent *Lion* in such squalid surroundings, and it was with something like a sense of shame that, coming round a bend in the black and narrow stream, I saw my poor old ship, heavily listed to one side, tied up outside Armstrong's yard. She looked incredibly small and mean; it was as though one could see some wild animal, accustomed to the freedom of the forest and the desert, cooped up in a cage in some slum, lame and mangy, a target for brickbats and orange peel. I am glad indeed that it was not my last view of her, but that I saw her again as lordly as ever, quartering the great North Sea; glad indeed to think that she lived to fight another day and to come home again, battered indeed, but covered with glory. She lies now in that 'Northern harbour which was her lair in the fighting days, in the repose of the Reserve and a nucleus crew; dreaming, I hope, of the chase and of the days when she was launched like a grey thunderbolt at the enemy. She and her two great sisters were noble examples of the ship designer's art. Their lines below water were sweet and wonderful; they steered like boats, and never failed to respond when the impossible in the way of speed was asked of them. And one of them has found a sea grave where the ignominy of the disposal list and the ship-knacker can never overtake her.

The theory of the Admiralty appeared to be that after the battle of the Dogger Bank the Germans would not come out again. The Dardanelles expedition was apparently occupying all the attention of the directing powers, and a period of comparative stagnation ensued—

Unlearned Lessons

the time when all the lessons learned should have been studied and applied. But the North Sea, in the official mind, sank for a time into insignificance, while the enemy submarines increased and multiplied. Time and again Admiral Beatty agitated for the means with which to keep them down, but no notice was taken. We went out to sea for Fleet exercises with the same totally inadequate monthly allowance of ammunition to be expended, and the same exercises, laid down in memoranda from the Commander-in-Chief at Scapa, exactly as they had been before the battle of the Dogger Bank was fought. Our gunnery people in the battle cruisers worked hard at applying the lessons they had learned, and valuable developments were achieved here—thanks chiefly to the enthusiasm of the men concerned, and a good deal also to Captain Chatfield's sound knowledge, which he was only too eager to revise in the light of experience. The *Lion* was fitted with a tripod mast, Director fire control, and other improvements; but in the elaborate P.Z.'s we performed with the Grand Fleet there was no development or modification of tactics, and the reliance was still on the fallacy that all was well with our material, and that we had more of it than the enemy. The result was that, although our gunnery got better and better, the effect of our ammunition showed the same disappointing results at Jutland as it had at the Dogger Bank.

I had made an effort to get a real Fleet Intelligence Service established, and had consulted Captain Hall when I was in London, who had promised every kind of help. But it was of no use. The high command set themselves steadily against anything in the way of an independent Intelligence Service. No one felt the need of it; it was not taken seriously, and if it had been established would not have been used; for even in our own Fleet the Admiral's secretary went so far as to utter the remarkable opinion that, at the stage which the war had now reached, he considered the need for even the embryo Intelligence Service we had at an end. For the time being there was nothing to be done, and my thoughts, stimulated by what I had seen and heard from Winston Churchill in London, turned towards the Dardanelles, where Admiral de Robeck had recently taken up his command, and it was thought that I might go out there, see the campaign through, and still be in lots of time for the grand finish in the North Sea. But I was too late for the Dardanelles. I went up to the Admiralty to see about it, but already the failure and abandonment of the campaign was being foreshadowed and the Admiralty *régime* which had inaugurated it was coming to an end. Before it finished, however, I was to assist at one interesting and historic scene which turned my thoughts in a new direction.

Having been sent to the Admiralty with further despatches in April, I was told to wait in town until the First Lord sent for me, as he wished to see me. When he received me, Winston Churchill told me that he had for long been considering the advisability of giving the public some closer insight into the life of the Fleet in all its manifold activities. No one knew better than he with what difficulties the job was beset; but he very kindly said that I was in a unique position and could perhaps do what would otherwise be impossible. What he wanted was a kind of "eye-witness" for the Navy; someone who could go about, see everything, and yet who

An Historic Interview

had sufficient training in the essential intricacies of naval life both to understand the significance of what he saw and to know what could and could not be made public with discretion. We had a long and interesting talk. He was very keen on the idea, and I became so, since I felt that whatever qualifications I might have for that work were enormously increased by my sea experience.

He asked me if I had seen Lord Fisher, and when I replied that I had not, he said, " We must have his approval; I will send for him." He rang the bell, and told the messenger to " Ask the First Sea Lord to come in." It was all strictly correct, but it made me uncomfortable that I should be thus made a witness of the fiery old man's forced acknowledgment of the superior civil authority. Presently the door was opened. " The First Sea Lord," said the messenger, and Lord Fisher walked in, looking rather surly. He greeted me with a word or two and then turned expectantly to Winston, who, rather nervously, I thought, but very mildly and tactfully, explained his suggestion. But the old man broke out at once as though he were present at a conspiracy.

" I object," he said.

Winston renewed his argument, which of course was a very sound one, and which was acted upon afterwards with a great deal less intelligence and purpose behind it; I saw him now in a new aspect in which I could not but admire him, for he was gentle, sympathetic, diplomatic, and even soothing to his hostile colleague. Something more than the mere point at issue lay behind Lord Fisher's sensitiveness and opposition; we know now what it was, but I did not know then that the parting was

Aftermath

coming so soon, although I felt that trouble was in the air.

"Besides," continued Lord Fisher, "the Commander-in-Chief would never consent."

"Of course he would have to be consulted," said Winston. "I don't know what his views would be; but supposing that he did approve, would you still object?"

"Yes," said Lord Fisher, retiring on his second line of defence. "The Press would never stand it; they'd be jealous, and say we were showing partiality and allowing one writer special privileges."

"Oh, I think I could manage the Press," said Winston, with a wave of the hand.

"Oh, *I* could manage the Press," said Lord Fisher, "if that were all." And for an amazing moment these two potentates boasted to one another as to their respective powers of "handling" the Press.

"So if that is all," continued Winston, "I do not think it would be a serious difficulty."

Then Lord Fisher, at bay, was driven into his last stronghold, and giving the table a mighty thump, he thundered, "I shall object as First Sea Lord!" and burst out into a great tirade. The Navy was everything we had in the world; it stood between us and defeat and destruction; the whole of the Army might be wiped out to-morrow, and it would make no difference to the Empire, but if we touched the Navy—— and so on, with a great deal of anger and eloquence. To my embarrassment he suddenly turned to me at the end of his address (for it amounted to that) and asked, "Don't you agree with me?" I said I did, but added that I did not quite

236

Born Violent

see how the existence of the Navy depended on the people being kept in ignorance of its life and services, upon which he turned upon me, apparently boiling with wrath : "Oh, you don't, don't you; and who asked you for your opinion, sir?"

"You did, sir."

"Well, I'll rub your nose in your opinion, sir, and let me tell you that a certain person has got his eye on you; he does not at all approve of you being where you are—remember that!"

I felt that this was becoming childish, as well as rude; and as the First Lord hastily interposed with a red herring which drew the old man's attention off me, I waited for a lull (I had been edging towards the door all the time) and said to Winston, "If you do not want me any more, sir, perhaps I may be allowed to retire." Upon which the old man, like one emerging from a nerve-storm, turned to me, walked over and put his hand on my shoulder.

"I didn't mean anything personal against you," he said. "I entirely agree that if anyone were to do this work, you are the right man for it, and I shouldn't consent to anyone else; but I know it would never do; the Press would never stand it. And don't mind what I said just now. I am always violent! I was born violent; I wouldn't be weaned!"

And under cover of the laughter I retired to the less electrical society of Masterton Smith and Eddie Marsh in the next room. When I got home to my house I found two telephone messages; one from the First Sea Lord, asking me to lunch with him, and the other from the First Lord, saying that if I received an invitation to

Aftermath

lunch with the First Sea Lord he hoped I would go, as Lord Fisher was distressed lest he might have appeared rude to me, when he really meant nothing of the kind. I could not, as it happened, go to lunch, and I felt far from happy that, at such a juncture of the war, the First Lord and the First Sea Lord of the Admiralty should have time to concern themselves with so infinitely trifling a matter. I mentioned this to Winston some years afterwards, when we were recalling the scene, and he replied with amusing candour, "Oh, it wasn't the feelings of a Lieutenant R.N.V.R. that we were thinking of; it was the voice of history." And the Voice of History has now duly uttered itself.

Who was the "certain person" referred to by Lord Fisher (if indeed he existed) I do not know; but in any case he need not have worried. Other certain persons had their eye, if not on me, on my coveted place; and their combined forces were irresistible. In any case, the spell was broken. The increasing complications involved by a larger command and a larger staff made my curious undefined position, which I had made for myself, more difficult to hold; absence in London, waiting the pleasure of the First Lord, did the rest—"his place let another take" being an eternal rule in the Navy. The time came when the best service I could render my Admiral was to yield the space which I occupied near him to others of whom he had more need. It was the most difficult service of all to render; but my bit of duty was done. From the moment when it ceased to be active and real it would have been an anti-climax to continue in an imitation of it. The eddies of the war caught me up and whirled me off in other directions.

The late Captain Cecil Prowse.

(Captain of *Queen Mary* 1914-1916.)

A Reward

I was far from finished with the Navy yet, and could easily fill another volume with another side of its war life. But I had to begin again and learn new kinds of technique; the antique administration of a great Naval depôt in war-time, the organization and doings of the fighting armies on the Western front, the mediæval convolutions of Spanish politics. Each experience is a history in itself; they were all war service and lasted until long after the Armistice; but the end of the glorious part of the war for me was when I laid aside my coveted aiguilettes and gave them, not without a sigh, to a friend who was hastily proceeding to take up an appointment as Flag-Lieutenant. But I had my reward, which I would not willingly exchange for any that can be expressed in ribbon. It took the form of a few words written by one who never lavished verbal praise on men for doing their best, because he expected it of them. They were contained in a letter to me from the Admiral after I left him, in which he spoke with envy of my going to the sunshine of the Dardanelles (that being still the idea), and assuring me that I should be " back in lots of time for the final show, when we will manage to find a place for you somewhere and somehow." And then came the award which, as I cannot wear it on my breast, I may perhaps be allowed to exhibit here :

" *I shall miss you; it was refreshing to have someone to talk to who was not of the Navy, and your advice was good.*"

CHAPTER XV

THE FIRST SPRING

NO one who served in the North Sea during the first year of the war is likely to forget the coming of the first spring. Things had not then begun to repeat themselves in annual cycle, and the ever cheerful and optimistic mind of the Navy had not got used to the idea that there might be the Jordan of a second and third winter and spring to be crossed before the Canaan of peace should open out in halcyon prospect. The first winter had indeed been long and dark, and in many respects disappointing. Spring brought with it the prospect of better conditions, and of course the ever-increasing hope that the great naval day of days would have arrived before the summer. In the meanwhile how weary was the eye of that eternal monochrome! Even in harbour there was little or no variation of the everlasting grey—grey sea, grey skies, grey hills, and grey ships, with often a grey mist or a grey drizzle to thicken and depress the heavy atmosphere. Even for those who went ashore in those sombre northern harbours there was little to look for but a tumbling trip in the grey picket-boat, to land on the grey stones of the jetty, and walk up the grey road into the grey hills until it was time to turn back towards the grey sea. The only relief of colour that Nature afforded us was in the grand, smoky sunsets, that sometimes burned up the remnants of the day in the scroll of scarlet flame.

And yet these conditions were at no time stable, but were always moving towards a happier state. Long before there had seemed to be much change in the dim morning light one began to notice the gradual retreat of the sunset bugle into the evening hours. At the worst it found one at tea in the wardroom; but day by day it fell a little later, moving through the dog watches until at midsummer it had fairly moved out of them altogether. But almost the first realization of the coming spring was when the sunset bugle caught one in a constitutional on deck between tea and dinner—the sudden flourish ringing out across the profound silence; when every moving figure became rigid in its tracks and stood at the salute facing aft while the ensign fluttered slowly down. And then one would realize that the sky was still quite light, that it was getting on for six o'clock, and that the days were indeed lengthening.

You had to make your observations of Nature on board ship in a very restricted field. There were no tips of branches to watch becoming peppered with green; no early dandelions or groundsel in some sheltered hedgerow to advertise the advent of spring; no changing colour of moss or grass to tell you what was happening. But one morning I noticed, crossing the deck before breakfast, that the dew on the guns was shining with a new lustre, not like a mere deposit of misty condensation, but like an incrustation of jewels; and realized that for the first time at this hour the sun was fairly up and shining, and that there was a faint warmth as well as light in its rays. Dew on the guns—the words in themselves contain a

The First Spring

whole picture gallery and commentary on our position at the coming of spring.

The grimness of that first winter and the coming of the first spring are each of them identified in my memory with a *leit-motif*. That of winter is a certain strain heard in the small hours of the freezing darkness in Cromarty Firth. One would be awakened, apparently in black midnight, by sounds afar off, but drawing nearer, and gradually recognizable as the voices of the Boatswain's mates bellowing out their *réveillé* along the mess decks, turning out the hands. " *Hea—ve out, heave out, heave out! Lash up and stow, lash up and stow! Show a leg, show a leg, show a leg! Rouse and shine, you've had your time!* " These and similar quaint exhortations, breaking the dead silence of night, echoed through the steel walls with a dreadful harshness, recalling the sleepers from their wanderings in the country of dreams to the hard facts of discipline. They had had their " time "—a few hours packed in hammocks close together, in an atmosphere and odour that only the breath of the salt sea could blow away; and in gratitude for that they were to " rouse and shine " ! Something of the sense of doom and prison, of awaking to death, seemed to sound in those hideous shouts, and tinged one's own remaining slumbers with a guilty compunction.

And so spring likewise when it came had a strain of music to accompany its march down the avenues of memory.

This is the bugle call for searchlight crews, mustered every evening in harbour to test the gear and circuits;

A Truant Morning

and I associate it with those early spring evenings in the *Princess Royal*, with the cold silver of the arc lights

set in the gold of sunset, and the jolly figure of " Torps," observing his minions, standing against the background of twilight sky.

To everyone there comes a day, probably long before the actual arrival of spring, which speaks of it with promises, and breaks, if only for a moment, the spell of winter. I remember one such day, which must have been very early in the year indeed (for there was a long interval of winter between it and the actual coming of spring), that was for me the earliest indication that the great horologe of the seasons had not run down and stopped. It was very rare indeed for anyone to leave the ship and go ashore in the forenoon. But on this day the Admiral, for whom even the formidable task of daily routine was by no means sufficient to work off his superfluous energy, and who was given to long and swift-striding constitutionals ashore, decided for once to forsake his desk in the morning, and had summoned me in attendance. One had a real sense of truancy in this going ashore for a walk in the morning; it was like playing a game of cricket in school hours; it had only happened once before, and it never happened again. The swift trim barge shot forward with us away from the grey hulls and the unending traffic of the Fleet, and landed us on a little promontory where we could turn our backs to the sea and, after

The First Spring

a climb of a mile up the bare windy road, turn into the shelter of the woods.

It was a day of high wind and gleams of pale sunshine, cold and invigorating; over our heads as we walked was the roar of the wind in the branches; beneath our feet the crackle and race of the dry leaves. And the sudden change from the bleak salt element to the cathedral-like aisles of the wood, with moss under foot and the smell of earth instead of the tingle of spray in one's nostrils, came like a sudden reminder that there was another life silently going on—something that would bring spring and victory and peace and all good things in their appointed time, whatever deserts or shadowed valleys might have to be crossed first. On our left, as we walked, we could always see the silver glint of the sea between the crowded branches of the trees; but there was also a little woodland stream running beside us to remind us that there was a more kindly water than that of the salt sea; water that was not a mere harbour and hiding-place for mines and submarines, but was even then nourishing the roots of the primroses that in a week or two would be flowering in the shelter of the hollows. And although we spoke of sea matters and war matters, there was in the mind of one of us at least an agreeable subconsciousness of those other things and a readjusted sense of their importance. When we came out from the shelter of the wood and back to the seashore it was blowing harder than ever, and the barge bruised her planks against the stones of the pier, and we got drenched with spray on our return to the ship. And we went out to sea that night against a rising gale and a falling barometer, and the dashing and slopping of the waves

Tiger raising steam.

H.M.A.S. *Australia.*

against my scuttle soon drowned the memory of the rustling leaves; but one had heard it, and the promise in it was in due time fulfilled.

For even at sea, and in so monotonous a water as the North Sea, the changes of the seasons and the coming of spring are experienced. Although no green blades sprout over these fields, and though the waves break only into one perennial blossom of foam, spring will come to you there as everywhere in creation. It is not the sense of colour that tells you of his coming; his heralds are the increasing softness of the wind, the light on the sky and sea, and the warmth of the sunshine. The day when it is a positive joy, even on the deck of a swiftly moving ship, to be out in the sunshine, when you are not cold, however strongly the wind blows, and when you can enjoy the air and the breezes without having to keep violently in motion, is the day when spring first finds you at sea. We had had such days in March, but in April again the weather had been colder. In the week before Easter we had been at sea in circumstances that had promised to be more than usually exciting; but once more the enemy had disappointed us by the exercise of that part of valour which is said to be the better part and in which he had shown himself an adept. It had been misty and grey, although spring had been coming on fast ashore, and we had come back to harbour with that slight sense of anti-climax that always follows a time of tension and strenuous expectation that has not been fulfilled.

But Easter Sunday broke mild and sunny; I had nothing to do till the middle watch that night, and I decided once more to play truant and forsake the ship. By tactful treatment of the Commander at exactly the

The First Spring

right moment I got a boat, and was safely ashore before ten o'clock. I have never enjoyed such a sense of contrast. There was not a breath of wind; the sky was blue and the sun hot, and the world lay still in that Sabbath silence and peace that is so great a reality in Scotland. The stillness was intense and almost conscious, as if it were a natural Sabbath, and as if the morning were the evening of a celestial day. I was reminded of Thorow's Sunday on the Concord, when " the air was so elastic and crystalline that it had the same effect on the landscape that a glass has on a picture, to give it an ideal remoteness and perfection. The landscape was enveloped in a mild quiet light, in which the woods and fences checkered and partitioned it with new regularity, and rough and uneven fields stretched away with lawn-like smoothness to the horizon, and the clouds, finely distinct and picturesque, seemed a fit drapery to hang over fairyland. The world seemed decked for some holiday or prouder pageantry, with silken streamers flying, and the course of life to wind on before you like a green lane into a country maze at the season when fruit trees are in blossom." Everywhere, on either side as I walked, crocuses decked the little gardens with purple and gold; and in that walk of an hour along the valley of the little river one encountered all the flowers of spring.

And suddenly I heard the sound of a bell and came upon an ancient kirk, lying with its little kirkyard in a blaze of sunshine and of golden crocuses. I joined the stream of villagers at the door of the kirk and went in, glad of the cool shade of the little building after my hot walk. Although the service followed the austere Scottish ritual, it had dignity and fitness for

246

The End of Winter

the day and place; and to these simple rustics their minister preached a powerful, scholarly and brilliant discourse which had it been preached in an English cathedral would have been talked about long afterwards. And when it was over I went out again, and by field paths and wooded ways walked until I was tired, and until the railway took me back, with a great bunch of Easter flowers for the wardroom table, to the life and the conditions of the sea. I can never think of Heaven as a place where "there shall be no more sea"; but after that day there was no more winter.

CHAPTER XVI

FOUNDATIONS OF THE FUTURE

" In England the Navy has hitherto treated the past, except for the voluntary efforts of young officers who work under an almost offensive official discouragement, as though it were negligible wreckage at the bottom of the sea."

CARLYON BELLAIRS.[1]

THE reader who has made acquaintance with the life of the Navy through the medium of these pages shares already, I hope, something of the writer's feeling for it, not only as an expression of organized human power, but also as the nursery and seedfield of some of the highest human qualities. For that alone its existence as an element in the life of a modern state would, I think, be justified. Courage and discipline, by which alone a community can be defended and preserved from dangers within and without, are apt to become dormant in times of peace and prosperity. Courage is in the blood of our race, and awakes again at the call of danger; but discipline is an artificial growth which, if neglected, dies in the individual. Without it strength is dissipated, and force becomes a weapon that recoils on the user. Having as a nation been under stern discipline for several years, we have experienced the inevitable reaction in which the individual, weary of a state of affairs in which he was of no account, flies to

[1] "The Battle of Jutland," p. 27.

A School of Discipline

the opposite extreme in which he attempts to dismiss the common interest from any claim to his consideration. No state of greater unhappiness, for the individual or the community, can be imagined. The well-being of each is dependent on the good of the other : so we state the first principle on which the most primitive attempt at self-government must be founded. Discipline may be defined as the instruction in that principle by which is made possible a mode of life in accordance with rules. As a mere school of discipline the British Navy is probably incomparable; the essence of the thing is there, with the sea as an eternal menace to the neglect or decline of it; and although it may seem narrow and archaic compared with the broader discipline involved in any life of toil or effort, it is chiefly because it is more intense. The plant grown for use or ornament is allowed to flourish in its branches; that grown for propagation is kept strong and vigorous by ruthless cutting back; its strength is retained in its roots so that it may burst forth when the increase is required. So with the Navy, and its value to the nation in peace time as the nursery wherein the strong stock of discipline may be kept alive against the day of necessity.

But this being granted, the reader may still ask himself whether, in order to preserve the tradition of discipline, it is necessary to spend millions a year on building ships that in the nature of things become obsolete and have to be replaced. Of course it is not. Whether we require a Navy or not depends on the state of the world and on the degree of perfection to which common human nature has attained. Alas! no dove sent out from our ark of England at this time is likely to return with an olive branch in her mouth. The waters of unrest still surge over the world, and the harbinger of good will finds no resting or nesting place yet. Granted, therefore, that a Navy has to be kept up, you get the discipline thrown in, so to speak, as an asset to be set off against the apparently unproductive expenditure. And is the expenditure unproductive? The Navy is the insurance policy of the Empire; and if anyone has discovered a better or cheaper insurance, now is the time to come forward with it. Otherwise the old policy must be renewed. The premium is bound to be a heavy drain; but if it is not paid, if even one year is allowed to go by, the policy will lapse, in the sense that in naval construction you can never make good a lost year, and you lose your place, won by effort and sacrifice in the past, in relation to other Powers. Most of us are driven to a severe economy in these years; but our insurance premiums are the last form of expenditure we dare give up.

In its human composition, and in the spirit that inspires it, the Navy remains practically unchanged from one generation to another. On the mechanical and material side it changes greatly and continuously. So much so that certain voices have been raised to say that the " capital ship " has been rendered obsolete by this war, and that naval war in future will be conducted under the sea or in the air. Intelligent readers of this book will have some material at least from which they may form their own opinion on that strange idea. It is not the idea of the majority of those who have experience either of capital ships or of submarines in warfare.

Big Ships or——?

There is, strictly speaking, no such weapon as the submarine; it is an extension or variety of the torpedo-carrying vessel. The capital ship is the surface, gun-carrying vessel in its most powerful form. The submarine craft is such only for purposes of concealment, and must come to the surface to fight. In the late war, in spite of the immense scale on which it was used, it was driven under and destroyed by the surface vessel; while capital ships when handled properly did their business without interference from submarines. In the battle cruisers we scoured the North Sea by day and night without their being able to hinder us. Of course their existence caused anxiety, just as the existence of the gun, or the aircraft, or the fact that we were at war at all, caused anxiety. But sea warfare cannot be decided by either of the combatants flying into the air or descending to the depths. The aeroplane must ultimately come down and the submarine must ultimately come up, and it is there, on the surface, that the capital ship is waiting to settle conclusions with them both. What form it takes depends on the particular use to which it is likely to be put; and that again depends on the interpretation of the world-situation in military terms by an educated staff.

Let us repeat it, at the cost of tedium : *the principles of war do not change.* In the primitive quarrel between two unarmed men the one who can strike quickest and hardest stands the best chance. And the one who can so strike will be most anxious to get nearer, to keep nearer, to the enemy. It is not by hiding or going away that he will win. And the most elaborate modern warfare conceivable is only an extension of the prehistoric duel. Fist, flint or stone to be thrown, stick to be wielded,

Foundations of the Future

bow and arrow, knife, sword, catapult, gun, bullet, shell, disease-bringing germs—they are all extensions of man's arm and fist, and of his will to damage and destroy his enemy. Capital ships fighting at sea no longer do so by ramming one another, but by firing with guns at the limit of visual distance; and so far the gun is the dominating factor in sea warfare, and the capital ship is its mobile platform.

Confusion of thought has arisen on this subject through failure to discriminate between the principles of war, which do not change, and the applications of them, which do. The idea that because certain elements have modified war in a certain way on land, they must modify war at sea in the same way, is fallacious. The sea is, and forever will be, an inimical element for man. The land, the earth, is his home; he plants his feet on it, draws his whole life from it, can exist upon it in a state of nature. That is not true of either the sea or the air, neither of which are elements in which mankind as a race can abide. And this is an eternal law, that will last as long as the world and men's quarrels in it. In resorting to the inimical element for purposes of warfare, the one who can keep nearer to his enemy in it, who can best master it, use it, be at home in it, breathe and see and fight in it, will be in the best position to apply the unchanging principles of war. And it is not beneath the sea or above it that man can best and most powerfully use his faculties, but on its surface.

The events recorded in this book are already things of the past, and if they are not to become "negligible wreckage" it behoves the citizen of the British Empire,

The Principles of War do not Change

as well as the naval officer, to come to some conclusion as to their bearing on the present and the future. The Navy is typical of our race in this: that owing to the peculiar human qualities of the men who compose it it manages to survive the most astounding muddles, mistakes, and lack of imagination on the part of those administering it, and to come through undefeated in the end. Undefeated; but can we say victorious? Its existence, backing the effort of the whole united manhood of the Allies, won the war for us; but it did not end the war, as it conceivably might have done, by fighting and destroying the enemy at sea. And this because at certain critical moments those who had its destinies in their hands were infected and paralysed by the idea that its supreme function was not to fight, but to be.

A study of the neglected "wreckage at the bottom of the sea" shows this view to be a fallacy. The principles of war do not change; and the way to get the highest efficiency out of a fighting machine is to fight with it. To fight is not to threaten, but to destroy and overwhelm; and our enemies, not having been destroyed or overwhelmed, shrewdly decided that although they could not win the war they might win the peace; and they are now preparing to do so. And the war which was to end war may conceivably be but a prelude to a prolonged condition of enmity and warfare that will purge mankind to its very vitals.

If this or anything like it be so, the people that has the will to exist must continue to learn, and to learn from the immediate past. In the light of this study. as applied to naval warfare, the first thing to go down

Foundations of the Future

is that terrible complacency which assured us that " all was well with the Navy," that it was " perfectly equipped down to the last detail." It was not. ₁ The Navy was ill-equipped for the task it had to perform ; its equipment had to be learned and improvised under the immediate peril of war, at an inconceivably wasteful cost of human and material resources. It was only our surprising immunity in the early days resulting from a similar lack of imagination on the part of our enemies that gave us the time to make good, towards the end of the war, all the deficiencies which study and foresight should have supplied. In the period covered by this book the deficiencies were revealed. The battle of the Dogger Bank contained the essence of all North Sea warfare, with the exception of night fighting ; but its lessons were never effectively studied or applied until after Jutland, when nothing happened that was new or could not have been foretold. And now, five years after Jutland, it is left to a mere onlooker like myself to make public for the first time the essential facts of the Dogger Bank battle ; while the essential truths of Jutland are still hidden in the cloud of official reticence and secrecy. The Admiralty has its official records, which in time become mistaken for true records ; but sometimes they have little relation to historic fact. About nothing that went at all wrong in the naval war did the Admiralty tell the truth ; and one danger of that system is that the untruth becomes material for history, and is somehow believed just because it is official. Yet everyone knows that access to the truth must be the basis of all sound learning. The groundwork of Admiralty reform should be a department in which records would be sifted, copied, digested and preserved, not necessarily by people whom it is desired to reward for sea services with a shore appointment, but by people qualified by nature and training for that very work. Until that is done the Navy must continue to rely on accident for the record of some of its most glorious deeds and the preservation of some of its greatest traditions.

The faults of the Navy are known to itself, and perhaps for that very reason there has always been a certain amount of sensitiveness and resentment in the Service on their being referred to by people who might not perhaps understand the causes of them. That was one reason, no doubt, why the Navy so long resisted the obviously necessary admittance into some of its fastnesses of amateur and volunteer service, however enthusiastic. It was a very close club, which was not prepared to explain matters perfectly understood within itself to outsiders lacking the necessary experience and intuition to grasp their significance. But the most serious disadvantage under which it laboured lay precisely in the system which made it so single-hearted and, up to a point, miraculously efficient. To take a little boy of thirteen away from his home and isolate him from all the thought and development of his generation, with the one idea of getting out of him every ounce of specialized efficiency, was an austere method of ensuring the survival of a certain kind of the fittest; but it was probably the most wasteful method that could be employed. There were many other kinds of fitness which could not survive that ordeal, and so through the years that this fierce winnowing went on the survivors, as they proved, were

Foundations of the Future

undoubtedly fit. But how much splendid material was not rendered useless, not only to the Navy, but to the community and itself, in the process? The miserable pay which officers in the Navy received was a further cause of this wastage of fine human material. For the ideas and traditions of the Navy are of the old upper class, while the ranks of its officers are largely drawn from the middle and professional classes. To the little boy, wrested from an ordinary home at the tender age alluded to, life unfolded and developed itself even in the Navy; life with its urgencies, its desires, its dreams. Hence the marriage of the average naval officer was too often an affair of haste, opportunity, or convenience; his married life was too often a mockery; and too often it was utterly impossible for him to hand on to his children the proper heritage of the fine habits and ideals with which his training, however narrow and specialized, had endowed him. All these things represented a serious and tragic waste. Collectively they account in a great measure for the narrowness of point of view, and the lack of that experience of the world gained only in contact with a great many sides of human life and activity to which the Navy as a service must plead guilty; and they account also for mistrust of outside thought or criticism, and a preference for submitting to the faulty rule of an obsolete authority rather than for opposing it in an organized effort towards self-improvement.

These things are being put right now; the breath of the sea and the smoke of war are blowing through the Admiralty again, and the Young Navy is in power there. The extent of its success will depend precisely on the extent to which it remains young and in touch with the naval generation born of the war. Many things age and change rapidly in Whitehall—among them Points of View; and the Neptunes who one after another have come blowing in from the sea to grasp the trident ashore have often been astonished to find how soon it could change into a walking-stick, or even into a pair of crutches.

In the course of this narrative the temptation to essay some portrait of the chief figure in it has been constant, and has had to be resisted, if only because any such attempt would necessarily fail in its object. It is impossible to write of a man, one's contemporary, to whom one has stood in the relation both of friendship and of service, who is still in the prime of life, as though he were dead; to attempt to sum him up and assign him a place in the Valhalla of departed heroes would be both futile and absurd. It is possible that Lord Beatty has still his greatest work before him. His own merits and the accidents of war have placed him in the highest position which a sailor can occupy in his profession; a position in which, coming fresh from active service and from the command of the Navy in war, he can so influence the Admiralty administration that the lessons of the war shall be learned and understood. According to his success or failure in that task history will no doubt write its final verdict upon him. But one who has served him and observed him closely in the stress of war may at least bear this testimony to his conduct in the chapter of his life which is already over: that in every-thing that he did or attempted he showed forth in

R   257

himself and evoked in others the fighting spirit that made England invincible in the past. The common view of him as a dashing leader trusting largely to luck, which so much endears a man to the ordinary English mind, is singularly untrue. It was not the mere instinct of the hunting-field, strong as it was in him, that brought him to the head of the Navy. His caution and his sense of responsibility were just as remarkable as his enterprise; but they were never allowed to obscure or dominate the fighting spirit. Even a mere glance at his portrait should be enough to dispel the common delusion. You may read sensitiveness there, inspiration, fullness of life; but you read also a sense of what responsibility really means. Burdens and problems, you feel, are not intolerable to one who does not rely on mysteries, but has his own clear light by which burdens can be borne and problems solved.

Perhaps the greatest tribute one can pay to him and to the Navy is to say that in the qualities in which he proved supreme he was not exceptional, but typical; and it was because he was a product of the modern Navy and contained in himself all its most characteristic qualities, that the Navy would have trusted and followed him anywhere. Thus he was exceptional, not in the nature, but in the extent of his qualities. If you were to take a hundred captains of destroyers, give them his war service, his opportunities, his early promotion, and his power of devoting himself to the essentials of his profession, you might very likely find a dozen Beattys; and his career gives one some idea of what kind of material may have been wasted in the past. Such a career, however brilliant, gives one

Spe·ight, Ltd.

Admiral of the Fleet Earl Beatty,
O.M., G.C.B., G.C.V.O., D.S.O., D.C.L.

The Mantle of Nelson

much to think about. For a man like Beatty to achieve the highest attainable position, to command the British Navy in war, to be loaded with honours, and yet to have missed through no fault of his own the chance of exercising his genius in its fullest capacity, and to the most telling effect, is a destiny almost tragic; yet it is a destiny common to all but the fortunate among men of genius. If Nelson[1] had not died at Trafalgar, it is extremely likely that he would have lived to know indifference and hostility, and to experience the neglect from which his own dramatic end saved him, from which those dear to him suffered; and it is only recently that the lessons of his great work have been seriously studied. Lord Beatty is at once more and less fortunate than his great predecessor. If he had died at Jutland he would have passed unchallenged into the company of the supreme masters of sea warfare; and although nothing he can do at the Admiralty can affect the verdict of history upon his sea leadership, his warfare there lies still before him; he has still a reputation to make as an administrative reformer; and he still has either to fail or succeed in giving to the Navy an administration worthy of it. The spirit of the Navy, which was seen in him at its best, needs no reform. But the spirit of the Admiralty, of the machine which administers, equips, and uses the Navy, does need reform; and if he can achieve that reformation he will have deserved better of his country than if he had fought and sunk every German ship on the seas. As it is, he has both deserved and won a supreme position among those who

[1] I thought it might be possible to write a book about sea warfare without mentioning that great name, if only because in the things of which I have written his mantle was worthily worn by another; but it will creep in.

Foundations of the Future

are England's strength and defence in the hour of danger.

I came to the Navy from an angle in life quite opposite to that of my shipmates, with everything to learn, many things to forget, and little besides love of the sea in common with them; and life has swept me away from them again. I had a very short time in which to know them, but it was enough to make me sure of their qualities. It has been my lot to drag life with a very wide net, to know many kinds of society, in many countries, and in many fields of human activity; and to not a little of this experience did five years of war contribute. But the greatest certainty that the war brought me was this: that in those days and nights of adventure, of sea emergency and sea routine, in excitement sometimes, in weariness often, in sun and in cloud, in danger and in serene security, I was in good company; the best, perhaps, and for me the most congenial, that those years of storm afforded.

APPENDIX A

THE DOGGER BANK DESPATCH

ON arrival at Rosyth on January 26 Sir David Beatty sent a brief telegraphic despatch to the Admiralty and to the Commander-in-Chief. A paraphrase of this despatch was issued to the Press with the heading " The following preliminary telegraphic report has been received from Vice-Admiral Sir David Beatty." In addition to several minor additions and alterations the following change was made, which has caused up to the present a great deal of misunderstanding.

Paragraph 8 in the published telegram read as follows:

> " The presence of the enemy's submarines subsequently necessitated the action being broken off."

The actual sentence in Sir David Beatty's telegram was:

> " In view of unknown condition of *Lion* and presence of enemy submarines, Admiral Moore considered retirement desirable at noon and gave orders accordingly."

In February, 1915, Admiral Beatty wrote a detailed despatch describing the action. After some time this was returned to him in proof by the Admiralty, seventeen out of its thirty paragraphs either altered or omitted altogether. Even the report as thus edited, however, was not published. The despatch which has been given

Appendix

to the public, which hitherto has been the only authoritative guide as to what really occurred at the **Dogger Bank** battle, was a further edited version of the revised proof. The alterations were so numerous and so remarkable, and presented such an essentially different account in some vital matters from that written by the Vice-Admiral, that no naval student can possibly understand this action in the light of Sir David Beatty's report as published. As I prepared at the time a comparative analysis of the three versions of this report, I am fortunately able to publish here, for the first time, the original despatch as written by Sir David Beatty. For purposes of comparison I have added to it the despatch as published, with notes as to the effect of the principal alterations.

I remember that when the telegraphic report was published containing the entirely fictitious sentence, "The presence of the enemy's submarines necessitated the action being broken off," an American naval writer published an article analysing the action, and saying that Admiral Beatty, on the evidence of his published report, ought to be shot. I showed this article to the Admiral at the time, and his only comment was, " I quite agree with him."

ORIGINAL DESPATCH.

"H.M.S. *Princess Royal,*

" SIR,—   " *February* 2, 1915.

*" I have the honour to report that at 7.0 A.M. on January 24, 1915, I passed through the position 55.18 N. 8.12 E. with the following vessels in company :

"The First Battle Cruiser Squadron, consisting of

.* Altered in published despatch.

The Dogger Bank Despatch

Lion, flying my flag, *Tiger* and *Princess Royal*, in the order named.

" The Second Battle Cruiser Squadron, consisting of *New Zealand*, flying the flag of Rear-Admiral Sir Archibald Moore, K.C.B., C.V.O., and *Indomitable*.

" The First Light Cruiser Squadron, consisting of *Southampton*, flying the broad pennant of Commodore W. E. Goodenough, M.V.O., *Nottingham*, *Birmingham* and *Lowestoft*, were disposed 5 miles on my port beam.

" The whole force was steering S. 12 W. at 18 knots.

† " 2. Having passed through the position referred to, I ordered the First Light Cruiser Squadron to spread for look-out duties N.E. by N.

* " 3. Commodore (T) R. Y. Tyrwhitt, C.B., in *Arethusa*, with a half flotilla, was sighted ahead at 7.10 A.M., and at 7.25 A.M. the flash of guns was observed S.S.E. Shortly afterwards a report reached me from *Aurora* that she was engaged with enemy's ships. I immediately altered course to S.S.E., increased to 22 knots, and ordered L.C.S. and Flotillas to chase S.S.E. to get in touch and report movements of enemy.

" 4. This order was acted upon with great promptitude; indeed, my wishes had already been forestalled by the respective Senior Officers, and reports almost immediately followed from *Southampton*, *Arethusa* and *Aurora* as to the position and the composition of the enemy, which consisted of 4 Battle Cruisers, 6 Light Cruisers and a number of Destroyers steering N.W. The enemy had already altered course to S.E. From now onwards the

* Altered in published despatch.

† Omitted in published despatch.

Appendix

Light Cruisers maintained touch with the enemy and kept me fully informed as to their movements.

* " 5. The Battle Cruisers worked up to full speed, steering to obtain the leeward position and if possible to get to the Southward between the enemy and their base, with the object of forcing them to the Northward away from it. The wind at the time was N.E., light, with extreme visibility. At 7.50 A.M. the enemy Battle Cruisers, 4 in number, were sighted on the port bow steaming fast, steering approximately S.E., distant 14 miles.

* " 6. Owing to the prompt reports received, we had attained our position on the lee quarter of the enemy, and so altered course to S.E. parallel to them, and settled down to a long stern chase, gradually increasing our speed until we reached 28.5 knots. Great credit is due to the Engineer Staffs of *New Zealand* and *Indomitable* —these ships greatly exceeded their normal speed, and actually reached 27 and 26 knots respectively.

" 7. At 8.52 A.M. we had closed to within 20,000 yards of the rear ship, and the Battle Cruisers manœuvred to keep on a line of bearing so that guns would bear; *Lion* fired a single shot, which fell short. The enemy at this time were in single line ahead, with Light Cruisers ahead, and a large number of Destroyers on their starboard beam.

* " 8. Single shots were fired at intervals to test the range, and at 9.9 A.M. *Lion* made her first hit on the *Blücher*, No. 4 in the line. The *Tiger* opening fire at 9.20 A.M. on the rear ship, the *Lion* shifted to No. 3 in the line, at 18,000 yards, this ship being hit

* Altered in published despatch.

264

The Dogger Bank Despatch

by several salvoes. The enemy returned our fire at
9.14 A.M., scoring their first hit at 9.28 A.M. on *Lion*.
Princess Royal, on coming into range, opened fire on
Blücher.

* " 9. Three of the enemy ships were now concentrating on *Lion*, the range of the leading ship being
17,500 yards, so at 9.35 A.M. I made the signal, " Engage
the corresponding ships in the enemy's line." By this ·
time *New Zealand* was within range of *Blücher*, which
had dropped somewhat astern, and opened fire on her.
Princess Royal shifted to the third ship in the line,
inflicting considerable damage on her.

* " 10. Our Flotilla Cruisers and Destroyers had
gradually dropped from a position broad on our beam
to our port quarter, so as not to foul our range with their
smoke; but the enemy's destroyers threatening attack, I
ordered Commodore (T) to take station ahead. This he
was unable to do without passing between us and the
enemy and masking our fire with his smoke. The *Meteor*
and " M " Division succeeded later in passing ahead of us
by virtue of their great speed, and I fully concur in the
remarks of the Commodore (T) as to the able and gallant
manner in which Commander Hon. H. Meade handled
this division.

* " 11. About 9.45 A.M. the situation was as follows :
Blücher, the fourth in their line, already showed signs
of having suffered severely from gun fire; their leading
ship and No. 3 were also on fire. *Lion* was engaging
No. 1, *Princess Royal* No. 3, *New Zealand* No. 4, while
the *Tiger*, who was second in our line, fired first at their
No. 1 and, when interfered with by smoke, at their

* Altered in published despatch.

265

Appendix

No. 4. This was unfortunate, as it left the second enemy ship unfired at, and she concentrated on *Lion*.

" 12. The enemy's destroyers emitted vast columns of smoke to screen their Battle Cruisers, and under cover of this the latter now appeared to have altered course to the Northward to increase their distance, and certainly the rear ships hauled out on the port quarter of their leader, thereby increasing their distance from our line. The Battle Cruisers, therefore, were ordered to form on a line of bearing N.N.W. and proceed at their utmost speed.

* " 13. Their destroyers then showed evident signs of an attempt to attack, and I signalled to the Squadron to that effect. *Lion* and *Tiger* opened fire with 4-inch and 6-inch guns respectively, and caused them to retire and resume their original course. The 6-inch guns of *Tiger* performed very useful service at a long range, and certainly succeeded in placing 2 salvoes among them at 12,000 yards.

† " 14. Any attempt on our part to close the enemy by altering course to port was met by the enemy's torpedo craft steering more to starboard, and so putting us in a position of having to cross their track—this had to be avoided owing to the danger of their minelaying. We had, therefore, to depend on maintaining our speed and establishing an overlap ahead before we could close sufficiently to force them to the Northward or bring them to close action.

† " 15. The First Light Cruiser Squadron maintained an excellent position on the port quarter of the enemy's

* Altered in published despatch.
† Omitted in published despatch.

The Dogger Bank Despatch

line, enabling them to observe and keep touch or attack any vessel that might fall out of the line. They were also in a good position to mark the effect of our fire and the fall of the shot. *Southampton* reported that one ship, probably *Tiger*, was firing consistently 'over.' This might have enabled her to correct her range.

† " 16. From 10.0 A.M. onwards *Lion* suffered considerably from the concentrated fire of the enemy's two leading ships, and two alterations of one point inwards were made accordingly, ships turning together. *Lion* then zigzagged to throw out the enemy's range. About 10.40 A.M. *Lion* received heavy punishment. By 10.51 A.M. her port engine was stopped, all lights were out, she was making water rapidly, listing heavily to port, and was unable to maintain her place in the line.

* " 17. At 10.48 A.M. the *Blücher*, which had dropped considerably astern of enemy's line, hauled out to port, steering North, with a heavy list, on fire, and apparently in a defeated condition. I consequently ordered *Indomitable*, which was astern, to attack enemy breaking to the Northward.

* " 18. At 10.54 A.M. submarines were reported on the starboard bow, and I personally observed the wash of a periscope, 2 points on our starboard bow. I immediately signalled, 'Turn 8 points to port together'—this signal was hauled down at 11.0 A.M. As this turn would take us across the track of enemy destroyers, it was important that it should be sufficiently large to take us clear of it before we reached the position they were in at this moment so as to avoid the mines which they would

* Altered in published despatch.
† Omitted in published despatch.

267

Appendix

probably take the opportunity of dropping. *Indomitable* subsequently reported that a torpedo had been fired at her, crossing her bows 40 yards ahead after leaving the vicinity of the sinking *Blücher*—so it may be assumed that the enemy submarines had closed and attacked her.

† "19. It was now clear that *Lion* could no longer remain 'Guide' of the Fleet, and as our zigzagging might have caused doubt as to the actual course to be steered, I hoisted the signal, 'Course N.E.,' at 11.2 A.M. This course would have cut the enemy Battle Cruisers off from *Blücher* should they turn to support her, as I anticipated they would. Should they leave her to her fate, our ships could have again turned to a parallel course when clear of track of their torpedo craft.

† "20. At 11.5 A.M. I hoisted the signal, 'Attack the enemy's rear,' hauled down the course signal, and hoisted 'Keep nearer to the enemy.' At this time *Lion's* wireless apparatus was out of action and only two signal halliards remained, preventing me from informing Admiral Moore of the reason for my sudden 8-point turn or from exercising any further command. I kept the signals, 'Attack the rear' and 'Keep closer,' flying till the remainder of the Squadron had passed out of sight.

* "21. At 11.8 A.M. the injury to the *Lion* being reported as incapable of immediate repair, I semaphored to Commodore (T) to close and to detail destroyers as a submarine screen and directed *Lion* to shape course N.W. At 11.20 A.M. I called the *Attack* alongside, shifting my flag to her at about 11.35 A.M. I proceeded

---

* Altered in published despatch.

† Omitted in published despatch.

The Dogger Bank Despatch

at utmost speed to rejoin the Squadron, and met them at noon retiring N.N.W.

* " 22. Having made a signal to turn 16 points, to resume pursuit of the enemy, I boarded and hoisted my flag in *Princess Royal* at about 12.20 P.M. Captain Brock acquainted me of what had occurred since *Lion* fell out of the line, viz. that *Blücher* had been sunk and that the remaining enemy Battle Cruisers had continued their course to the eastward in a considerably damaged condition. He also informed me that a Zeppelin and a seaplane had endeavoured to drop bombs on the vessels which went to the rescue of the survivors of *Blücher*. Realizing then that the opportunity of effecting the total destruction of the enemy had passed, I re-formed the Squadron and proceeded to pick up *Lion*.

* " 28. The good seamanship of Lieut.-Commander Callaghan in placing his vessel alongside the *Lion* and subsequently the *Princess Royal*, while both ships were under way, enabled the transfer of flag to be made in the shortest possible time with the minimum risk of submarine attack.

* " 24. At 2.0 P.M. I closed *Lion* and received a report that her starboard engine was giving trouble owing to priming, and that possibly she would not be able to steam for more than 12 hours. At 8.88 P.M. I ordered *Indomitable* to take her in tow, which was accomplished by 5.0 P.M.

† " 25. I directed the Destroyer Flotillas to surround the two ships to form a submarine screen. Throughout the homeward journey this duty was performed under

* Altered in published despatch.
† Omitted in published despatch.

269

Appendix

the direction of the Commodore (T) in a most masterly and skilful manner, providing almost complete security from submarine attack.

* " 26. The greatest credit is due to the Captains of *Indomitable* and *Lion* for the seamanlike manner in which the *Lion* was taken in tow under difficult circumstances and brought safely to port.

† " 27. The Second Light Cruiser Squadron, which had now joined me, was stationed S.E. 10 miles, and First Light Cruiser Squadron E. 10 miles, to act as screen from destroyer attack, the Battle Cruisers taking station to be in a position where necessary.

† " 28. Before concluding this report, I desire to remark that during the critical moments of uncertainty as to the condition of *Lion* the officers and men of that ship exhibited a coolness and indifference to danger worthy of the best traditions of the Service.

" 29. The excellent steaming of the ships engaged in the operation was a conspicuous feature.

* " 80. I attach an appendix giving the names of various officers and men who specially distinguished themselves. I also enclose reports from officers under my orders.

" I have the honour to be,
" Sir,
" Your obedient Servant,
" DAVID BEATTY,
" *Vice-Admiral.*"

---

* Altered in published despatch.
† Omitted in published despatch.

Appendix

THE DESPATCH AS PUBLISHED

The following is the form in which the despatch was published by the Admiralty :

H.M.S. *Princess Royal*, 2nd February, 1915.

1. SIR,—I have the honour to report that at daybreak on 24th January, 1915, the following vessels were patrolling in company :—The battle cruisers *Lion* (Captain Alfred E. M. Chatfield, C.V.O.), flying my flag, *Princess Royal* (Captain Osmond de B. Brock, Aide-de-Camp), *Tiger* (Captain Henry B. Pelly, M.V.O.), *New Zealand* (Captain Lionel Halsey, C.M.G., Aide-de-Camp), flying the flag of Rear-Admiral Sir Archibald Moore, K.C.B., C.V.O., and *Indomitable* (Captain Francis W. Kennedy). The light cruisers *Southampton*, flying the broad pennant of Commodore William E. Goodenough, M.V.O.; *Nottingham* (Captain Charles B. Miller), *Birmingham* (Captain Arthur A. M. Duff), and *Lowestoft* (Captain Theobold W. B. Kennedy) were disposed on my port beam. Commodore (T) Reginald Y. Tyrwhitt, C.B., in *Arethusa*, *Aurora* (Captain Wilmot S. Nicholson), *Undaunted* (Captain Francis G. St. John, M.V.O.). *Arethusa* and the destroyer flotilla were ahead.

    Position omitted, and names of C.O.s inserted. " Daybreak " substituted for 7.0 A.M.

2. *Omitted.*

3. At 7.25 A.M. the flash of guns was observed S.S.E. Shortly afterwards a report reached me from *Aurora* that she was engaged with enemy's ships. I immediately altered course to S.S.E., increased to 22 knots, and ordered the light cruisers and flotillas to chase S.S.E. to get in touch and report movements of enemy.

    Commodore's name omitted.

4. This order was acted upon with great promptitude; indeed, my wishes had already been forestalled by the respective senior officers, and reports almost immediately followed from *Southampton*, *Arethusa*, and *Aurora* as to the position and composition of the enemy, which consisted of three battle-cruisers and *Blücher*, six light cruisers, and a number of destroyers steering N.W.

Appendix

The enemy had altered course to S.E. From now onwards the light cruisers maintained touch with the enemy, and kept me fully informed as to their movements.

Unaltered.

5. The battle cruisers worked up to full speed, steering to the southward, the wind at the time N.E., light, with extreme visibility.

Leeward position and reason for course steered omitted. Composition of enemy force omitted.

6. At 7.80 the enemy were sighted on the port bow steaming fast, steering approximately S.E., distant 14 miles. Owing to the prompt reports received, we had attained our position on the quarter of the enemy, and so altered course to S.E., parallel to them, and settled down to a long stern chase, gradually increasing our speed until we reached 28.5 knots.

Great credit is due to the engineer staffs of *New Zealand* and *Indomitable*. These ships greatly exceeded their normal speed.

Leeward position omitted. Actual speed of New Zealand and Indomitable omitted.

7. At 8.25 A.M., as we had closed to within 20,000 yards of the rear ship, the battle cruisers manœuvred to keep on a line of bearing so that guns would bear, and *Lion* fired a single shot, which fell short. The enemy at this time were in single line ahead, with light cruisers ahead, and a large number of destroyers on their starboard beam.

Unaltered.

8. Single shots were fired at intervals to test the range, and at 9.9 A.M. *Lion* made her first hit on the *Blücher*, No. 4 in the line. The *Tiger* opened fire at 9.20 A.M. on the rear ship. The *Lion* shifted to No. 8 in the line at 18,000 yards, this ship being hit by several salvoes. The enemy returned our fire at 9.14 A.M. *Princess Royal*, on coming into range, opened fire at *Blücher*, the range of the leading ship being 17,500 yards.

First hit by enemy and time omitted.

9. At 9.85 A.M. *New Zealand* was within range of *Blücher*, which had dropped somewhat astern, and opened fire on her. *Princess Royal* shifted to the third ship in line, inflicting considerable damage on her.

The Official Version

Concentration of three ships on Lion omitted.

Signal to engage corresponding enemy ships omitted, and sentence recast.

10. Our flotilla cruisers and destroyers had gradually dropped from a position broad on our beam to our port quarter, so as not to foul our range with their smoke, but, the enemy's destroyers threatening attack, the *Meteor* and " M " division passed ahead of us, Captain the Hon. H. Meade, D.S.O., handling this division with conspicuous ability.

Order to Commodore (T) and his inability to fulfil it omitted. Paragraph altered so as to suggest that " M " division passed ahead at once, instead of " later " in original. Reference to Commander Meade slightly altered.

11. About 9.45 A.M. the situation was as follows :

Blücher, the fourth in their line, already showed signs of having suffered severely from gunfire. Their leading ship and No. 8 were also on fire. *Lion* was engaging No. 1, *Princess Royal* No. 8, *New Zealand* No. 4, while the *Tiger*, who was second in our line, fired first at their No. 1, and when interfered with by smoke at their No. 4.

Reference to Tiger's failure to fire at No. 2 omitted.

12. The enemy's destroyers emitted vast columns of smoke to screen their battle cruisers, and under cover of this the latter now appeared to have altered their course to the northward to increase their distance, and certainly the rear ships hauled out on the port quarter of their leader, thereby increasing their distance from our line. The battle cruisers therefore were ordered to form a line of bearing N.N.W., and proceed at their utmost speed.

Unaltered.

13. Their destroyers then showed evident signs of an attempt to attack the *Lion*, and the *Tiger* opened fire on them and caused them to retire and resume their original course.

Signal to squadron omitted. Reference to secondary armament omitted. Reference to Tiger's salvoes omitted.

14. *Omitted.*

15. *Omitted.*

16. *Omitted.*

17. At 10.48 A.M. the *Blücher*, which had dropped considerably astern of the enemy's line, hauled out to port, steering

north with a heavy list, on fire, and apparently in a defeated condition. I consequently ordered *Indomitable* to attack the enemy, breaking northward.

Position of Indomitable, astern, omitted.

18. At 10.54 A.M. submarines were reported on the starboard bow, and I personally observed the wash of a periscope two points on our starboard bow. I immediately turned to port.

Number of points of turn to port omitted.

Reference to track of enemy destroyers omitted. Reference to likelihood of mine-dropping omitted. Submarine attack on Indomitable omitted. Explanation of 8-point turn omitted.

19. *Omitted.*

20. *Omitted.*

21. At 11.8 A.M. injury to the *Lion* being reported as incapable of immediate repair, I directed the *Lion* to shape course north-west. At 11.80 A.M. I called the *Attack* alongside, shifting my flag to her at about 11.85 A.M. I proceeded at utmost speed to rejoin the squadron, and met them at noon retiring N.N.W.

Signals to Commodore (T) and Lion omitted.

22. I boarded and hoisted my flag in *Princess Royal* at about 12.20 P.M., when Captain Brock acquainted me of what had occurred since the *Lion* fell out of the line—namely, the *Blücher* had been sunk, and that the enemy battle cruisers had continued their course to the eastward in a considerably damaged condition.

He also informed me that a Zeppelin and a seaplane had endeavoured to drop bombs on the vessels which went to the rescue of the survivors of the *Blücher*.

Word "remaining" omitted. Reference to reasons for re-forming Squadron omitted.

28. The good seamanship of Lieutenant-Commander Cyril Callaghan, H.M.S. *Attack*, in placing his vessel alongside the *Lion*, and subsequently the *Princess Royal*, enabled the transfer of the flag to be made in the shortest possible time.

Reference to risk of submarine attack omitted.

24. At 2 P.M. I closed the *Lion*, and received a report that her starboard engine was giving trouble, owing to priming, and

The Official Version

at 8.88 P.M. I ordered the *Indomitable* to take her in tow, which was accomplished by 5 P.M.

Lion's probable steaming endurance omitted.

25. *Omitted.*
26. The greatest credit is due to the Captains of *Indomitable* and *Lion* for the seamanlike manner in which the *Lion* was taken in tow under difficult circumstances.

    Fact that Lion was brought safely to port omitted.

27. *Omitted.*
28. *Omitted.*
29. The excellent steaming of the ships engaged in the operation was a conspicuous feature.
80. I attach an appendix, giving the names of various officers and men who specially distinguished themselves. Where all did well it is difficult to single out officers and men for special mention, and as *Lion* and *Tiger* were the only ships hit by the enemy, the majority of these I mention belong to those ships.

    Reasons for majority of names being from Lion and Tiger inserted.

> I have the honour to be, sir,
> Your obedient servant,
> (Signed)   DAVID BEATTY, Vice-Admiral.

Out of 80 paragraphs only 4 are unaltered.

The chief effect of the omission of certain paragraphs is as follows:

Par.

15. *To conceal Tiger's failure to hit.*
18 and 19. *To leave the 8-point turn to port unexplained.*
20. *To conceal the fact that a general signal was made which was not carried out.*
22. *To conceal the fact that what had happened (whatever it was) between 11.20 and 12.20 had rendered the " total destruction " of the enemy impossible.*

APPENDIX B

FORCES ENGAGED IN THE BATTLE OF THE DOGGER BANK

(I.) BRITISH

FIRST BATTLE CRUISER SQUADRON

Ship	Speed Knots	Armament
Lion (Flag)	28	
Vice-Admiral Sir David Beatty, K.C.B., M.V.O., D.S.O.		Eight 13·5-inch Sixteen 4-inch
Princess Royal	28	Eight 13·5-inch Sixteen 4-inch
Tiger	30	Eight 13·5-inch Sixteen 6-inch

SECOND BATTLE CRUISER SQUADRON

New Zealand (Flag)	26	Eight 12-inch Sixteen 4-inch
Rear Admiral Sir Archibald Moore, K.C.B.		
Indomitable	25	Eight 12-inch Sixteen 4-inch

FIRST LIGHT CRUISER SQUADRON

Ship	Speed Knots	Ship			Speed Knots
Southampton (Broad Pennant)	25	*Birmingham*	.	.	. 25
Commodore William E.		*Nottingham*	.	.	. 25
Goodenough, M.V.O.		*Lowestoft* .	.	.	. 25

FLOTILLAS

Arethusa (Flag) . . .	28·5
Commodore Reginald Y. Tyrwhitt, C.B.	

TENTH DESTROYER FLOTILLA

Meteor	34	*Mentor* .	.	.	. 34
Commander Hon. H.		*Mastiff* .	.	.	. 34
Meade		*Minos* .	.	.	. 34
Miranda	34	*Morris* .	.	.	. 34
Milne	34				

Forces Engaged

Third Destroyer Flotilla

Ship	Speed Knots	Ship	Speed Knots
Undaunted	29	Liberty	29
Captain Francis G. St. John, M.V.O. (Captain D.3)		Laertes	29
		Lucifer	29
		Lawford	29
Lookout	29	Lydia	29
Lysander	29	Louis	29
Landrail	29	Legion	29
Laurel	29	Lark	29

First Destroyer Flotilla

Ship	Speed	Ship	Speed
Aurora	27	Druid	27
Captain Wilmot S. Nicholson (Captain D.1)		Hornet	27
		Tigress	27
Acheron	27	Sandfly	27
Attack	27	Jackal	27
Hydra	27	Goshawk	27
Ariel	27	Phœnix	27
Forester	27	Lapwing	27
Defender	27		

IN SUPPORT

Third Battle Squadron

Ship	Ship
Dominion (Flag)	Hibernia
Vice-Admiral Bradford, C.V.O.	Hindustan
Africa	King Edward VII.
Briton	Zealandia

Second Cruiser Squadron

Shannon (Flag)	Hercules
Rear-Admiral the Hon. Somerset Gough Calthorpe, C.V.O., C.B.	Cochran

Third Cruiser Squadron

Antrim (Flag)	Argyle
Rear-Admiral William C. Pakenham, C.B., M.V.O.	Devonshire

Second Light Cruiser Squadron

Falmouth (Flag)	Gloucester
Rear-Admiral T. W. D. Napier, M.V.O.	Yarmouth
	Dartmouth

Appendix

(II.) GERMAN

FIRST SCOUTING GROUP

Ship		Speed Knots	Armament
Seydlitz (Flag)		26*	Ten 11-inch
Rear-Admiral Von Hipper			Twelve 5·9-inch
Moltke		25	Ten 11-inch
			Twelve 5·9-inch
Derfflinger		27	Eight 12-inch
			Twelve 5·9-inch
Blücher		24	Twelve 8·2-inch.
			Eight 5·9-inch

SECOND SCOUTING GROUP

Ship		Speed	Armament
Stralsund		25	Twelve 4·1-inch
Graudenz		27	Twelve 4·1-inch
Rostock		27	Twelve 4·1-inch
Kolberg		25	Twelve 4·1-inch

Torpedo-boat Flotilla V. 2nd and 18th Half-Flotillas.

EXPENDITURE OF AMMUNITION ON THE 24th JANUARY, 1915.

The five Battle Cruisers present expended between them 1,154 heavy shells, of which 708 were armour piercing, and 365 were lyddite, the remainder being C.P.C. and shrapnel.

No regulation was laid down as to how, or when the different kinds of shells were to be used, this matter being decided by the Captain of each ship. I believe there were about 700 six-inch and four-inch shells used.

On the German side 976 heavy shells were used, and as far as can be made out from the available figures, about three or four hundred shells of the secondary armaments. Of course no figures are available as to the Blücher expenditure, which must have been heavy, as she was practically in action all the time until she sank. We may take it, however, that the expenditure on both sides was, roughly speaking, about the same. The Lion received eighteen hits, and two other hits were recorded on the other battle cruisers; and if one puts the expenditure of ammunition at 2,000 shells, it will be seen how great is the proportion required to be expended in a modern long range action of this kind; and that the hits recorded were, in the case of the Germans, about one per cent. of the ammunition expended.

* All the German ships exceeded their official speeds.

278

APPENDIX C

PERSONNEL OF THE BATTLE CRUISERS ENGAGED ON 24th JANUARY, 1915

(From the Navy List for January, 1915.)

H.M.S. LION

26,350 *Tons.*   *H.P.* 70,000 *N.D.*

Guns—8-13·5 *inch*, 16-4 *inch*, 4-3 *pr.*

Vice-Admiral (acting) ... *Sir* David Beatty, KCB, MVO, DSO ... 1 Mar 13

Personal Staff.
Secretary .... Frank T. Spickernell   1 Mar 13
Flag Lieut. Com. Ralph F. Seymour ... 1 Mar 13

For General Staff Duties.
Commander ......The Hon. Reginald
A. R. Plunkett ...24 Feb 13
(For War Staff Duties.)
Lieutenant ......Edward R. B. Kemble 5 Aug 14
Lieut. R.N.V.R. Filson Young ...... 9 Nov 14
Eng. Capt. ......Charles G. Taylor,MVO13 Sept 14
(Accommodated in ' Tiger.')
Lieut. R.M.A. ...Harold M. Franks ... 4 June 12
(18 Nov. 11)
(For duty as Assist. for W.T. Duties.)
Clerk to Sec. ......Leslie N. Sampson ... 1 Mar 13
Reginald H. Pearce... 3 Mar 13
Artif. Eng. ......William K. Bodycomb31 Oct 12
(To assist Eng. Capt.)
(Accommodated in ' Tiger.')

Captain ....Alfred E. M. Chatfield,
CVO............... — Mar 13
Commander ......(N)Herbert L. Edwards
26 Dec 12
Charles A. Fountaine 30 Nov 14
Lieut.-Com. ......(T)Evan O. Bunbury 31 Dec 13
Francis H. Brabant...— Oct 13
(G)Gerald F. Longhurst
3 Jan 14
Lieutenant ......John B. Glencross ...31 Oct 13
Guy P. Bowles......... 4 June 13
Arthur L. Harrison... 4 June 12
Charles M. R. Schwerdt
31 Apr 13
Lieut. R.N.R. ...Ernest H. Thornton
(act.) .... 7 Feb 14
Eng. Com.........Donald P. Green ...25 Feb 10
Eng.Lieut.-Com. George Preece .... 9 Aug 13
Eng.-Lieut. ......Ralph P. Janion(tempy) 6 June 14
John O. Flint ......16 Aug 11
Asst. ....{ A. K. Stephens ......— Apr 14
Constructor (*With rank of Eng. Lieut.)*
Major R.M. ......Francis J. W. Harvey 12 Feb 13

Lieut. R.M. ......Francis E. Jones......23 Dec 12
(And for Physical Training Duties.)
Chaplain ....Rev. Cecil W. Lydall,
MA .... 4 June 12
Fleet Surgeon ...Alexander Maclean, MB 10 Dec 13
Staff Surgeon ...Alfred B. Cox, MB ... 4 June 12
Fleet Paym. ......Charles H. Rowe ...26 Apr 12
Surgeon ....Maurice C. Mason ...— Aug 14
Sub-Lieut. ......Lord Burghersh ...... 6 May 14
Mate (E) ......Harry E. LePoidevin 19 Dec 14
Asst. Paym. ......James Dean ...... 6 June 12
James G. Johnson ...— Aug 13
Ch. Carpenter ...Frederick E. Dailey 12 July 10
Ch. Artif. Eng. ...Edward C. Phillips ... 1 Oct 12
Gunner ....Nathaniel Mitchell ...16 June 14
(T) Joseph H. Burton14 Apr 13
Robert Purdie .... 4 June 12
(For Instructional Duties.)
Boatswain. ......William H. Olver ......6 Oct 13
William H. Macey ......4 June 12
(For Q.D. Duties.)
Martin Norsworthy... 4 June 13
(For Q.D. Duties.)
Sig. Boatswain ...Edward Downing ... 4 June 13
R.M. Gunner ...George W. Comley ...— Sept 12
Art. Eng. ....James L. Crawford... 4 June 12
Daniel Humpherson 8 Oct 12
Arthur J. Rice ...... 7 Nov 13
William O. McLean
(act.) ....12 May 14
Wt. Electrician ...Edwin G. Goad ...... 2 Apr 13
Midshipman ......Robert L. Moore ...15 Jan 13
R. E. Lewis-Lloyd ...15 Jan 13
William E. Steele ...15 Jan 13
The Hon. Alan B. de
Blacquiere ....15 Jan 13
William G. B. Hartley15 May 13
Patrick F. Cooper ...15 May 13
Richard F. Fegan ...15 May 13
Philip E. Vaux ......15 May 13
Sterling N. Cobbold 15 May 13
John R. S. Haines ...15 May 13
Alastair G. M. Small 15 May 14
Frank H. Alderson ...15 May 14
John P. F. Turner ...15 May 14

(Commissioned at Devonport on the 4th June, 1912.)

279

Appendix

H.M.S. TIGER

28,350 Tons.   H.P. 90,000 N.D.

Guns—8-13·5 inch, 16-6 inch, 4-3 pr.

Captain   ...   Henry B. Pelly, MVO.

Commander	...Arthur J. Davies
	(N)Edward R. Jones
Lieut.-Com.	...James Bayley (ret.)
	(T) Walter N. Lapage
	(G) Evan Bruce-Gardyne
Lieutenant	...Theodôre K. Elmsley
	Henry E. O. Blagrove
	Leonard H. White
	Charles S. Lockhart
	(E) John P. Charley
Lieut. R.N.R.	...Alexander S. Mackay
Lieut. R.N.V.R.	Kenneth G. Reid
Lt. R.N.V.R.(ty.)	Arthur J. L. Darby
Eng.-Com.	......Cecil H. A. Bermingham
Eng. Lt. Com.	George E. McEwen
Eng. Lieut.	......Harold T. Evans
Eng. Lieut. (ty)	Henry O. Hill
Chaplain.	.........Rev. Wilfred H. Gibbins, MA
Capt. R.M.A.	...Alan G. B. Bourne, MVO
Lieut. R.M. (act.)	Charles W. Adair
Staff Surg.	...John B Muir, MB!
Fleet Paym.	...James E. V. Morton
Surgeon	.........James C. Kelly, MB, BA
Ty. Surg.	.........Douglas Ross, MB
Sub-Lieut.	......Robert R. Gibbons
Asst. Paym.	...Herbert L. M. Bamber
Asst. Paym. R.N.R. (act.) }	John W. Sells
Ch. Gunner	......Frederick S. Farlow
Ch. Boatswain	...Arthur Adams

Ch. Carpenter	...John N. Matheson
Ch. Artificer Engineer }	Thomas Lowrey
Gunner	.........(T) Joseph E. Hamley
	William H. Lake (act.)
	George Wood (act.)
	Crispin G. B. Taylor (act.)
Boatswain	......Richard Sullivan (act.)
B.M. Gunner	...Reginald J. Gunsm
Sig. Bosn.	.........Harry E. Wellman
Artif. Eng.	......Robert Douglas
	William A. Pickup
Wt. Mech.	.........Samuel E. Gray
Midshipman	......Patrick H. W. Ferguson
	David Gilmour
	Arthur G. T. Grier
	James A. C. Forbes
	Henry C. Holmes
	Dyson S. Hore
	John G. D. Ouvry
	Cecil W. V. Gooding
	Hugh E. Holland
	Ian M. R. Campbell
	Ronald A. Macdonald
	Sidney M. Raw
	Donald A. Willey
Midshipman (R.N.R.) {	John W. Lamble (proby.)
	Arthur H. H. Griffiths (proby.)
	Henry R. Wilkinson (proby.)

H.M.S. PRINCESS ROYAL

28,350 Tons.   H.P. 70,000 N.D.

Guns—8-13·5 inch, 16-4 inch, 4-3 pr.

Captain   ...   Osmond De B. Brock, AdC   ...   1 Aug 12

Commander	...Alister F. Beal ......10 Aug. 12	
	Roland C. S. Hunt ...16 Aug. 11	
	(In lieu of Lieut. (G))	
Lieut.-Com.	......(T)Charles D. Burke — Feb. 13	
	(N)Douglas B. LeMottée	
	31 July 12	
	Noel E Isemonger ...13 Jan 14	
Lieutenant	......Kenneth J. Duff-Dunbar	
	14 Nov 12	
	Arthur G. Harris ...14 Nov 12	
	John M. Boyd ......14 Nov 12	
	Herbert C. Mayo ...25 Apr 13	
	(E) Guy F. B. Ottley 1 Oct 14	
Lieut. R.N.R.	...William L. Wilson	
	(act.) ....27 Jan 14	

Lieut. R.N.V.R.	The Hon. Guy Colebroke	
	— Dec	14
Eng. Com.	......Thomas H. Wallice	24 Mar 10
Eng. Lieut.	...Albert A. G. Martell	17 May 11
	Albert K. Dibley ...21 Apr	14
Capt. R.M.A.	...Frederick G. Tanqueray-Willaume ....14 Nov	12
Chaplain	...Rev. Richard H. O'Donovan	
	BA ....28 Aug	13
Fleet Surg.	......Arthur R. H. Skey, MB 31 Mar.	14
Fleet Paym.	......Harold Rodham ...12 Aug	12
Surgeon	.........Malcolm M. Melrose	14 Nov 12
Tempy. Surgeon	Hugh W. Bayly ...... — Aug	14
Sub-Lieut.	.........Henry Clanchy	6 Feb 14
	Henry F. Scholes(act.)14 Nov	12

(Continued on next page)

280

Personnel

H.M.S. PRINCESS ROYAL—*(Continued from previous page)*

Sub-Lieut. ...... Alexander D. Gibson-
Carmichael (act.) ...14 Nov 12
Geoffrey J. Landale (act.)
14 Nov 12
Frank A. Hall (act.) 1 Jan 14
John B. Cole Hamilton
(act.)14 Nov 12
Asst. Paym. ...Herbert C. Waldron — July 13
Ch. Gunner ....Samuel Mallin .... 3 Aug 11
Ch. Sig. }
Boatswain } Henry J. Wayling ...14 Nov 12
Gunner ....(T)Arthur H. Cruft.. 4 July 11
John W. J. Draisey 28 Apr 13
(For Instructional Duties.)
Albert W. Wildbore — Oct 13
(For Instructional Duties.)
Boatswain ......Henry J. Bailey ......14 Nov 12
R.M. Gunner ...John Masterton ......14 Nov 12
Carpenter ......John W. Sparks ......29 Apr 11
Artif. Eng. .....John Lippiett ....14 Nov 12

Artif. Eng. ......George W. Redgate...14 Nov 12
William E. Ross ......12 Aug 12
Ernest Thaxter ......14 Nov 12
Joseph House .... 7 Nov 13
Wt. Electrician ...Joseph Berry .... 2 Apr 13
Midshipman ...Edward C. Bindloss 14 Nov 12
Henry J. Johnstone 14 Nov 12
Frank L. C. Butcher 15 Sept 13
Stephen S. Palmes ...15 Sept 13
George L. C. Briggs 15 Sept 13
Colin Buist ....15 Sept 13
Andrew J. Paton ....15 Sept 13
Midshipman }
R.N.R. } William P. Lillie...15 Sept 13
Cyril J. West ....15 Sept 13
William C. A. Robson
(proby.) ....15 Sept 13
Tom Parker (proby.) 15 Sept 13
Clerk ....Frederick W. Bayley 9 Aug 13

(Commissioned at Devonport on 14th November, 1912.)

H.M.S. NEW ZEALAND

18,800 Tons. H.P. 44,000 N.D.

Guns—8-12 inch, 16-4 inch, 4-3 pr.

Was built at the charge of the New Zealand Government.

Rear-Admiral ... Sir Archibald Gordon Moore, KCB ... Jan 15

Personal Staff.

Secretary .... R. T. Johnson ... Jan 15.
Flag-Lieut. ... Herbert F. Pott ... Jan 15.

Captain ....Lionel Halsey, CMG ...21 Sept 12
Commander ......Henry E. Grace ......15 Sept 12
Lieut.-Com. ......(D)Dudley B. N. North20 Jan 13
(N) Kenelm E. L.
Creighton ....24 June 14
(T)Archibald A. Lovett-
Cameron ....— Oct 12
(G)Cecil B. Prickett...27 June 14
Lieutenant ......Alexander D. Boyle 18 Nov 12
Cyril Gore.............— Nov 12
H.S.H. Prince George
L. V. H. S. of
Battenberg ....— Feb 13
Penrose L. Barcroft
(tempy.)...........9 Jan 13
Thomas A. Benskin — Dec 13
Lieut. R.N.R. ...James Irvine (act.) ... 2 Dec 13
Joseph K. Chaplin (act.)
29 July 14
Eng. Com. ......Thomas H. Turner ...19 May 11
Eng. Lieut. ......John D. Grieve ...21 Oct 11
Ernest McK. Phillips 12 Nov 12
Harry G. Marshall ... 9 Jan 13
Temp. Eng. Lieut. Thomas Orr ....19 Dec 14
Capt. R.M.A. ...Harold Blount ......19 Nov 12
Chaplain and } Rev. William G.
Naval Inst. } Litchfield, MA ...... 1 Jan 14
Fleet Surgeon ...Cecil H. Rook ....19 Nov 12
Staff Surgeon ...James R. A. Clark-
Hall ....15 Nov 13
Fleet Paym. ...Frank P. E. Hanham 11 Nov 12
Tempy. Surg. ...Hildred B. Carlill,
MA, MD ....— Sept 14

Sub-Lieut. ......George E. M. O'Donnell
6 May 14
Hugh B. Anderson ...15 Jan 13
Clare G. Vyner (act.) 15 Jan 13
Asst. Paym. ...Arthur C. A. Janion 7 Jan 13
(D)Denzil R.Thurstan 19 Nov 12
Ch. Gunner ...Jesse H. Mack ......16 Nov 12
Ch. Carpenter ...Robert Laitt ....18 July 11
Gunner ....(T) Harry Joynes....25 Mar 14
Vincent S. Robinson 19 Nov 12
(For Instructional Duties.)
Boatswain ......Sydney C. Legg ....27 Feb 12
William J Reynolds — Nov 12
(For Q.D. Duties.)
William R. Head ...13 Jan 13
(For Q.D. Duties.)
Sig. Boatswain ...Albert Lewis ......19 Nov 12
R.M. Gunner ...Albert E. Elliott ......19 Nov 12
Artif. Eng........William J. Cater ... 1 Jan 14
Robert K. Weir ......24 Sept 12
Percy E. Brooker (act.)13 Nov 12
Midshipman ...The Earl of Carlisle...15 Jan 13
Geoffrey T. A. Scott 15 Jan 13
Thomas A. W. Robertson
15 Jan 13
John C. Annesley ...15 Jan 13
Oliver J. L. Symon...15 Jan 13
Albert L. Poland......15 Jan 13
Cecil S. Miller ....15 Jan 13
Edmund G. B. Coore 15 Jan 13
Cuthbert F. B. Bowlby15 Jan 13
Harry N. Sanctuary 25 Oct 14
Horace T. Day.........25 Oct 14
Philip H. Baker ......25 Oct 14
Charles E. Payne......25 Oct 14
Edward H. Kitson ...25 Oct 14
William P. Carne......25 Oct 14

(Commissioned at Govan 19th November, 1912, and completed to full crew at Devonport on 23rd November, 1912.)

281

Appendix

H.M.S. INDOMITABLE

17,250 Tons. Turbine. H.P. 41,000 N.D.

Guns—8-12 inch, 16-4 inch.

Captain ... Francis W. Kennedy ... 11 Dec 1912

Commander ......John A. Moreton......20 Dec 12
Lieut.-Com. ......(T)William B. Rowbotham
                  6 Jan 13
      (N) Morgan Tindal ... 4 Oct 13
      (G) Lachlan D. I. Mac-
        Kinnon .... 5 Apr 13
      Stuart E. Holder......— May 13
Lieutenant ......*The Hon.* Roger Coke15 Oct 13
      Reginald H. Ransome10 Feb 14
      Noel M. F. Corbett... 2-Mar 12
      Daniel de Pass...—...10 Feb 14
Lieut. R.N.R. ...George B. Bray (act.) 9 Apr 14
Eng. Com. ......James Mountifield ...12 Nov 13
Eng. Lieut. ......Albert Knothe ......10 Feb 12
      George B. Allen ......15 Oct 13
      Henry W. Ascott ... 3 Apr 13
Capt R.M.A.......Lancelot D. Briscoe 11 Dec 12
Chaplain ....*Rev.* Paschal C. Gough.
         BA ....10 Feb 14
Fleet Surgeon ...George Gibson ......11 Aug 13
Fleet Paym. ......Augustus P. Hughes 29 Oct 12
Surgeon ....Alfred R. Price, MB...11 Aug 13
Tempy. Surg. ...William H. S. Hodge 14 Sept 14

Sub-Lieut. ....Hugh A. Taylor ...... 6 Feb 14
      Humphrey D. Tollemache
                  5 May 14
      Thomas H. Troubridge
              (act.)15 Sept 12
      Basil J. Dugdale (act.)— Aug 12
      John P. Money (act.) — Aug 13
      John G. Y. Loveband
            (act.)— Aug 13
      Cecil C. A. Allen (act.)15 Sept 12
      Lionel G. C. Thompson
            (act.)— Aug 13
      Humphrey R. Brand
            (act.)15 Sept 12
Asst. Paym. ......William P. B. Cormac 10 Feb 14
Ch. Gunner ......George B. Hasell......27 Jan 14
Gunner ....(T)Arthur V. Tedder 16 June 13
*Bandmaster R.M.*Herbert Reely ...... 5 Nov 12
Midshipman ......John I. Macnabb......26 Nov 12
      Alexander G. C. Smith— Sept 12
      Reginald G. Frances 15 Jan 14
      John O. Chadpole ...15 Jan 14
Clerk ....Crichton F. Labordel31 July 13

(Re-commissioned at Chatham, 5th November, 1912.

APPENDIX D

CORRESPONDENCE WITH THE ADMIRALTY, 1920

BEFORE beginning the actual writing of this book, I had the following correspondence with the Admiralty :

October the twelfth, 1920.   124, Ebury Street,
    SIR,—   S.W.

      I should be obliged if you would bring the following matter to the notice of the Board of Admiralty.

      1. I have been asked to write a book on the work of the Battle Cruisers in the North Sea, especially during the period (Nov. 1914 to May 1915) when I had the honour of serving as Lieutenant (tempy.) R.N.V.R. on the staff of the Vice-Admiral commanding the Battle Cruiser Fleet.

      2. There are two ways in which this commission can be executed, and I have hesitated between them. One is to make my book virtually an account of the Battle Cruiser Fleet from its beginnings in the Battle Cruiser Squadron until the end of its work in the war. The other is to write a narrative concerning my personal experience, not only of the operations which I witnessed, but of persons and relationships in the Fleet and in the Admiralty in its relation to the Fleet. In the second case the book would be a record of my own experience ; in the first the method would be impersonal and historic.

      3. For the second I require no assistance ; for the first I should have to consult documents of which I have no record, although many of them passed through my hands in the Intelligence Office of the Battle Cruiser Fleet. If their Lordships would see fit to allow me to consult at the Admiralty, and under any necessary supervision, the documents essential for ensuring accuracy in this first method, I would, on behalf of myself and my publishers, agree to submit for their Lordships' censorship such material of my book as should be based on these documents, and not to make any use of them of which they might not approve. . . . I have the honour to be,
                               Sir,
                                  Your obedient servant,
                                (Signed) FILSON YOUNG.

To the Secretary of the Admiralty,
    Whitehall, S.W.

Appendix

\
                                                        Admiralty,
Sir,—   30*th October*, 1920.

I am commanded by My Lords Commissioners of the Admiralty
to inform you that they have had under consideration the proposal
contained in your letter of the 12th instant that you should be allowed
access to official documents concerning the war in order to enable
you to write an account of the work of the Battle Cruiser Force.

2. Their Lordships regret that they can make no exception to
the rule which has been laid down, that only Sir Julian Corbett, who
has been appointed under the Committee of Imperial Defence on
behalf of H.M. Government to write the official History of the War,
can be granted permission to see official documents relating to the war.

                          I am, Sir,
                    Your Obedient Servant,
Filson Young, Esq.   W. W. Baddeley.

This reply indicates a state of affairs that is highly
characteristic both of the Admiralty and of our national
official attitude towards anything in the nature of history
and literature. On making inquiries, I found, to my
amazement, that the Board of Admiralty has actually no
control over the original documents on which any true
history of the events of the naval war must be based.
These documents have been handed over to a department
called the Historical Department of the Committee of
National Defence. This department has simply to receive
what is given to it and assume that the material is
complete. The Admiralty, on the other hand, gets rid
of all responsibility by handing over a mass of papers to
the department and saying that they are complete. As
a matter of fact they are not complete; vital material
has been lost or destroyed, and no one is in a position
to fix the responsibility or to be made responsible.

My own position in the light of this letter is a very
simple one. Some of the material which I have used is
technically confidential, and I am technically liable to

Correspondence

all kinds of penalties for having either preserved or published it. That is a risk which I cheerfully take. On the other hand, with regard to the Dogger Bank battle at any rate, it seemed probable that my material was not less valuable than that likely to be in official hands, and that some of it would probably not be available to them at all unless I published it. There may be a few inaccuracies as to actual times and positions, which would have been avoided if I had been allowed access to the logs of ships, but I do not think that they are in any case material to the main purpose of this book.

My chief regret is that, being thrown back entirely on my own resources, the doings of the battle cruisers, and of the *Lion* herself, occupy what may seem to some a disproportionate share of the picture. There are many incidents in the work of our light cruisers and destroyers which I remember as being recorded in unpublished despatches, and which ought to become a part of history. But I have no record of them; and until the documents in which they are buried are made available to someone who knows what to look for and where to look for it, some of the most gallant incidents of the war must go unrecorded, since the record of them would form no part of official history.

INDEX

Index

Index

T

Index

Index

Index

Index

Index

Index

Index

PRINTED BY CASSELL & COMPANY, LIMITED, LA BELLE SAUVAGE, LONDON, E.C
10 ʳ21